P9-DEZ-549

14⁹⁹

HINDU WIFE, HINDU NATION

TANIKA SARKAR

Hindu Wife, Hindu Nation

Community, Religion, and Cultural Nationalism

INDIANA UNIVERSITY PRESS
BLOOMINGTON AND INDIANAPOLIS

This book is a publication of

Indiana University Press
601 North Morton Street
Bloomington, IN 47404-3797 USA

http://iupress.indiana.edu

Telephone orders— 800-842-6796
Fax orders— 812-855-7931
Orders by email—
iuporder@indiana.edu

© 2001 by Permanent Black

All rights reserved

No part of this book may be reproduced
or utilized in any form or by any means,
electronic or mechanical, including
photocopying and recording, or by any
information storage and retrieval
system, without permission in writing
from the publisher. The Association of
American University Presses' Resolution
on Permissions constitutes the only
exception to this prohibition.

The paper used in this publication
meets the minimum requirements of
American National Standard for
Information Sciences—
Permanence of Paper for Printed
Library Materials,
ANSI Z39.48–1984.

Manufactured in the United States of
America

Cataloging information is available
from the Library of Congress.

ISBN 0-253-34046-2 (cloth)
1 2 3 4 5 06 05 04 03 02 01

For Aditya

Contents

Introduction

This book comprises chapters that were originally essays written over more than a decade. It reflects the shifts and breaks in my interests in some ways, but the chapters are, all the same, unified by their focus upon the development of Hindu cultural nationalism, largely in nineteenth-century Bengal. A final chapter leads from there into Hindutva in the Hindi belt, and into the Hindu cultural chauvinism of our own time.

This is not to suggest that Hindutva is the logical fulfilment of all the other kinds of politics I discuss elsewhere in the book, nor that there is a historical inevitability to its power. I certainly do not argue that Hindutva has vanquished or will oust other nationalist and Hindu imaginaries. Yet there are historical connections among the themes of the Bengal chapters which open up a space for the final chapter. Since most of the book focuses on a very fundamental transformation in the structures of political-cultural sensibility that occurred in late-nineteenth-century Bengal, I shall here try to collate certain changes in relations of property, land and enterprise in those times. These developments relate to the abandonment of liberal reformism in favour of Hindu cultural nationalism.

But first let me spell out the limits of this book. Almost all of it deals with Hindu middle-class people in late-nineteenth-century Bengal, when they were turning quite decisively towards a Hindu cultural indigenism and nationalism, from a more socially-questioning and self-critical earlier era. At the same time, this narrow limit is relative, for the people whom I discuss act always in response to, in reaction against, or together with, people who are Muslim, low castes, peasants and labourers, and the colonial ruling classes. What they do, how they change over time, depends largely on these relationships. Nor are they a unified group among themselves. They include large tenure-holders and very petty landowners; or solvent, protected tenants. They also include struggling clerks in government and mercantile offices; as well as a dim and floating world of unknown artists, hack-writers, actors and actresses. They also, equally, feature erudite reformers, powerful politicians, and famous literary figures, as also a growing pool of castes ranging from the twice-born to those claiming at least Shudra status. And, of course, these people include men as well as women, the latter emerging as allies, partners, as well as interlocutors of the upper-caste and middle-class values and interests of their men.

I begin with studies of the 1870s, when the public sphere registered a broadening of liberal commitments, as well as the emergence of a hard and closed nationalistic culture. I then exemplify the direction and extent of the later shift in the chapters which focus on the two phases of Bankimchandra's writings. I develop these themes in the chapters on the Age of Consent Bill, its responses within the public sphere, and its import in the making of a militant Hindu cultural nationalism. As a contrast, as well as a sequel, I look at the religious imagining that structures the cultural production of Gandhian nationalism.

I conclude with a chapter on the cultural politics of contemporary Hindutva. This relates not merely to a fundamentally transformed postcolonial context and predicament, but also to a very different North Indian political formation based on a social milieu of urban traders and manufacturers and the service sector. Its cultural politics has been historically bred on the tensions between Arya Samaj reformist chauvinism and Sanatani conservatism, each trying to grapple with the development of low-caste separatist sects and cults, their defection from Hindu caste controls, their cultural and political self-assertiveness. The Samaj and the Sanatanis eventually converged on a shared anti-Muslim politics and sought to short-circuit internal faultlines within the Hindu community via the image of a threatening Muslim. More distant from a cosmopolitan English education than the Bengali middle classes, refusing the established Urdu-based cultural style of North India, and equally distant from rural–popular cultural traditions, the emergent politics may be usefully categorised as emanating from the 'vernacular elite.'[1] This formation shares not so much its material-cultural experiences with the Bengali middle classes as certain discursive and ideological terrains. Here the continuities and departures in the sensibilities that used the hymn 'Bande Mataram'—so central to both its author, Bankim, and to Hindutva today—constitutes the mediating link.

II

Some chapters on the nineteenth century and early Gandhian nationalism—i.e. the first chapter, on the Hindu nation and Hindu wives; the two pieces on Bankim; and the essay on nationalist iconography—deal with distinct discursive traditions and their larger political and ideological negotiations. In the chapters on the Elokeshi–Mohunt scandal, on Rashsundari, and the two on the Age of Consent debates, in contrast, I begin with a small and bounded local event. I unravel its texture and follow the different threads into different, seemingly discrete histories that, nonetheless, connect within the event. This use of small beginnings to explore larger historical processes has the advantage of relocating the enquiry from reified structures to actual men and women engaged in concrete activities and relationships: i.e. from nationalism and colonisation of Culture by post-Enlightenment knowledge, and Middle-class Formation or Patriarchy, to people with their own names, faces and histories; from abstraction and category to specifics of collective existence, social relationships, struggles over domination and exploitation where each individual or group seems capable of a personal utterance within an inherited structure of language uses.

The reference to individual utterance is not fortuitous in a study

---

[1]For a study of the progenitor of this political formation, see Christopher R. King, *One Language, Two Scripts: The Hindi Movement in Nineteenth-century North India* (Bombay: Oxford University Press, 1994). Also, Vasudha Dalmia, *The Nationalization of Hindu Traditions* (Delhi: Oxford University Press, 1997).

that begins with the nineteenth century. In his book of Bengal proverbs, S.K. De makes the point that pre-nineteenth-century linguistic expressions were made up largely of fragments of earlier authoritative sayings, of which proverbs are an important part. From the mid or late nineteenth century, however, this bricolage was reduced, clearing a space for more individuated enunciations which aspired towards originality and uniqueness of expression.[2] Building on this, we may perceive a language-use that moves towards innovative self-expression, articulating a sense of selfhood that is different from others rather than composed of, or a replication of, others.

Indeed, through new nineteenth-century resources such as popular vernacular prose, print, newspapers and cheap chapbooks, we have authors, both highbrow and lowbrow, writing in major and minor keys and appending signatures to their compositions. This is in radical contrast to an earlier expressive convention in pre-print manuscript literature, where minor authors sought to insert their voices into the public domain by slipping anonymous compositions into a text written by a great name.

Signatures came from all sorts of people whose opinion or arguments had never been earlier heard within a broad public sphere. In the latter half of the century, lower-caste associations bring out journals, poetry, and autobiographies, as well as religious tracts of caste-based sects. Peasant and tribal movements do not as yet throw up their own authors, but their political activities and their religious worldviews—their sense of a moral economy—are reported and discussed with great anxiety as well as with occasional sympathy by the middle-class press. At the same time, a Bengali Muslim religious authorship emerges to debate various Islamic theological stances that are locked in bitter combat.[3] Even earlier, there was a flourishing genre of Christian evangelising literature in Bengali that had, in fact, created a rudimentary prose as well as the first Bengali printing press of the early nineteenth century. The earliest work of Bengali fiction emerged via missionary writing— Mrs Mullens' *Phulmoni O Karuna*, in the 1820s.[4]

[2]S.K. De, *Bangle Prabad* (Calcutta, n.d.).

[3]See Rafiuddin Ahmad, *The Bengal Muslims: A Quest for Identity* (Delhi: Oxford University Press, 1981).

[4]See Kanchan Basu, ed., *Dushprapya Sahitya Sangraha* (Calcutta, 1992, reprint).

In a sense, the emergence of submerged and subaltern voices in the realm of public discourse eventually created rather hard boundaries and identities—more insistent, perhaps, about a singular and unified collective self than were older authorities, who had not faced the possibility of contested identities to this extent. At the same time, the cheapness and ubiquity of print allowed for the stratification and individuation of opinion, so that the possibilities of identity formation remained open-ended.

Dialogues via the print medium enabled an accumulation of plural, multiphonal opinion, as well as their continuous circulation and dissemination. This process led towards the production of even larger pluralities, and a public sphere emerged out of this arena from the middle of the century. Here individuals unconnected with the state apparatus talked about economic, social, religious, political and intimate matters. Up to the 1870s, I find that this sphere possessed a variegated and growing sprawl. The presence of a racially arrogant and discriminatory state, a growing awareness of economic drain, and gender-related controversies among liberals, the orthodox, and Hindu nationalists registered themselves through the press, in public oral debates, and in the social-satirical farces and drama of new public theatres. The subjects for discussion included religious dogma, ritual norms, customs, as well as new urban landscapes, rural and peasant problems, revenues, factory and gender law, schools and governance. What is significant about the form of the debates is that almost all the opinion articulated here came under critical scrutiny from others within the same arena. Self-justification constantly required a display of rational arguments, marshalled according to certain known and accepted procedures. In the process, colonial laws as well as religious prescription could no longer rely comfortably upon authoritarian command alone.

The book begins with two events in the 1870s. Each was a scandal in its own way—that is, each transgressed the limits of the normal, and therefore gave rise to interpretive communities which reflected upon these exceptional occurrences. In one, a young wife was seduced by the mohunt of a great Shaivite pilgrimage and then subsequently killed by her husband. The other was the publication of an autobiography by a housewife whose family held extremely strict views against female literacy. The autobiography added the perception and opinions of a woman on the controversies about the mode-of-being of upper-caste Hindu women. It was also living proof of how a woman, finding received wisdom and prescription unsatisfactory, insisted on developing an individual social and theological understanding for herself. I wrote this out of dissatisfaction with the parameters of feminist cultural studies which seemed to me to reiterate the recast presence of patriarchy within male discourses in the form of very similar images of women across history and geography.

The second event deals with a case of murder and adultery. Through this modern legal-judicial processes, as well as custom and religion, were put on trial in public performances, cultural productions and writings. They were discussed from a variety of finely-graded differences in perspective on Hindu marriage and pilgrimage, religious and state authority, morality and law. This chapter, again, came out of my fatigue with certain radical interpretive schemes that remain motionless between the two grand and stagnant narratives of domination and resistance, without an adequate sense of the innumerable small historical shifts that alter the terms of debate and discourse when connected with the new media, involved in the production of opinion.

The two chapters on Bankim capture two distinct and opposed discursive-ideological moments in the writings of the same individual. This master of satire and polemic against class, gender and the caste power of the Hindu educated gentry, this novelist experimenting with transgressive forms of love across religious divides, later came to found a Hindu imaginary of disciplined, warlike, chauvinistic nationbuilders reared on a pedagogical apparatus of martial, scriptural and nationalistic values. He himself put this together in a sort of syllabus devised by his last few novels and polemical essays. I look at the changes as well as at the internal fractures within Bankim's later writings that implicitly blocked the operations of this change.

I then take up a later and very different moment in nationalism— one connected with Congress mass movement and the popular literature and iconography that it produced. Gandhians believed in an ideology of the separate spheres of male and female activities, of upper- and lower-caste functions. However, they insisted that social asymmetries of class, caste and gender implied a moral vision of trusteeship for the privileged as much as they enjoined obedience for the subordinated. Moreover, the practical experience of mass struggles opened up fairly equal political functions for men as well as women, for low-caste peasants and upper-caste proprietors. The woman and the peasant were, moreover, valorised as ideal satyagrahis, as already-constituted ideal political subjects by virtue of their nurturing functions, their moral resistance strategies, and their meekness. Ironically, this privileging doubly confirmed their social subordination and submissiveness. At the same time, such idealisations of their functions came into conflict with their new-found political activism, and with the many breaks with convention and prescription that this required in practice. Discursive images thus need to be qualified by the realities of political practice, especially among women themselves, whose initiative often overran the boundaries set by the Congress leadership.[5]

In the chapter on Hindutva discourse, I go back to the beginnings that Bankim had tried to make but which had faltered at the hurdle set up by his own rich and complex sensibility. This final chapter suggests a contrast between two versions of communalism, even though the hard and closed contemporary Hindutva version of it borrows from the earlier tradition.

III

Some years back, when I was teaching a class of undergraduate students at St Stephen's College in Delhi, a student asked me with some perplexity: How is it that the Bengali intelligentsia turned away so firmly from liberal reformism to Hindu revivalism later in the century? I sensed that any attempt at a response would need to draw upon multiple, disjunct sources of nineteenth-century historical developments in a number of thinly or implicitly connected fields. The rest of this Introduction is a belated attempt at a partial answer.

If the public sphere was expansive and adventurous in its discussion

[5]See my 'Woman is a Political Animal: Women's Histories, Feminist Writings', Indian History Congress, Delhi, 1999.

of prescription and custom upto the early 1870s, the introspection gave way to a more authoritarian conservatism and nativism in the next decades.[6] Not that the entire middle class turned unanimously to Hindu revivalism, nor that self-questioning and self-criticism dried up entirely. But the dominant tone changed from satire and self-irony to ponderous traditionalism. I would like to indicate certain long-term changes in the larger material experiences of the middle classes that, I suggest, put a closure to their earlier willingness to question the bases of their social power.

Various levels of the middle class derived various portions of their income from landowing of different kinds. From the last decade of the eighteenth-century, the Permanent Settlement had generated a permanent gap between landowners' access to peasant rent, which was elastic, and the revenue that they paid to the state, which was fixed in perpetuity. There is much controversy about whether or not the harsh sale laws and insistence on absolute punctuality of revenue payment drove traditional landowing classes out of business, clearing a space for non-rural new proprietors; or whether the new land market made much of the land circulate among established landowing groups.[7] It is certain, however, that in the course of the nineteenth century, especially after the steady growth in agrarian prices from the middle years, landowners and tenure-holders found the high revenue assessment rates much mitigated by the rents and cesses that tenants provided and upon which there was no ceiling. The colonial state retained a stance of careful non-interference in landlord–tenant relations for a long time. Even the extraction of extra-legal cesses was overlooked. The burden of regula-

[6]See Amiya P. Sen, *Hindu Revivalism in Bengal: 1872–1905* (Delhi: Oxford University Press, 1993).

[7]See Ranajit Guha, *A Rule of Property for Bengal: An Essay on the Idea of Permanent Settlement* (Paris: Mouton and Company, 1963); Also Ratnalekha Ray, *Change in Bengal Agrarian Society, 1760–1850* (Delhi: Oxford University Press, 1980); Asok Sen, 'Agrarian Structure and Tenancy Laws in Bengal', in Sen, *et al.*, eds, *Three Studies on Agrarian Structure in Bengal, 1850–1947* (Calcutta, 1982); B.B. Chowdhury, 'Agrarian Economy and Agrarian Relations in Bengal, 1859–1885', in N.K. Sinha, ed., *The History of Bengal* (Calcutta, 1967); Dietmar Rothermund, *Government, Landlord and Peasant in India: Agrarian Relations Under British Rule, 1865–1935* (Wiesbaden, 1978).

tion was passed to the revenue courts. Here a huge pressure of litigation over claims to peasant rental among various categories of tenure-holders and landowners ushered in a 'lawyers' paradise' without, however, providing protection to a largely Muslim and low-caste tenantry from rent hikes and cesses, or from eviction on charges of non-payment of rent.

Peasant smallholding, the basis of Bengali agrarian economy, survived with great difficulty, its boundary from landless labour or shareholding being precarious. The introduction of jute as a cash crop, commanding a global market, did consolidate the upper stratum of peasant smallholding on a stronger and more secure basis from mid-century.[8] Cash-cropping and closer connections with provincial, Indian and world markets stimulated brisk local trading, petty manufacture and local financial networks. It produced a stratum of rural or small-town *byaparis* or businessmen who ran parallel to or overlapped with small peasants. At the same time, this did not significantly alter land relations nor produced a surplus which was adequate for investment into bigger capitalist ventures.

The Permanent Settlement, on the other hand, provided comfortable cushioning to landlords against an initially heavy revenue burden. Contrary to Cornwallis' expectations about 'improving' landlords of the English variety, the rent–revenue gap bred parasitic tenureholding of fairly infinite gradations rather than agrarian entrepreneurship. Men with surplus capital from land chose to plough back the profits into landholding again, partly because of the amenities that the Settlement provided in its unrevised form, partly also because of an absence of alternative investment opportunities. Foreign trade was virtually closed to Indian capital in these parts by a combination of powerful European mercantile organisations and governmental discriminatory policies. Nor was the capital available from land adequate for independent industrial ventures, since the big financial agencies were in European hands and discriminated relentlessly against Indian ventures. Landholders themselves were often not interested in exploring profit-making ventures. The Court of Wards records of the Mahishadal Raj in Midnapur shows

---

[8]See Sugata Bose, *Peasant Labour and Colonial Capital: Rural Bengal since 1770*, New Cambridge History of India (Cambridge: Cambridge University Press, 1993).

that with a 15 per cent surplus in their annual budget, the preferred form of investment was not moneylending, trade or manufacture, but the purchase of petty and scattered zamindaris and of fairly low interest-bearing government securities.[9]

It is notable, though, that upto the 1840s Bengali capital—whether accumulated within the interestices of compradore collaboration with European capital, or generated out of the agrarian surplus—was not entirely unenterprising. Nor was the maximisation of feudal rent through increased landholding the only form of investment. Even though the extent of Indian capital in the European agency-houses cannot be exactly assessed, it seems that, at each occasion of business depression and panic till 1830, the houses suffered considerably from the withdrawal of Indian investments. Higher rates of interest were offered to tempt them back, since their investment was in the form of short-term loans, whereas Europeans invested on a partnership basis.[10] Such inducements would suggest that the value of Indian investments could not have been insignificant. A few independent commercial and manufacturing ventures like shipping had also begun to appear under Bengali auspices, which again reveals an initial period of the buoyancy of Bengali entrepreneurship even in the face of highly unfair conditions of competition from European capital. A certain cautious measure of vitality was also expressed by some landowners who were, at this time, experimenting with agrarian improvement measures like the introduction of new crops and rationalised land management.[11]

The financial disasters of the 1840s put paid to hopes of modest Bengali enterprises of investment in financial ventures: even the survivors of the crisis struggled entirely on their own, while European capital

[9]Chitta Panda, *The Decline of the Bengal Zamindars: Midnapore, 1870–1920* (Delhi: Oxford University Press, 1996), pp. 46–7.

[10]Amales Tripathi, *Trade and Finance in the Bengal Presidency, 1793–1833* (Calcutta, 1979); Sabyasachi Bhattacharya, 'Eastern India', in Dharma Kumar, ed., *The Cambridge Economic History of India, 1757–1920*, vol. 2 (Cambridge: Cambridge University Press, 1983), p. 294.

[11]Nilmoni Mukherji, *A Bengal Zamindar: Joykrishna Mukherjee of Uttarpara and His Times* (Calcutta, 1975), chapters 5–12. Also S.C. Nandy, *The Kassimbazar Raj* (Calcutta, 1987).

was eventually bailed out by state help. While some studies have taken note of the long-term implications of the financial crisis upon an aborted Bengali entrepreneurship, they have not linked it with wider dimensions of the agrarian situation. A major consequence was redoubled dependence on landholding as the only safe form of investment. The concept of 'banijye basati Lakshmi' or 'Fortune Smiles on Trade' generated both nostalgic and utopian literary visions of seafaring adventurers and muscular Bengali entrepreneurs; it created an emotional and moral vision for later Swadeshi enterprises. Actually, however, land became the real resort for enterprise, shielded as it was from the uncertainties of revenue assessments. In fact, so blatant was the elasticity of rent and cesses that, upto the 1870s, the nationalist press as well as polemicists like Bankim studied in detail and expressed grave concern about peasant exploitation. Ricardian theories of rent found a productive soil among self-critical sections of a middle-class intelligentsia that combined professional opportunities with rent income in varying proportions. Also, there were efforts to transform landowning from a parasitic dependence on the passive extraction of rent to the active creation of surplus through improvements.

Here lie the long-range implications of what I would designate as the second crisis of investment for middle-class Bengalis who commanded a certain amount of surplus capital. The conjoined effects of two kinds of blockage also need to be studied against larger moral and political values. For landownership does not entail a pure economic role or property relationship: it involves a moral economy of paternalistic relationships where extraction and expropriation are masked and softened by personal encounters and caste-based, normative values associated with labour, services and ritual activities. It also depends on a self-image of local sovereignty that finds an appropriate resonance in normative and prescriptive gender relations. And it is here that I would see many of the roots of the transformation of a self-critical and self-changing liberal intelligentsia into a closed, status-quoist, chauvinistic one. It closed itself off to intellectual challenges and clung to the surviving bases of power with tenacious authoritarianism—that is, the typical forms of Bengali Hindu revivalism of the upper-caste gentry cum educated middle class.

If landowning was solace and reprieve, then this was also a threatened haven from about the 1860s.[12] In 1859, the first Rent Act was passed to secure the claims of a small upper category of occupancy tenants. The results were minimal, affecting a minority. Landlords managed to offset it by moving tenants from plot to plot so that none could claim continuous occupancy over the same plot for the stipulated period. Yet its significance lies in the fact that this was the first major step by a hitherto complaisant government in intervening and altering land-lord–tenant relations, and that too in favour of the tenant. More, the government had been persuaded to a large extent in this by Christian missionary pleas on behalf of tenants. Landlords pointed this out, com-plaining bitterly that missionaries incited peasants against rent and cess payments. In the 1840s, Christian villagers had, indeed, withheld rent payment in south-western Bengal and there were fears of Christian peasant 'rebellions'.[13]

The land question and the caste and religious question converged. The Lex Loci Act of 1850 had stipulated that Hindus converting to other religions (and thereby losing their caste status) would still retain their share of ancestral properties. The tightly structured cage of eco-nomic, caste and religious authority suddenly seemed to have sprung a few significant leaks. This was conjoined to the great fears generated by the currents of Wahhab and Faraizi reform movements in the 1830s and 1840s that assumed the shape of resisting the authority and de-mands of Hindu zamindars, with considerable violence, by Muslim ten-ants. In the case of the Islamic reform movements among peasants, the state had helped out Hindu men of property. But now that symbiosis—in social, religious and economic senses—began to look precarious.

This was only the beginning. From the early 1860s Calcutta High Court judges began a prolonged discussion on the tenant question. Of course, the immediate context was massive peasant resistance against the enforced cultivation of indigo and the oppressions of European planters. Here, of course peasants often worked together with local *taluqdars*. But so did Christian missionaries work on behalf of tenants against planters—of whom only the contributions of Reverend Long

---

[12]See Dietmar Rothermund, op.cit., pp. 100–5.

[13]See B.B. Chaudhury, op.cit., also G.A. Oddie, *Missionaries, Rebellion and Nationalism: James Long of Bengal, 1814–87* (London: Curzon Press, 1999).

are somewhat familiar to us. The ryot now assumed a new reality as a conscious, determined and autonomous political subject. The state stood amazed by the spectacle of tenant resistance. Let me cite the impact of the 'Blue Mutiny' against indigo planters upon a senior Bengali police officer who later wrote his memoirs:

> None could force ryots to desist from their pledge—we won't plant indigo. What a marvellous commitment ... Planters used to have such arrogance, wealth and power ... now all melted away like thin air ... Ryots went to prison in their thousands but they would not give in ... on their way to prison, they would be met by men, women and children of entire villages who would feed them and bless them ...[14]

Note the separate and exclusive stress on the heroic 'ryots' rather than on *taluqdars* or small zamindars—who also sometimes joined the movement.

Since this defiance was directed against racist European planters, the Bengali middle classes and the intelligentsia were, on the whole, sympathetic. But peasant defiance is always a double-edged weapon and the state began to pay a little more attention to the problems of this ryot.[15] An amendment to the 1859 Tenancy Act in 1869 removed the trial of rent cases from revenue to civil courts. Zamindars could earlier demand summary trials for a cluster of related cases together in the revenue courts, but in the civil courts each case against the tenant had to be individually settled—thus committing landlord litigants to vastly increased expenses and trouble. Lt.-Governor George Campbell was a man who had decided to ponder on the ryot question very seriously. He had made an earlier study of the Irish land question and had served for a period in North India, where the state had decided to settle revenue matters with groups of cultivators rather than through the mediation of landlords. Moreover, he was influenced by Ricardian economic thinking, which condemned rent as unearned income. All of this had predisposed him against the Permanent Settlement and the untrammelled power of Bengali landlords.

[14]Girishchandra Basu, *Sekaler Darogar Kahini,* in Kanchan Basu, ed., *Dushprapya Sahitya Sangraha* (Calcutta: Reflect Publications, 1992).

[15]See Dietmar Rothermund, op.cit.

Campbell imposed a road cess upon landlords, the proceeds of which were to go to fund elementary education—a field entirely neglected by the government, which relied on 'filtration effects' of higher education on mass levels: if the government sets up schools and colleges for a small 'creamy' layer, the educated classes will educate the masses on their own initiative. This Macaulayan conviction had, however, proved illusory. As late as 1888–9 higher education, funded primarily by Bengalis themselves, had seen a marked expansion, while the proportion of illiterates remained constant. The increase in colleges was 15 per cent over the previous year, English high schools by 8 per cent, middle schools by 4 per cent, while upper primary schools had increased only at the rate of 2 per cent and lower primary ones had actually declined by 9 per cent.[16] The colonial ruling class and the Bengali middle class were equally resistant to mass education. Campbell's scheme now seemed to suggest disturbing changes in the pattern of this happy complicity. Moreover, he also suggested that Bengali should be made the medium of instruction at the Guru Pathshalas set up for rural elementary education. These new schools were meant for the poorer social classes. The *Somprakash* expressed deep resentment at this use of a noble language for the edification of the vulgar masses. All kinds of privileges and distinctions seemed to be at stake.[17]

Moreover, the cess was based on rent rolls which would now be opened up to governmental scrutiny. This boded ill for landlords and increased their nervousness. 'The Lt. Governor's name has become a byword for whatever is unjust or crude,' threatened *Somprakash* at the beginning of 1873.[18] All these apprehensions were more than fulfilled later in the year when tenants—largely Muslim and low caste—combined in an extremely stubborn and powerful movement against Pabna landlords. The middle classes accused Campbell of masterly inactivity instead of determined repression, which, they said, sent dangerous signals to peasants.

Again, the aftermath of the uprising was followed not by renewed disciplinary powers in the hands of zamindars but by the appointment

---

[16] *Report on the Administration of Bengal, 1888–9* (Calcutta, 1889), p. 327.
[17] *Somprakash*, 4 January 1873, *Report on Native Papers* (Bengal, 1873).
[18] Ibid.

of the Rent Law Commission, which submitted its report in 1880. On its basis a further amendment was made to expand the category of protected tenants in 1885. Campbell, in the meantime, had been succeeded by Richard Temple who subscribed to his predecessor's views on the tenant question. The Liberal Viceroy Lord Ripon was also in favour of extending the rights of tenants to land under their cultivation. Ultimately, however, the proposals were much moderated on the advice of Sir Henry Maine, who pointed out that the principle of social justice would violate custom and prescription, which should be accorded priority.[19] This was an extremely significant argument, for in the next decades the same authority for custom and prescription would be claimed by Hindu revivalists against all notions of gender justice. Even though Maine managed to save much for the rural *pater familias*, the long years of waiting—as pro-tenant suggestions flew around official quarters—told on the loyalism of the middle classes who combined professional incomes with rent from land. Security of property was part of a larger complex of confidence bred out of caste, educational and gender privileges, all of which were threatened by liberal reformism, missionary initiative, and state legislation. Missionaries and reformers had earlier colluded in opening up education for girls, for controlling sati, and legalising widow remarriage, while missionaries had also argued for enlarging rural primary education for peasants and low castes. Much earlier the missionary, William Adam, had wanted this to be the major invetment area for government spending on education.[20] Macaulay had overruled his proposals in favour of elite education, and at higher levels. Now the favour seemed to be on the point of being withdrawn, or at least more equally distributed. Hunter suggested an equalisation of Muslim educational opportunities. Again, promises and suggestions did not bear actual fruit, but they certainly aggravated the nervousness of a proprietorial class of men who liked their monopoly on education to be seen as natural advantages and passports to power over women, non-Hindus, low castes and peasants.

The Pabna riots, I feel, finally did for Bengali gentlemen what 1857 had not been able to accomplish: it made nationalists out of them,

[19]See Dietmar Rothermund, *op.cit.*

[20]William Adam, *Second Report on the State of Eduction in Bengal, 1836,* edited by Anathnath Basu (Calcutta, 1941).

nationalists of an exceedingly strident and extremist variety. Educated unemployment was growing as consequence of a top-heavy educational structure that looked like an inverted pyramid, and which overpopulated the limited field of middle-class employment in the colonial world. Upon this fell the double crisis of investment. The Bengali *bhadralok* felt their last secure privileges slipping out of control with the Pabna riots.

There were significant dimensions to the representations of the riots in bhadralok discourse. Class anxieties were expressed as anxieties about the collapse of an entire order of privileges, most powerfully articulated through the motif of loss of caste and the loss of virtue in women. In June 1873 the *Amrita Bazar Patrika*, while still admitting zamindari coercion and oppression, compared rioters with Genghiz Khan. Their intention was, it said, 'To insult and destroy the caste of respectable men, to violate the chastity of females of gentle blood, to break into pieces the images of idols ...'[21] The *Halishahar Patrika* pointed out that most of the rebels were Muslim and the few Hindus who had joined them had done so reluctantly. 'Government stood by as properties were ruined, caste insulted ... the chastity of hundreds of females has been outraged.'[22] A letter to the editor of the *Amrita Bazar Patrika* written by a 'gentleman from Pabna' said that unless Hindu villagers joined rebels, 'female member of his family are carried off, some are dishonoured and others are made to submit to *neka* marriage.'[23]

The 1870s were also a time when the government began to discuss the situation of the lower castes as a separate issue in the context of census operations. A minimal amount of ameliorative gestures—especially in education, which had thus far been an upper-caste bhadralok preserve and source of distinction—could not be ruled out. It was also a time when the condition of Bengali Muslims was studied widely by senior officials like W.W. Hunter, who formulated the thesis of Muslim backwardness and urged the government to rectify it. If the Pabna riots had attacked the undue privileges of landlords, in the 1870s low-caste *chandal* peasants of East Bengal began to defy the scripture of caste Hindus, and

[21] 26 June 1873, *Report on Native Papers* (hereafter *RNP*), 1873.
[22] 4 July 1873, *RNP*, 1873.
[23] 26 June, *op.cit.*

organised a sect of their own under their chandal guru Haridas Thakur. Religious dissent was subsequently extended into a boycott of upper-caste landlords and a withdrawal of labour services to them.[24]

If lowly people threatened the bhadralok with insubordination, and if women, too, had been encouraged by reformism towards social questioning, then the state both aided them—however mildly—and further undercut the existing privileges and claims of Bengali gentlemen. Viceroy Lytton was outspoken in his contempt for 'baboos' whose education, he said, had made them get above themselves. He took every opportunity of curbing their freedom of expression in the late 1870s through a series of legislative infringements of civil rights. Lord Ripon, in contrast, as a Liberal, made efforts to equalise the functions of officials—Indian and European magistrates both being allowed to judge cases involving Europeans—thereby arousing great hopes of justice. Yet the Ilbert Bill backfired and released fumes of racial hatred from Europeans of a kind rarely expressed, and never so concentratedly and nakedly since the days of 1857. In fact, my argument that the Pabna riots made nationalists out of the bhadralok is somewhat unfair and partial. It was the astounding racism of the Lytton–Ilbert Bill years that led to that accomplishment. What the Pabna riots and the new missionary-reformist-state initiatives for mass education and rectification of some aspects of land relations did was destroy an earlier sense of impregnable securities written into the state structure. This had been a confidence that would even allow some amount of self-criticism and self-reform.

Middle-class fears and apprehensions now sedimented into a deposit that provided the soil for a new political sensibility. Structures of social authority—whether upper caste, gentry or masculine—could not bear any more injury, certainly no longer from within. Where introspection and self-correction had made some progress earlier—in the realm of thinking about gender relations, in particular—the trend now was to not only conserve tradition, prescription and custom but also to construct elaborate arguments in their defence. What was most important—as is evident from the Age of Consent controversies—was that this defence

[24]See Sekhar Bandyopadhya, *Caste, Protest and Identity in Colonial India: Namashudras of Bengal, 1872–1947* (London: Curzon Press, 1997).

relies on indigenism. The will to change or interrogate custom was accused of mimicking Western colonial knowledge, while status-quoism was linked to the survival of authentic norms.

While tradition was formally worshipped as both an absolute good and as the Absolutely Authentic, it was renovated by cultural nationalists to accommodate spaces for dangerously dissident lower orders. The late nineteenth century was a time of ardent Vaishnavism in Bengal, which denied the spiritual privileges of the brahman without significantly questioning the social dimensions of *varnashram* or caste hierarchies. Print was used to strengthen popular knowledge of key Hindu scriptures, which were also translated on a wide scale. Religious manuscripts were compiled—under the auspices from 1871 of Rajendralal Mitra—from villages, royal and zamindari collections, and households of pandits. The searches yielded a few surprises. While Bansberia in Hooghly, a noted old centre of Sanskrit learning, could provide nothing new, the household of Hitalal Mishra, an obscure landlord in the small village of Mankar at Burdwan, offered 500–600 volumes of rare manuscripts of Vedanta literature—even though Bengal had never been considered a fertile field for Vedantic studies.[25] We find that religious works—both annotated commentaries as well as Bengali popularisations of important Sanskrit texts—constituted a very large share of Bengali publications: as many as 171 works in 1887–8 and 249 in 1888–9.[26] The intelligentsia was trying to create a community out of enormously stratified Hindus on the basis of congregational devotion and a comprehensible and shared religious textual tradition. Prescription and custom would still provide the basis for a caste and class order, but now a willed embrace of that order was solicited from women, low castes, peasants.

IV

Under the Dayabhaga system of Hindu law that prevailed in Bengal, women neither inherited their father's land nor had a definite right to

[25] *Proceedings of the Asiatic Society of Bengal*, December–January 1873 (Calcutta, 1873).

[26] Reports on the Administration of Bengal, 1887–8 and 1888–9 (Calcutta, 1888 and 1889), pp. 302 and 328.

the land of their husbands. At most, they had usufruct rights on behalf of minor sons if they were widows.[27] If for daughters and wives of land-owners the absence of property rights led to a somewhat ambiguous class status, it was compounded by larger ambiguities about the notions of land and home. Women, given away in marriages that were made without their consent in early infancy, were ousted from the lineage they were born into and implanted upon a new one, of which they knew nothing at first. Patrilocal marriages similarly took them away from their natal homes and grafted them onto the household of complete strangers who might live far away.[28] Women's autobiographies express the sense of a rather thin integration with family and lineage, and with the land that these women possessed on both sides of the line. They would remain somewhat incomplete class and caste subjects, permanent refugees, in a sense, in both households.

E.P. Thompson has argued that notions of class derived from the categories of a fully industrialised society would be misleading were they applied to a different social formation. If nineteenth-century Bengal presented a more fluid and inchoate picture of class relations than those that obtain in an established capitalist structure, then we may have something to learn about the ways of understanding the social perspectives of subordinated groups in as-yet weakly industrialised societies from his study of eighteenth-century England. 'For what may define the consciousness of these groups more clearly will be such factors as their degree of dependence: that is, their dependence on or independence of the lines of interest, influence, preferments, and patronage which structured society from top to bottom.' Thompson also argues that tradesmen and artisans enjoyed a large degree of occupational independence from interest and patronage and were thereby able to nourish 'a more robust anti-court and sometimes republican consciousness.'[29]

[27]See R.L. Choudhury, *Hindu Womens' Right to Property: Past and Present* (Calcutta: Firma K.L. Mukhopadhyaya, 1961), pp. 1–6.

[28]See Rashsundari Debi, *Amar Jiban* (Calcutta, 1876); also my translation and discussion, *Words to Win: The Making of Amar Jiban, A Modern Autobiography* (Delhi, 1999).

[29]E.P. Thompson, *Witness Against the Beast: William Blake and the Moral Law* (New York: New Press, 1993), pp. 110–11.

With an upper-caste, affluent gentlewoman like Rashsundari, who published the first autobiography in the Bengal language in 1876, we find a far more complicated and compromised relationship with the distribution of social and economic power and influence. On the one hand, they were women of high caste, important families, enjoying economic security and solvency that fell to the lot of relatively few Bengalis of their times. They had power over their servants and even over their tenants and labourers. On the other hand they had little money to dispose of on their own. The Dayabhaga system had since the sixteenth century reduced the woman's access to *stridhan* or bridal gifts considerably.[30] Nor did they have absolute ownership rights over any form of property. They were people without incomes, more economically dependent on their families than labouring women. Within their families they were subjected to severe discipline and constraints on mobility, they provided service and deference through signs that were quite similar to those that low castes and classes expressed towards their social superiors. They were certainly not as implicated in the relations of class and caste domination and in the exploitation of tenants and labourers as their husbands and fathers.

The woman was, moreover, required to provide heavy unpaid and often unacknowledged labour at home. Rashsundari's memoirs show that she was as familiar with enforced starvation as the poorest labourer would have been. Such subordination within the family—to the same men who stood above low castes and peasants—ensured a space of relative autonomy, unmarked by the vested interests of the family. The autonomy was another name for sharing some of the marks of subordination with men and women of other castes and classes. Here men guarded more jealously against her education than they could against the literacy of poor people. Liberal reformers were mocked, lampooned, outcasted and physically attacked for starting schools for girls. The autonomy gave a somewhat different slant to the writings of women, after the 1860s, on the theme of the Hindu family. Precisely at a time of cultural nationalism that valorised the non-reformed woman as the resi-

---

[30]Sureshchandra Bandyopadhyaya, *Smritishastre Bangali* (Calcutta, A. Mukherjee, 1959), pp. 1–18.

due of past freedom and the nucleus of the future nation, women were sometimes outspoken in their criticism of past custom and in their celebration of modernity and its resources for women like themselves.[31]

However, the power and powerlessness of the woman made up a changing cycle, depending on the status of her husband, her possession of sons, her fertility, looks, health and capacity for domestic labour. The middle-aged mother of grown-up sons could be a powerful matriarch and elderly mothers-in-laws could command and oppress young wives. The woman would get more securely stitched into the fabric of lineage, caste and class at a later stage in her life cycle. We tend to absolutise male and female domains—this is so in much feminist writing—and see them as seamless blocs, forming opposites of total power and total powerlessness. Patriarchy, however, operates through far more complicated trajectories, with crisscrossing power lines that fracture both domains and that, at times, unite segments across the blocs. The same woman, depending on the presence of sons, her husband's status and fortune, and her age, gets to know both subjection and rule. This is why, and how, perhaps, women are, much of the time, complicit subjects of patriarchy.

V

Finally, a few acknowledgments. Neeladri Bhattacharya has spent a great deal of his time reading, encouraging and criticising virtually all that I have written over several years. I cannot thank him enough for his generosity. I am also most grateful to Jasodhara Bagchi for her friendship and helpfulness; and to Dr Jyotindra Jain, Senior Director, Crafts Museum, for help with the book jacket. Rukun Advani has been patient, kind, long-suffering and stimulating—and yet ruthless when editing. P.K. Datta provided criticism and suggestions of great value.

I have always found that research improves from the added responsibility of teaching, and I thank my students for coming up with questions that made me carefully consider my statement and positions.

I deeply appreciate the fact that, these days, Aditya tries seriously and thoughtfully to bring me up better. Had he started much earlier, he

---

[31]On nineteenth-century womens' writings, see my *Words to Win*, op.cit.

would have made a good job of it, I'm sure. Sumit, as always, makes thinking and writing possible for a person who, left to herself, would do little of either. The responsibility for the flaws and errors that remain in this book is entirely mine.

Earlier versions of some chapters within this book appeared in various journals: chapter one in *Studies in History*, N.S., vol. 8, no. 2, July–Dec. 1992; chapter two in (the same journal) N.S., vol. 13, no. 1, Jan.-June 1997; chapter three in *History Workshop Journal*, no. 36, Autumn 1993; chapter four in *Oxford Literary Review*, vol. 16, 1–2, 1994; chapter five in David Ludden, ed., *Making India Hindu* (Delhi: OUP, 1996); chapter six in Ratna Kapur, ed., *Feminist Terrains in Legal Domains* (Delhi: Kali for Women, 1996); and chapter eight in Alice Thorner & Maithreyi Krishnaraj, eds, *Ideals, Images and Real Lives: Women in Literature and History* (Hyderabad: Orient Longman, 2000).

CHAPTER ONE

Hindu Wife, Hindu Nation
Domesticity and Nationalism in Nineteenth-century Bengal

In nineteenth-century Bengal the intelligentsia was engaged in a convoluted critical exercise. This exercise involved interrogating power relationships within indigenous customs and traditions—especially gender norms within such customs—though there were definite patriarchal limits to this interrogation. The exercise involved, simultaneously, questioning the connections established between the local and the metropolitan—in short Bengal's overall colonial connection. The problems so interanimated and complicated one another that, far from reaching a resolution, Bengal's intelligentsia was unable to set itself an agenda with any absolute certainty. Emergent nationalist consciousness, which straddled a complex range of forms and possibilities, posed yet more questions and doubts to settled convictions instead of offering any clear answers.

It is perhaps time to remind ourselves that colonisation did not necessarily simplify the range of questions and problems for the colonised. Recent historiographical and cultural studies sometimes tend to reduce the whole complex enterprise of colonialism to the manageable yet impoverished proportions of a crude binary framework: whether the local assented to or refused the structures of colonialism. Further surgeries displace these structures from the realm of colonial political economy into a conveniently attenuated rump of the epistemological and ontological aspects of colonial mastery—these are now to be regarded as the *real* structures. The recent historiographical shift further simplifies its task by locating these structures in a single form of Western power-knowledge with monolithic and fixed signs. A flat, uninflected, deductive, structural determinism then reads the consciousness of the colonised mechanically off these signs. Moreover, since these signs are vested with totalitarian powers, the consciousness of the colonised is divested of all claims to an autonomous life and made parasitic upon the master discourse of colonialism. This discourse supposedly constitutes the iron cage of language and meaning within which the colonised mind may only perform mimetic gestures.[1]

There is no denying that colonialism spawned the nineteenth-century intelligentsia. It is equally true that the history of the new middle classes was marked by many absences and voids—the absence of economic and political leadership being dominant and constitutive. The aftermath of 1857 left little doubt about the coercive and violent aspects of colonial rule. The sense of racial discrimination was heightened steadily through Lyttonian repression in the 1870s: the vernacular press and the theatre were muzzled, the Indian population was forcibly disarmed. The rabidly racist rhetoric during the Ilbert Bill agitation of the 1880s and a relatively moderate government's capitulation to it constituted crowning proof. Given the new political conditions, which largely demystified colonial myths about their non-discriminating fairness and the existence of a rule of law, Bengal's earlier reformism soon got over its hopeful youth. The Brahmos were split right down the middle and Vidyasagar spent his last few days in bitter disillusionment over his own agenda.[2] Earlier creative innovations within the new arena of education lost their initiative: a standardised and officialised uniform education policy proceeded to unfold itself from the 1880s.[3] The initiative would not be recovered till the time of the Swadeshi Movement.

[1] Edward Said's *Orientalism* (London, 1978) has acquired enormous canonical value for recent perspectives on the colonial period. For an equally influential application of Saidian dicta, see Partha Chatterjee, *Nationalist Thought and the Colonial World: A Derivative Discourse?* (Delhi, 1986).

[2] See Asok Sen, *Iswar Chandra Vidyasagar & His Elusive Milestones* (Calcutta, 1977). In fact, the presumed naive faith and hope of the early reformers can be looked at very differently. For a more pessimistic reading of that phase, see Sumit Sarkar, 'The Complexities of Young Bengal', *A Critique of Colonial India* (Calcutta, 1985).

[3] All experimentation with courses and pedagogic methods gradually dried up

The formation of a nineteenth-century political sphere is usually located within the religious and political associations that began to acquire pan-Indian aspirations from the 1870s. An alternative and often opposed area is seen as constituted by mass protest movements—tribal revolts, the Indigo mutiny, the Pabna riots, the post-1870s agrarian unrest within which sections of the bhadralok could participate as critical/sympathetic observers, active sympathisers and sometimes even as leaders. In the late-nineteenth-century middle-class context, however, the politics of associations, of self-government bodies and of lower-class protest acquired immediacy and substance largely through the mediation of vernacular printed journals which described these developments in close and vivid detail, and opened up such activity to widespread debate and comment.[4] The debate did not stop there. The public sphere, at this stage, remained integrally linked to domestic issues. A substantial number of journals and newspapers came into existence to debate issues of sati, kulin marriage, widow remarriage[5]—domestic issues which generated a wide range of authors and readers, from Bankimchandra to Battala farces.

Bengali prose, contrary to established belief, was not the creation of the Serampore Baptist Mission or the Fort William College: it had a longer and authentically home-grown lineage. Certainly, starting from the sixteenth century, and particularly in the eighteenth century, Bengali prose developed a number of crucial features and reasonable fluency through the exercise of an epistolary tradition; through Vaishnavite

---

after the Despatch of 1854 which introduced a drab uniformity through a systematic examination system. See Romesh Chandra Mitra, 'Education: 1833–1905', in N.K. Sinha (ed.), *The History of Bengal, 1757–1905* (Calcutta, 1967). See also Kissory Chand Mitra, *On the Progress of Education in Bengal* (July 1887), reprinted in *Nineteenth Century Studies* (January 1975).

[4]See Swarajit Chakraborti, *The Bengali Press, 1818–1868—A Study in the Growth of Public Opinion* (Calcutta, 1976). According to Rev. Long's evidence before the Indigo Commission, in 1860, the controversy on widow remarriage alone gave birth to twenty-five new publications in the vernacular press and the issues of early marriage and female education were similarly widely discussed. Benoy Ghose, 'The Press in Bengal', in N.K. Sinha (ed.), *The History of Bengal*, op.cit., p. 227.

[5]Ibid.

theological expositions; and through descriptions of pilgrimage.[6] Missionary and colonial efforts contributed a significant but by no means formative moment in this much larger process. Print culture, far from displacing earlier traditions and freezing writing habits into cultural translations of foreign norms, actually continued and expanded many of the earlier conventions. Vaishnavite literature, for instance, continued to form a substantial part of the new printed material. Nor were the new print forms a displacement and marginalisation of earlier popular oral-performative traditions, substituting for them a single line of new, largely derivative and sanitised, educated-middle-class values. Much of the recent work on nineteenth-century new Bengali culture, which is eager to brand this culture as alienated and elitist, chooses to wander only within elitist productions, counterposing this with a rather utopian, healthy, sensual, earthy, popular pre-colonial cultural past.[7]

Not only were there very substantial popular writing traditions even before the entry of print, the fact is that print itself stimulated new expressions of urban popular culture—the theatre, woodcut prints, Battala literature. Battala groups of minuscule yet numerous and highly solvent publisher-printers produced a large corpus of cheap booklets, tracts and pamphlets—mostly pulp, but also a significant volume of serious religious work.[8] These were written by and for a literate but little-educated, sprawling readership and authorship which rarely read or wrote anything else. Up to the 1940s these presses had a rapid turnover, enormously brisk sales, and continuous production.[9] Cheap woodcut prints, and later oleographs, similarly carried pictures of religious matters, of current scandal, and of the new city elite into a much larger number of lower-middle-class and even rural homes.[10]

[6]Asit Kumar Bandyopadhyay, *Bangla Sahityer Itibritta*, vol. IV (Calcutta, 1985). See also vol. V (Calcutta, 1985).

[7]This seems to constitute the consensus about the new printed prose in several articles in Svati Joshi (ed.), *Rethinking English: Essays in Literature, Language, History* (New Delhi, 1992). See also Sumanta Banerjea, 'Marginalization of Women's Popular Culture in Nineteenth-century Bengal', in Kumkum Sangari and Sudesh Vaid (eds), *Recasting Women: Essays in Colonial History* (Delhi, 1989).

[8]Asit Kumar Bandyopadhyay, *Bangla Sahityer Itibritta*, vol. V.

[9]See Bireswar Bandyopadhya, *Heto Bai, Heto Chhara* (Calcutta, 1984).

[10]William G. Archer, *Bazar Paintings of Calcutta* (London, 1953). Regarding

The new Calcutta theatre, again, boomed largely through lower-middle-class patronage, and, in its turn, stimulated the growth of print through the continuous turnout of play scripts. In the Battala areas of North Calcutta, even today, small printing presses and tiny theatre groups (called 'operas') jostle with each other, creating an unbroken circuit of script publishers and playhouses and even of actors and actresses. The red light area of Chitpur Road borders on it and this, in the nineteenth century, was the main source for the supply of actresses. The success of the theatre depended significantly upon lower-middle-class themes and preferences. While the classical themes and chaste language of Madhusudan Dutt's early plays were displayed to depressingly empty halls, the fortunes of the lately established Bengal Theatre picked up and flourished in the early 1870s with the performance of a popular farce—*Mohanter Ei Ki Kaj*. This play enacted a scandal that had rocked the popular imagination when the mohunt of the Tarakeswar pilgrimage seduced a young girl who was, later, murdered by her husband—an employee, interestingly, at a printing press.[11]

Print revolutionised reading habits and possibilities. It penetrated into all sorts of times and spaces within everyday life by its sheer portability. Earlier, manuscripts were extremely rare commodities with a slow and thinly spread-out circulation. Moreover, the reading time and space devoted to them had to be carefully selected and limited: they were inscribed on heavy yet fragile paper which was pressed together between flat wooden covers and not sewn because sewing would have strained the delicate material. Each page had to be carefully extracted from between the wooden pattas, read, and then restored to its proper place. This whole complicated, delicate and time-consuming reading exercise could be carried out only at special times and places and involved fixed postures. The new, plentiful, cheap, portable and replicable printed books, in contrast, inserted themselves into all kinds of times and spaces effortlessly. This unprecedented and easy availability was augmented by the

---

the circulation of reading matter, visual and art objects, and cultural performances within a popular circuit, see Jyotindra Jain, *Kalighat Paintings: Images from a Changing World* (Ahmedabad: Mapin, 1999).

[11]See Brajendranath Bandyopadhyay, *Bangiya Natyashalar Itihas, 1795–1876* (Calcutta, 1943), p. 151.

introduction of primers and textbooks in school and pathshalas. Earlier, pathshala training largely comprised oral arithmetic and the acquiring of writing skills, usually to the exclusion of reading matter of any sort. Students normally read only what they themselves wrote, following set pieces dictated from memory by the teacher.[12] New educational institutions reversed this process, and the proportion between reading and writing. Within the confines of a limited class, reading became a non-specialised, fluid, pervasive, everyday activity. This is why vernacular presses developed and proliferated, provoking comment from many observers of contemporary society.

The growth of vernacular prose and the press made possible the incorporation of a new range of themes within literate culture which neither the English works, nor classical Sanskrit/Persian education, nor theological and imaginative literature could have included within their scope: themes concerning everyday life. In the Bengali language catalogues of the Imperial Library holdings, for the three decades between the 1870s and the 1890s roughly half of all prose works deal with problems pertaining to the organisation of everyday living. Simultaneous with the entry of these new themes, an extended range of new authors was created. A cross-section of thinking men, and even a few exceptionally fortunate women, could, without formal learning, develop and express ideas within a public debate over the shape of their own daily lives. A vast range of 'non-authors' could at least follow the debates on themes involving themselves. Within this shared yet contested enterprise, the middle class could recuperate something of what it lacked, in terms of an articulated position, within the production process and the power structure. By marking out an autonomous discursive field of force, which drew within its orbit men as well as a few women, highly educated professionals as well as petty clerks, artists, artisans, hack writers and theatre persons, the Bengali middle class was certainly present at its own making.

This autonomy was expressed primarily through a paradox. A deep, pervasive awareness of political subjection did not elicit from this class

---

[12]See Kazi Shahidullah, *Pathshalas into Schools: The Development of Indigenous Elementary Education in Bengal, 1854–1905* (Calcutta, 1987).

of people, for a long time, any direct or explicit demand for independence. What it did was to make the middle class dourly deny its own
energies, to refuse any description of itself except those that were deeply
negative and bleak. Early reformist expectations of radical social improvement or Moderate nationalistic assertions about the 'providential
nature of the British connection' might indicate an optimism about
prospects under colonialism; yet the hopes were usually brittle and small.
They stemmed from sporadic, rather tentative, expectations of strictly
specific gains rather than from grand visions of emancipatory possibilities. The general run of popular observation as well as more erudite
literary production would equally characterise present time as degenerate, recasting the old trope of kaliyug to express new kinds of anxiety
about a modernity ushered in under alien direction.[13]

For a long time, unease about foreign rule would be obliquely
expressed through a critique of modern times. Spectacular changes,
technological growth and breakthroughs that were revolutionising their
own life and experiences—railways, electricity, telegraph, urban growth,
city crowds, street scenes—were steadfastly refused recognition into
the symbolic order of these sections of people, except in a tangential
and negative sense. It is disconcerting to find how scantily Calcutta
was being represented as a city, whether in Bankim's novels, or in bazaar
paintings, or in woodcut pictures which dwell on domestic situations
and interior scenes. The only comments on the city centred on a series
of bans that restricted public civic activities.[14] In 1829 the newspaper

[13]For the reorientation of this traditional myth under colonial conditions, see
Sumit Sarkar, 'The Kalki Avatar of Bikrampur: A Village Scandal in Early Twentieth-
Century Bengal', in Ranajit Guha (ed.), *Subaltern Studies VI: Writings on South
Asian History & Society* (Delhi, 1989).

[14]A survey of excerpts from a collection of mid-nineteenth-century newspapers—among other things—indicates that while most technological breakthroughs went largely ignored, Calcutta registered itself as a city which forced the
indigenous urban population into recasting their ingrained bodily disposition
and public activities according to strange, uncustomary norms imposed by the city's
rulers. A ban on religious processions with music was seen with apprehension:
'now our officials are publicly opposing Hindu religion.' The streets were to be
withdrawn from the sphere of religious activity. (*Sambad Prabhakar*, editorial, 12/
December 1858.) A similar reaction followed the ban on urinating in public places

Bangadoot had pioneered one of the first definitions of the new middle class. It was then described in terms of a marked increase in the size and circulation of wealth.[15] In the last few decades of the century, vernacular journals were unanimous in their description of a diseased, unproductive, morally decaying bhadralok.

II

Middle-class Bengalis chose to read certain features of their physical and economic environment obsessively, as symptomatic elements, as metaphors of their larger condition. It seems useful to point out some of the physical and economic changes which particularly engaged their attention, and the ways in which these were used as narrative devices to describe their lives and times.

Concrete physical reasons shaped much of the bleak mental landscape which the nineteenth-century middle class inhabited. The Hindu nationalists of these times belonged largely to Calcutta or to the western, southern and central parts of the province which had been, for the

---

by Indians. The ban was read as a forced Westernisation of bodily gestures as well as a sign of racial discrimination. 'We are poor Bengalis, much oppressed by officials . . . . Whenever Sahibs feel like urinating, they stand like palm trees, choose the wall of a (native) gentleman's house and then let go of a stream of piss . . . . The pissing law should be the same for everyone.' (Ibid., 2 August 1858.) A complexly inflected text uses the device of newly departed Bengali souls reporting on major changes in the city to ones long dead. While the obvious format is that of deadpan, factual reportage, the balance sheet carefully and unobtrusively stacks up very minor, unimportant gains on the credit side while the debit sheet reveals the loss of fundamental values. They start with the replanting of public parks with colourful but unfragrant Western flowers replacing the white, fragrant Indian varieties. At the end they build up to larger and more direct comments: 'The Legislative Assembly is displacing Dharmashastras. Now one freely retains ancestral property even while changing religion and adulterous widows inherit their husband's property without difficulty.' This refers to a new ruling that the widow's moral standing would not prevent her from inheriting the husband's property. It raised a storm of protest from the city's prominent gentlemen. Haranath Bhanja, *Suraloke Banger Parichay* (1875; rpt Calcutta, 1976).

[15] *Bangadoot*, 1829. Cited in R.C. Majumdar, *History of Modern Bengal, Part I, 1765–1905* (Calcutta, 1975), p. 253.

past several centuries, the key cultural zones of the region. This region as a whole was the home of Vaishnavite Bhakti as well as of Shakta music and poetry, of the Bengal school of Navyanyaya philosophy, of Tantric practices and Smarta orthodoxy, and of esoteric and syncretic popular religious sects. It saw, too, the rise of the Bengal school of temple architecture. Large zamindari estates provided patronage to art and manufacture, while the growth of foreign trade from the seventeenth century stimulated local artisanal, commercial and peasant economies.[16] The rise of the port of Hooghly bore testimony to the growth of new commerce.[17] Political turbulence and economic disasters over the eighteenth century, however, combined to fearfully destabilise the entire region. Eighteenth-century Shakta devotional poetry expressed these experiences in terms of existential uncertainties: coming back again and again to the unknowable countenance and the inscrutable intentions of the Divine Mother.[18]

From the late seventeenth century, and especially throughout the eighteenth century, the very land itself went through a major crisis.[19] The western arm of the Ganga, which bore most of the river's water-flow, gradually silted up, leading to the formation of a moribund delta in this region.[20] Productivity was lowered markedly due to frequent inundation: by the 1830s, some of the land which had yielded two crops a year was producing a harvest only every three or four years.[21] Low food-supply weakened the Bengali constitution and made it vulnerable to the fevers and epidemics of stagnant waters: the Burdwan or Hooghly fever which was a great killer; cholera epidemics from 1817;

[16]Hitesranjan Sanyal, *Social Mobility in Bengal* (Calcutta, 1981), pp. 36–44.

[17]See P.J. Marshall, *Bengal: The British Period in Eastern India 1740–1828* (Cambridge, 1987), pp. 25–9, 139.

[18]See a discussion on Shakta poetry in Shashibhushan Dasgupta, *Bharater Shakti Sadhana O Shakta Sahitya* (Calcutta, 1960).

[19]Frank, Perlin, 'Proto Industrialisation and Pre-Colonial South Asia', *Past & Present*, 1983, p. 56. Although he ascribes the major structural changes to a period well before the establishment of colonial rule, there is no doubt that colonial innovations and interferences sharpened the processes in the nineteenth century.

[20]Marshall, *Bengal*, p. 4. It is interesting that findings about the formation of the moribund delta became widely known by 1833.

[21]Ibid.

and the smallpox that raged once every seven years.[22] The silted-up waters, which became more stagnant with the construction of railway embankments from mid-century by the colonial state, produced the malaria-bearing anopheles mosquito, causing 'remittent' and 'intermittent' fevers which went undiagnosed till 1897.[23] Little children, women of childbearing age, and poor agricultural labourers were most prone to all of these,[24] but there was a marked and widespread decline of health.

A dread of prolonged and fatally weakening fevers, and of sudden and unexpected epidemics, structured the self-awareness of Bengalis. Enough ecological information had come in by the first three decades of the century[25] to build up a pessimistic picture of the land, the air, and the people. Contrasts between an earlier era and present times were most often made in terms of impaired health.[26] The woman in much of nineteenth-century literature presides over the sick bed.[27] Interestingly even though children, young women and agricultural labourers were the worst victims of fevers and epidemics, it was the vulnerability and degeneration of the body of the Hindu male babu which became the most significant sign of the times. One might even say that this is how the Bengali middle class sought to express its hegemonic aspirations; not by attributing to itself political or economic leadership roles, not through claims to power, but through ascribing to itself all the ills and deprivations that marked nineteenth-century Bengali society as a whole.

As the volume of water flowing down the Hooghly branch of the Ganga shrank, and as early colonial depredations shattered established economic and political patterns, a number of flourishing commercial, manufacturing and administrative centres went into decline. The decay

[22]Chowdhury, 'Agrarian Economy & Agrarian Relations in Bengal 1858–1885', in N.K. Sinha (ed.), *The History of Bengal*, pp. 241–3. Also Marshall, *Bengal*, pp. 5, 18–19.

[23]Ibid.

[24]Chowdhury, 'Agrarian Economy', pp. 243–4. Also Marshall, *Bengal*, p. 20.

[25]Marshall, *Bengal*, p. 4.

[26]See, for instance, Rajnarayan Basu, *Sekal O Ekal* (reprinted Calcutta, 1988), pp. 31–6.

[27]*Garhasthya* (monthly journal: Calcutta, 1884).

of the great port of Hooghly was dramatic. The ruin of Dacca—though this did not lie on the moribund delta—caused extensive comment. Malda, Murshidabad, Krishnanagore, Vishnupur—all were broken cities.[28] In course of his boat rides in the early years of the century, Diwan Kartikeya Chandra Ray passed along a whole string of ruined towns, decaying with disease and destitution and teeming with ghost stories: of how travellers would return home to find their once-flourishing habitations entirely taken over by the spirits of the dead.[29] Mid-century famines and ravages caused by forced indigo cultivation by white planters led to havoc and panic in rural areas. Bengali journalists agitated extensively over these issues.[30] The sense of depression produced by such sights and news came to make larger sense when they were fitted into a framework of systematic, critical knowledge shaped by theories of drain, deindustrialisation and poverty.

The growth of the colonial urban sector provided little comfort or hope. The higher reaches of the new liberal professions were racially structured and congested. The massive tertiary sector provided scope only for very small-scale investment. The larger part of the middle class found employment as petty clerks in foreign administrative or commercial establishments. In the discourse of the master race, manhood was defined not just through financial solvency but by the nature of relationship to property. A passive and subordinate working life produced, therefore, a deep sense of emasculation.

Yet, in the early decades, the bhadralok had seemed poised on the brink of a major entrepreneurial breakthrough when several wealthy Calcutta houses began to make substantial fortunes from shipping, insurance, mining and some foreign trade.[31] The boom was over by the 1840s, and after the 1860s hardly any new fortunes were made

[28]Marshall, *Bengal*, pp. 160–1.

[29]*Diwan Kartikeyachandra Rayer Atmajiban Charit* (Calcutta, reprinted 1956), pp. 36–9.

[30]Ghose, 'The Press in Bengal'. See also Chakraborti, *The Bengali Press*.

[31]See Nilmoni Mukherji, 'Foreign and Inland Trade' in Sinha (ed.), pp. 339–62. Also Sabyasachi Bhattacharya, 'Traders and Trade in Old Calcutta', in Sukanta Chaudhuri (ed.), *Calcutta: The Living City*, vol. I (Calcutta 1990), pp. 204–8. Also Marshall, *Bengal*, pp. 166–7.

that way. Hopes of business success had already formed a new economic vocabulary. Debendranath Tagore talks in his autobiography
about the failure of their business enterprise as the time 'when we lost
all our property',[32] even though the Jorasanko Tagores still retained
substantial rural estates and a solid Calcutta establishment. Property,
for some time at least, meant a specific kind of activity, i.e. business.
Significantly, an elegy to the lost golden era of Bengali entrepreneurship was composed in the early 1870s when a biography of a Bengali
business magnate described Ramdulal Dey's financial success as a condition of self-respect and even political equality.[33] Perhaps, even more
significantly, the book was reprinted in 1978 when a further round of
flight-of-capital had taken place in West Bengal.[34]

Bengali capital was to be tied up largely in urban real estate and rural
landholding, which did not require much acumen or entrepreneurship, and in local trade, which had little potential for growth.[35] By the
late nineteenth century the second rung in business activities had been
monopolised by Marwaris, the top rung having already long been an
European preserve. By the mid-nineteenth century Bengalis had only
a marginal presence in Burrabazaar—the heart of indigenous business
in Calcutta.[36]

Colesworthy Grant has left a vivid description of Burrabazaar in 1850.
It reveals that the bulk of goods circulating from here were foreign
imports.[37] What made matters worse was that these imports were most
often luxury articles or modern, household utensils that were replacing
indigenous products: Lal Behari Dey's novel on Bengali peasant life in

[32]Debendranath Tagore, *Atmacharit* (Calcutta, 1898), reprinted in *Atmakatha*
(Calcutta, 1981).

[33]Girish Ghosh, *Ramdoolal Dey: The Bengali Millionaire* (Calcutta, reprint
1978). The book, though undated, seems to have been published in 1878. Around
the same time Kissori Chand Mitra delivered a lecture on the life of Motilal Sil,
in a very similar vein, calling him the 'Rothschild of Calcutta'. See Pradip Sinha's
'Foreword' to *Ramdulal Dey*.

[34]See Sinha's 'Foreword' written in 1978.

[35]Marshall, *Bengal*, p. 13.

[36]Bhattacharya, 'Traders and Trade in Old Calcutta'.

[37]Ibid.

the 1870s noted their penetration into even tiny village fairs.[38] A late-nineteenth-century autobiography describes the disappearance of flint with the influx of foreign matchboxes. This was taken to denote the disappearance of honest labour and self-sufficiency—driven away by a laziness which led to enslavement.[39] *Sambad Prabhakar* complained in 1892: 'The Lakshmi of sound commerce has abandoned Bengal. Mother Bengal now produces coolies and clerks alone.' The tragedy was caused, said the paper, by a self-destructive inclination towards easier or more luxurious foreign alternatives.[40]

Women were primarily responsible for deciding household purchases. They, therefore, served as the target of both nationalist appeal and blame. A large body of tracts and folk art depicted the modern woman as a self-indulgent, spoilt and lazy creature who cared nothing for family or national fortune. This charge encompasses the triadic relationship between women, gold and servitude—*kamini, kanchan, dasatva*—that the nineteenth-century saint Ramakrishna was to engrave so deeply upon the Bengali moral order.[41] The archetypal evil woman of these times was not the immoral or the economically independent one, but one who, inspired by modern education, had exchanged sacred ritual objects (the conchshell bangle, the ritually pure fabric, sindur) for foreign luxury ones.[42] There was thus an interchange between economic compulsions and pleas for feminine commitment to ritual.

The rent–revenue gap that the Permanent Settlement had generated and guaranteed had constituted the major security area for Bengal's middle-class bhadralok. It had ensured a whole spectrum of fairly comfortable rentier incomes at many levels. Certainties of absolute

[38]Rev. Lal Behari Dey, *Bengal Peasant Life* (1878; reprinted Calcutta, 1970).

[39]Dinendra Kumar Ray, *Pallichitra* (Calcutta, 1904; reprinted Calcutta, 1981), p. 30.

[40]*Sambad Prabhakar*, 11.8.1892 in Ghosh, (ed.), *Samayik Patre Banglar Samaj-chitra* (Calcutta, 1978), p. 127.

[41]Sumit Sarkar, 'Kaliyug, Chakri and Bhakti: Ramakrishna and His Times', *Economic and Political Weekly,* 18 July 1992.

[42]See Tanika Sarkar, 'Nationalist Iconography: The Image of Women in Nine-teenth-Century Bengali Literature' in *Economic and Political Weekly*, 21 November 1987, reproduced with changes as chapter 8 within the present volume.

manipulative power over rent began to be breached—though in a very limited sense—from the mid-nineteenth century by the Rent Acts of 1859 and 1885. They intended to give a measure of security to upper tenants and curb some of the arbitrary coercive powers exercised by the landlord's kutcheries on unofficial courts-cum-dungeons. The Rent Act of 1859 had come about partly as a result of missionary pleas on behalf of the tenant.[43] Missionary-inspired colonial interference into the hitherto closed world of largely upper-caste Hindu zamindar and the lower-caste or Muslim peasant was curiously coextensive with very similar intrusions into the closed world of Hindu domestic practices. Both aroused a keen sense of the fragility of economic and domestic arrangements that had cushioned some of the traumas of the Hindu bhadralok. After the 1859 Act, landlords had been complaining that the loss of disciplinary power had eroded their moral authority and affected rent collection. The grievance closely parallels the dirges that were composed over each colonial or reformist suggestion for new conjugal laws. Clearly, the moral order of Hindu patriarchy was in peril.

If an alien, imposed modernity was represented as a series of deprivations, then nationalism could situate its emancipatory project only by enclosing a space that was still understood as inviolate, autonomous. Much of nineteenth-century nationalism identified this space as the 'Hindu way of life'. The fundamental distinction between reformers and Hindu nationalists of the nineteenth century did not lie in the fact that the former were less patriotic or that the latter were more rooted in indigenous tradition. It stemmed from two different readings of Hindu domestic practices and custom. While liberal reformers described them as a distortion of earlier purity and a major symptom of present decay, Hindu nationalists celebrated them as an excess reserved over and above colonisation, any change in which would signify the surrender of the last bastion of freedom. 'That household is our motherland, that family is our India', affirmed a tract on marriage, referring to the network of intimate human relationships into which lost independence had been folded back.[44] Colonisation had made it imperative to introduce an

[43]Chowdhury, *Agrarian Economy*, pp. 295–9.
[44]Chandra Kumar Bhattacharya, *Banga Vivaha* (Calcutta, 1881), p. 51.

absolute distinction between the Self and the Other, while emergent nationalism made it equally imperative to stake out claims to sole representational authority over the self.

It would be wrong to imagine that the middle class did not write about things beyond itself. Energetic enquiries were made into obscure religious cults and festivals; folk tales and poetic traditions were compiled; there were antiquarian and ethnographic surveys galore. Prizes were offered for writing plays on peasants and reports were written on peasant risings and Assam tea-plantation labourers. Yet at every point a troubled intelligentsia, keenly aware of the absence of organic links with any stable social formations in the past and the present, and of the fragility of its social moorings, felt unable to distinguish confidently the nature of its enterprise: was it anthropology or was it autobiography? What was being probed? The Self or the Other? It was in the representation of their own women that the tension was most acute and productive, the ambiguity at its richest. The object of investigation was enclosed within the Self, was immediately outside it, and was possibly opposed to it. The enquires were therefore endless.

The concern with domestic practice initiated much discussion and debate. The consequent transparency of concrete practices demystified the self-legitimising arguments around custom and, eventually, put far too many strains on the commitment to it. The Hindu nationalist agenda consequently moved out of the area of human relationships into the more public and reified domain of social service and patriotism towards the turn of the century. I would, then, relocate some of the vital beginnings of Bengali nationalism away from the recognised issues in the political sphere and into the politics of relationships within the family.

III

The Hindu home was the one sphere where improvement could be made through personal initiative, and changes wrought whereby education would bring forth concrete, manipulable, desired results.[45]

---

[45]A mechanical application of a simple divide between the home and the world is derived from an untenable extension of a mid-nineteenth-century Victorian

The home, then, had to substitute for the world outside and for all the work and relations there that lay beyond personal comprehension and control. 'Just as the King reigns over his dominion, so the head of the household (karta) rules over his household'[46]—began a mid-nineteenth-century tract on domestic management. 'The karta sometimes rules like a King, sometimes needs to legislate like the lawgiver and sometimes he adjudicates like the chief justice,'[47] said another. 'Whoever can run a Hindu family can administer a whole realm'[48] was an assertion frequently made within this body of writing. Yet another tract advised the karta on how to marshall his forces to face a rebellious woman within the family.[49] The karta, therefore, becomes within the home what he can never aspire to be outside it—a ruler, an administrator, a legislator or a chief justice, a general marshalling his troops. Apart from compensatory functions, the strategic placement of the home assumes other functions as well. The management of household relations becomes a political and administrative capability, providing training in governance that one no longer attains in the political sphere. The intention is to establish a claim to a share of power in the world, a political role that the Hindu is entitled to, via successful governance of the household. A possibly unintended consequence, however, is that in the process this renders household relations into political ones.

This was an unintended consequence because the Hindu nationalist

---

situation into a very different socio-political context. Partha Chatterjee argues along the lines of a series of binaries since he sees the nineteenth century 'nationalist' agenda as being a mimetic gesture. See Partha Chatterjee, 'The Nationalist Resolution of the Women Question' in Sangari and Vaid (eds), *Recasting Women*. The concept of the Victorian home and its separation from the public sphere, again, is an undifferentiated social construct, taking an active entrepreneurial segment as representative of the middle class. For a very different positioning of the domestic sphere within a less activist, non-entrepreneurial world of the clergy, see Howard M. Wach, 'A "still, small voice" from the Pulpit: Religion and the Creation of Social Morality in Manchester, 1820–1850', *The Journal of Modern History*, September 1991.

[46]Narayan Ray, *Bangamahila* (Calcutta, n.d.), p. 51.

[47]*Garhasthya* (monthly journal: Calcutta, 1884), p. 1.

[48]Monomohan Basu, *Hindur Achar Vyavahar* (Calcutta, *c.* 1872), p. 99.

[49]Chandrakanta Basu, *Sangjam Shiksha* (Calcutta, *c.* 1904), p. 81.

strategy centred its critique of colonialism primarily on the loveless, purely deprivational, unrequited nature of its political arrangement, an arrangement which endowed the dominant group with absolute power and profits and the subject people with helpless surrender— with no possibility of self-fulfilment. If the home was not merely an escape from this world but its critique and an alternative order in itself, then love and affect had to be the organising principle of this inner, hidden nation, and the exercise of power needed to be replaced with the notion of self-surrender and general self-fulfilment. Household relations had to be shown as supra-political ones, relations of power represented as purely emotional states.

Out of the entire gamut of household relations, conjugality was found to be ideally relevant to this project. Conjugality was based on the apparent absolutism of one partner and the total subordination of the other. As such, it was the one relationship that seemed most precisely to replicate colonial arrangements. Hence, this would best constitute the grounds for challenging and contesting colonial arrangements—i.e. by showing the supposedly real and radical difference between the two sets of relationships despite their apparently similar basis, and by establishing where the moral superiority of the one lay over the other. Success in this endeavour would then lend political strength to the opposition against reformist-cum-colonial-cum-missionary intervention into conjugality which had begun with renewed vigour from the 1870s—the Brahmo Marriage Act of 1873, proposals to introduce divorce in the 1880s, and the Age of Consent Act of 1891.[50]

Conjugality provided a variety of possible registers which could test, confirm or contest the Hindu's political condition. Conceived as an embryonic nation, this relationship could also define ingrained Hindu dispositions that might mirror or correct or criticise and overturn the values structuring colonialism. Virtues accumulated through proper expertise in conjugality could equip the man to a share of power in the world; equally, proof of the absence of moral leadership here would disqualify him and explain his subjection. The terms for describing

[50]See Tanika Sarkar, 'Conjugality and Hindu Nationalism', chapter six in the present volume.

Hindu marriage, then, also formed a language for rethinking relations in the political world and allowed Hindus to articulate both worlds simultaneously, even as they appeared to speak of only one or the other. A satirical poem conveyed this double message:

> The Bengali male goes out
> And gets thrashed everywhere he goes
> The Bengali male appears terrible only within his home.[51]

While its chief intention is to portray the husband's tyranny at home, the poem simultaneously refers to the colonial order which has deprived him of everything except the right to domestic tyranny.[52]

As we have already seen, Hindu nationalists needed to naturalise love as the basis for Hindu marriage, a higher form of love that excelled allegedly utilitarian, materialist and narrowly contractual Western arrangements. They argued that non-consensual Hindu marriages could, indeed, be more loving than the Western pattern of courtship based on class and property qualifications more than on love. In the Hindu case, a lifetime of togetherness beginning with infancy guaranteed a superior and more certain compatibility. Nationalists denied that the production of sons was the sole aim of Hindu marriage: they argued it was a complete spiritual union through perfect love. It was also kinder to women since it ensured not just a hold on the husband's affection but an integration with the family which gave her greater security. While the entire system of non-consensual, indissoluble, infant marriage was to be preserved intact and inviolate, each aspect of

---

[51]Surendranath Majumdar, *Mahila* (Calcutta, *c.* 1880), p. 4.

[52]The narrowly political intention is enriched by the admission of socio-political deprivations and emasculation of the Bengali male. Love within conjugality is evoked as a restorative, the wife confirming the male desirability of the husband:

> Our horrible labour is spiced with the discipline of clock time
> And with words like 'swine', 'nigger',
> Let that red face and grey eyes recede for a few days,
> Let my lotus-eyed darling take his place,
> And with her loving hands, clasp me to her bosom.

See Srinibas Basu, *Khokababu Prasange* (Calcutta, *c.* 1897).

the Hindu marriage needed to be written as a love story with a happy ending.[53]

Let us look at a very typical description of a child bride.

> People in this country take great pleasure in infant marriage. The little bit of a woman, the infant bride, clad in red silk. . . . Drums are beating and men, women and children are running in order to have a glimpse of that lovely face. From time to time she breaks forth into little ravishing smiles. She looks like a little lovely doll.

The key words are 'little, lovely, ravishing, pleasure, infant, doll'—inserted at carefully chosen selected intervals.[54] The community of 'men, women, and children' formed round this figure is bonded together by great visual pleasure, by happiness. Loveableness bathes the trauma of patrilocality in warm sensuousness and grounds non-consensual indissoluble infant marriage in mutual desire alone.

Given this sensual starting point, the absolute and unconditional chastity of the Hindu wife, extending beyond the death of the husband, was equally strongly grounded by this discourse in her own desire. This purity, since it is supposedly a conscious moral choice, becomes at once a sign of difference and of superiority, a Hindu claim to power. The politics of women's monogamy then is the condition of the possible Hindu nation: the one is often explicitly made to stand in for the other. 'We are but a half civilised, poor, sorrowful, subjected, despised nation. We have but one jewel and for us that is the treasure of seven realms, a priceless gem.'[55] Or, 'this so-called subjection of our woman produces this sacred jewel of chastity which still glows radiantly throughout the civilised world despite centuries of political subjection.'[56] Woman's chastity, then, has a real and stated, not merely symbolic, political value.

Willed chastity enables the widow to desire the austerities and sacrifices that her condition imposes on her. Since she still belongs spiritually to her husband in a transcendental sort of way, worldly comforts have

[53]See Tanika Sarkar, 'Conjugality and Hindu Nationalism'.
[54]Ibid.
[55]Basu, *Hindur Achar Vyavahar*, p. 31.
[56]Ibid., p. 60.

actually ceased to matter and her body and soul draw pleasure, not pain, from the rigours of material existence. Her life is not marked by loss or absence but by surfeit because her voluntary abdication of an earthly life is a form of sanyas within the household.[57] It not only gives her moral and spiritual energy but also ensures a reservoir of spirituality in each home and for the Hindu order as a whole. Also, strict ritual observances root the widow's body in ancient India, thus miraculously enabling her to escape foreign domination. The cloth she wears is necessarily indigenous, the water she drinks is to be carried from the sacred river and not through foreign water pipes, and the salt that goes into her food is special rock salt untouched by machines. Ergo, the nation needs ascetic widowhood.[58]

The final and highest test of the supremacy of Hindu conjugality was the proven past capacity for self-immolation by widows.[59] The sati was an adored nationalist symbol, her figure representing the moment of climax in expositions of Hindu nationalism. Bankimchandra saw in it the last hope of a doomed nation.[60] Jyotirindranath Tagore's patriotic plays reached dramatic finale with the song:

Flames burn higher, burn higher
The widow has come to immolate herself.[61]

[57]Pratapchandra Majumdar, *Stri Charitra* (Calcutta, n.d.). Interestingly, the model for the chaste Hindu widow is Queen Victoria. Also Kamakhyacharan Bandyo-padhyay, *Stri Shiksha* (Dacca, c. 1901). Interestingly, even Rev. Lal Behari Dey, who had converted to Christianity, became rather lyrical in his praise of chaste Hindu widows. The most unqualified admiration was evoked by Sister Nivedita. See *The Web of Indian Life*, first published Calcutta, 1904 (reprinted Calcutta, 1955).

[58]Ibid., p. 57.

[59]Sati was routinely evoked as the climax, the highest proof and the essence of the Hindu wife's chastity. 'The woman's chastity is the bright jewel of an Aryan family. The chaste wife is sitting at the heart of flames, with the feet of her husband clasped on her breasts. She is chanting Hari's name with a face radiant with love and joy. Whenever we think of that, we are filled with pride.' See Girijaprasanna Raychaudhury, *Grihalakshmi* (Calcutta, c. 1887), p. 67.

[60]Bankimchandra Chattopadhyay, 'Kamalakanter Daptar', *Bankim Rachanabali*, vol. II (Calcutta, 1954).

[61]Jyotorindhranath Tagore, 'Sarojini Natak', 1875, *Jyotirindranather Natyasangraha*, first published 1891.

Rabindranath's writings of the early Swadeshi period recall her glory.[62] An immense body of patriotic tracts routinely invoked the act as an unfailing source of nationalist inspiration and pride.

Yet another register for comparing and discussing and thereby masking power relations developed somewhat sketchily within Hindu nationalist discourses on the family. As *adhinata* was the crucial term on gender as well as political relations, so *dasatya* (slavery or servitude) became a key concept to explicate, or rather to deny, a third dimension of power—that of class and caste. Within this household-bound discourse a lower-class, lower-caste person could only assume the figure of the domestic servant whose servitude was constructed as willed surrender to enlightened paternalism, and thus provided yet another justification for Hindu patriarchy.[63]

It was the nature of the woman's commitment to the conjugal order that bound the system together. Moral initiative therefore passes on to the woman, uniquely privileging her activism. If the household was the embryonic nation, then the woman was the true patriotic subject. The male body, having passed through the grind of Western education, office, routine, and forced urbanisation, having been marked with the loss of traditional sports and martial activities, was supposedly remade in an attenuated, emasculated form by colonialism.[64] The female body, on the other hand, was still pure and unmarked, loyal to the rule of the shastras.

This construction of the Hindu wife could also bind wide-ranging social segments around her practices and norms in order to formulate a middle class which, in colonial Bengal, lacked a clearly articulated economic base.[65] Since the new economic man did not appear in Bengal,

[62]Sumit Sarkar, *The Swadeshi Movement in Bengal, 1903–1908* (Delhi: People's Publishing House, 1972), pp. 47–63.

[63]Basu, *Hindur Achar Vyavahar*, p. 51.

[64]See Tanika Sarkar, 'Conjugality and Hindu Nationalism'.

[65]This was enabled by the fact that, starting in the late seventeenth century, commercial and agrarian prosperity had generalised upper-caste conjugal practices among a wide spectrum of low peasant and trading castes as the inescapable mode of social respectability. See Sanyal, *Social Mobility in Bengal*. Conjugal norms, at the same time, were becoming more strict and inflexible. Raghunandan had made pre-pubertal marriage obligatory in the sixteenth century and, from the eighteenth century, the royal court of the Krishnanagore Raj enforced a Smarta orthodoxy,

it would be the new domestic woman who had to carry the image of a class.

IV

The image of the loving heart of Hindu conjugality was, understandably, more an act of heroic imagination and conviction than of lived experience. Paradoxically, the stronger the expression of conviction in the vision, the more strongly critical attention would focus on concrete aspects of the reality and render the project enormously complicated. Four developments problematised the Hindu nationalist discourse on conjugality in the last two decades of the nineteenth century. There was already an old and deeply influential counter-tradition of folklore and verse that described marriage and domesticity as a source of profound unhappiness for the woman.[66] Nineteenth-century discursive prose would extend these desperate sobs into critical argument, interrogation and frontal challenge: into a movement for change. From the 1860s women's own writings began to appear, further confirming this tradition.[67] And, finally, there were reformist campaigns for change that, from the mid-1880s under Malabari assiduously picked up and wove together all the material evidence on force and coercion within Hindu marriage. Two sensational events—Rukmabai's demand to be released from a marriage contracted at her infancy, and a little girl Phulmani being raped to death by her husband—seemed to abundantly

---

tightening the practices of austere widowhood. See Sibnath Shastri, *Ramtanu Lahiri O Tatkalin Bangasamaj* (Calcutta, 1903). From the early nineteenth century, foreign accounts reported the ubiquity of the ban on widow remarriage and customs of child marriage which were to be found even among the low caste. See Abbe Dubois' account of 1792–1823, Abbe Dubois, *Hindu Manners, Customs and Ceremonies,* translated by H.L. Beauchamp (Oxford, 3rd edition, 1906). Sati, similarly, was practised very widely by the Sudra castes of Bengal. Risley found infant marriage and ban on widow remarriage the two uniform practices even among untouchable castes. H.H. Risley, *Tribes and Castes of Bengal,* vol. I (Calcutta, 1891).

[66]Bhabataran Datta, *Bangladesher Chhara* (Calcutta, n.d).

[67]On this see Ghulam Murshid, *Reluctant Debutante: Responses of Bengali Women to Modernisation* (Rajshahi, 1983).

vindicate the reformist critique and added strength and urgency to their campaign.[68]

Women's voices had frequently been borrowed by male authors to express a profound sense of bleakness about her existence. Jayadev's Radha had remained implacably angry about sexual double standards.[69] A particular stream within eighteenth-century Shakta devotional po-etry—the Agamani songs—would use the mother's voice to mourn Durga's imminent parting at the end of her annual visit to her parent's home: 'Do not pass away the night of Nawami, leave her with me just a little longer.'[70] These songs, enormously popular throughout the nineteenth century, would find a double resonance from within a very wide-ranging age group among Bengali women. Thanks to the wide-spread custom of infant marriage, women, by their early twenties, might be daughters longing for their mothers, and, simultaneously, young mothers pining for their married daughters. In lullabies and folk verses, probably composed largely by women themselves, married sisters threatened to drown themselves unless their brothers came and took them away from 'this place of torture'. A little girl would plead with her playmate to play a last game with her, 'for the son of a stranger is coming to take me away and I shall never play again.' A young mother, hungry for the sight of her baby—from whom the endless duties of a joint family routine separate her—plans thus: 'I'll run away to the forest with my baby, and there, in solitude, I'll gaze upon the face of my treasure.'[71] A complicated variety of female rites—vrats—were evolved to eliminate the threat of the co-wife.[72]

The experience of their own subjection, however, gave to colonised men a fresh and acute sensitivity in relation to bondage. *Adhinata* became a peculiarly loaded word, fraught with a double guilt: the sin of submitting to foreign domination, which necessarily conjured up the associated

[68]See Tanika Sarkar, 'Conjugality'.

[69]On the importance of this twelfth-century text, see S.K. De, *Early History of the Vaishnava Faith and Movement in Bengal* (Calcutta, 1961), pp. 9–11.

[70]Rasikchandra Ray, 'Nabamir Gan', Prabhat Goswami (ed.), *Hajar Bachharer Bangla Gan* (Calcutta, 1969).

[71]Datta, *Bangladesher Chhara*.

[72]Nandalal Sil, *Vratakatha* (Calcutta, 1930).

guilt of submitting the woman to a state of subjection. The two senses of the word would continuously flow into each other, interanimate each other. They would sometimes be posed as cause and effect. 'When our white masters kick us, we return home and soothe ourselves by kicking our wives.'[73] Or, 'Our women lost their freedom when we lost ours.'[74]

Sometimes the order of cause and effect was reversed. A women's magazine published this poem in 1894:

Men, you have inflicted a terrible wrong
On the defenceless women of this land
    and because of that
You will forever remain exiles in your own
    land of birth.[75]

Reversal also introduces the theme of expiation.

Occasionally one kind of subjection was so closely linked to the other that they interchanged as metaphors. There is a poem on the caged bird and the title of this poem refers to the incarceration of women within the home:

Free bird, how do you hope to be happy within the cage?
Imprisoned, you have forgotten your own speech.
And you repeat the words of others mindlessly.[76]

Loss of one's language was also the most familiar trope for describing political subjection.

A whole alternative, contestatory description developed from the extended guilt over subjection, representing the Hindu home as the very antithesis of pleasure. 'Our home knows no joy, no pleasure. Our home is filled with a spirit more nightmarish than that which reigns over the cremation ground.'[77] It was the grave of pleasure, not its home.

The interrogation was not restricted to reformers. Hindu nationalists themselves, by relentlessly focussing on conjugality, problematised the

[73]Prasad Das Goswami, *Amader Samaj* (Serampore, 1896), p. 14.
[74]Bhattacharya, *Banga Vivaha* (Calcutta, *c.* 1881), p. 76.
[75]*Narishiksha*, part II (Calcutta, 1884), p. 210.
[76]Ibid., p. 194.
[77]Bhattacharya, *Banga Vivaha*, p. 60.

entire arena. Even the most status-quoist tracts, which conclude with very orthodox prescriptions, do so not with confidence and certainty but after a compulsive and obsessive probing of all the tension spots.[78] This endless preoccupation reveals continuous doubts rather than any final resolution, since excessive speech points at anxiety just as surely as silence does.

The alternative, challenging description gained in authenticity once Hindu women began to write about themselves from the 1860s. They wrote about the trauma and not the beauty of infant marriage, the deprivations of the widow, the absence of love in the lives of wives. 'Conjugal love has disappeared from our country,' wrote a Hindu woman in 1863. She also claimed that Hindu women suffered more than anyone else in the world.[79] The Hindu household was described as 'a most terrible mountain range, infested with wild beasts.'[80] Another woman said nothing in her life—not conjugal love nor children—could compensate for the deprivation of knowledge. 'Ignorant and cruel men have segregated us from this priceless and endlessly pleasurable jewel that is knowledge, and yet foolish women serve them and care for them like servants.'[81]

All varieties of women's writings unanimously identified and condemned two problem spots within the Hindu woman's existence— the pain of patrilocality and the longing for knowledge. Whatever the format and whatever the basic political stance towards patriarchy,

---

[78]See for instance, Saudamini Gupta, *Kanyar Prati Upadesh* (Dacca, third edition, *c.* 1918). Even though it teaches the daughter how best and most graciously she can submit to patriarchal discipline and demands in her married life, the text simultaneously undermines the patriarchal hegemonic claim by asserting, again and again, that this was going to be a life of sorrow and problems, 'All women must live out their lives without their relatives or close ones near them (p. 3) . . . My child, I cannot advise you on when or how much to eat, for whatever you do, you must know that, you will most probably be criticised.' (p. 41)

[79]Kailashbashini Debi, *Hindu Mahilaganer Heenabastha* (Calcutta, n.d.), p. 62.

[80]Ibid., p. 45. Also *Narishiksha*, part I (Calcutta, 1884: first edition *c.* 1868), p. 6.

[81]*Narishiksha*, part I, p. 134. See also Kailashbashini Debi, *Hindu Mahilaganer Heenabastha*, p. 67.

women's writings at this time agreed on these points of criticism. The longing for systematic learning was not a desire implanted by male reformers, missionaries and colonialists. A pious Hindu housewife, spending her life in a non-reformed domestic environment where no woman ever learnt to read, was so driven by this sharp desire that she taught herself the letters in great secrecy and with difficulty. When she finally started reading, a measure of her triumph was conveyed by her coining of a magnificent new word to describe her own achievement and 'mastery over the word'—*jitakshara*.[82] Instead of reducing the pain and the triumph of the whole process to yet another form of male patriarchal manipulation, we need to explore what historical conjunctures gave focus and direction to certain kinds of diffused experiences of deprivation among women themselves—why at this time, and why in this form.

In 1884 Rukmabai, a low-caste, educated, Maharashtrian girl sought to repudiate an unconsummated marriage contracted at her infancy with an illiterate, dissolute, sick husband.[83] Over this sensational challenge, Malabari mobilised reformers and renewed his campaign for the introduction of divorce and for a higher age of consent—demands that seriously eroded the principles of indissolubility and of infant marriage. A higher age of consent for the girl would also jeopardise the fundamental Hindu tenet of *garbhadhan*, that is, the obligatory ritual cohabitation as soon as the wife attains puberty—for otherwise her womb is tainted and her sons lose the right to serve up ancestral offerings.[84] Since in the hot climate of Bengal puberty may occur fairly early, a higher age of consent, it was feared, would interfere with this injunction.

For some time, in Hindu nationalist circles, Rukmabai became a name more dreaded than Malabari's or those of colonial legislators.[85]

---

[82]Rashsundari Debi, *Amar Jiban*, 1876, reprinted in *Atmakatha* (Calcutta 1981). See also Sarada Debi, *Atmakatha* (Calcutta, 1979), for a similar longing for the written word. In her case, however, it remained unfulfilled.

[83]Charles Heimsath, *Indian Nationalism and Hindu Social Reform* (Princeton University Press, 1964), pp. 91–4.

[84]Tanika Sarkar, 'Conjugality'.

[85]On folk poems about the Rukmabai episode sung on Calcutta streets, see Asit Kumar Bandyopadhyay, *Bangla Sahityer Itihas*, vol. V.

They would still valiantly argue that a true Hindu wife must find the husband desirable, irrespective of external circumstances—a problem that Rabindranath would continue to ponder on as late as the novel *Jogajog*.[86] Already, however, the basis of conjugality had shifted from love to prescription as soon as the imperative 'must' was introduced in the statement. A structured duality thus complicated the representation of conjugality. The two compulsions and possibilities of construction—preservation of conjugal discipline and accent on love—would inevitably prove incompatible.

Reformers had an easier time of it since they were willing to surrender the principle of sacrament to the principle of willed and regularly consummated conjugal love. Widows could remarry because the physical relationship was over for them and hence the marriage was over as well. Similarly, wives of endlessly polygamous Kulin Brahmins were really not married since, in their case, consummation was rare, if not impossible. Infant wives, thrown into a relationship not chosen by them, could similarly repudiate their marriage tie. Hindu nationalists, on the other hand, fused love into sacrament which, once performed, must reign supreme, irrespective of absence of consummation or consent. There were no gradations within marriage—a child widow who had not seen her husband was as meaningfully married to him as the wife of a monogamous, loving husband. Once love and willed surrender were separated out from the sacrament, however, Hindu nationalists had to take their stand on the latter alone in order to preserve the totality of the conjugal system.

They continued to sensualise the discipline of the sacrament—up to 1889 at least, when a more severe jolt occurred. Phulmani, a girl of ten, was raped to death by her twenty-nine-year-old husband Hari Maiti. Since she was beyond the statutory minimum age of ten, Hari Maiti could not be punished under existing Penal Code provisions. The event seemed to fully justify Malabari's allegations and a very

---

[86]It explores whether the marriage sacrament can or should generate love within a chaste Hindu girl, or if it must do so. Interestingly, the novel was composed at a time when yet another round of controversy about a higher age of consent was going on over the Sarda Bill proposals. *Rabindra Rachanabali*.

hesitant government was at last inclined to give in to proposals for a higher age of consent.[87]

The narrative of Hindu marriage could no longer use the language of love; it had to be rewritten in terms of force and pain. If the element of difference from other systems was so obviously seen to lie in discipline, then Hinduism had to be celebrated as a superior coercive power. 'The Hindu is truly very severe, even cruel,' exulted Chandranath Basu in 1892 in his rejoinder to Rabindranath on the question of 'Hinduvivaha'.[88] Self-fulfilment and pleasure were now demoted to a rather lower order of values. If infant marriage led to violence, even to bloody death, then it was the unique privilege and strength of the Hindu woman to accept the risk. Its practice could lead to weakened progeny and racial degeneration. But 'the Hindu prizes his religion above his life and short-lived children.'[89] Hindu scriptures did impose harsh injunctions on the wife as well as the widow. Yet 'this discipline is the prize and glory of chaste women and it prevails only in Hindu society.'[90]

A typical argument on the age of consent would run thus:

The performance of the *garbhadhan* must be after the first menstruation. It means the first cohabitation enjoined by the Shastras. It is the injunction of the Hindu Shastras that married girls must cohabit with their husbands at the first onset of their menses and all Hindus must implicitly obey the injunction. And he is not a true Hindu who does not obey it. If one girl in a lakh or even a crore menstruates before twelve it must be admitted that by raising the age of consent the ruler will be interfering with the religion of the Hindus. But everyone knows that hundreds of girls menstruate before twelve. And the *garbhas* of hundreds of girls will be tainted and impure. And the thousands of children who will be born of those impure *garbhas* will become impure.[91]

Even in this translation, the power of the voice comes through. Re-

[87]See Tanika Sarkar, 'Conjugality'.

[88]Chandranath Basu, *Hindutva (Hindur Prakrita Itihas)* (Calcutta, 1892).

[89]*Bangabashi*, 25 December 1890, *Report on Native Papers* (hereafter *RNP*), Bengal, 1890.

[90]*Dainik O Samachar Chandrika*, 14 January 1891, *RNP*, Bengal 1891.

[91]*Bangabashi*, 25 December 1890.

petitive short phrases, joined by many 'ands', the frequency of the word 'must', the deployment of increasing numbers—all add up to an incantatory, apocalyptic mode of speech very typical of fundamentalist millenarianism. All external arguments have been chipped away and the bare mandate is repeated on rising notes of urgency. Hindu nationalism has learnt to speak the authoritative word in the appropriately authoritarian voice.

Yet the grounding of an imagined nation upon sheer pain could not proceed beyond this point. Hinduism has come far too close to its own description of the prescriptive, loveless, disciplinary regime that is colonialism. The discourse reaches its breaking point and begins to collapse into self-travesty, the beginnings of self-disgust. When Joygobinda Shome said in 1891: what if infant wives die in childbirth since female scorpions always do in any case—the limits of this discourse had been reached.[92] Rajendralal Mitra had earlier raised a laugh at a Shobhabazaar Raj palace meeting when he described the Hindu wife as 'an article of gift . . . she is given away even as a cow or any other chattel.'[93] I suspect that the laugh was uneasy. The hegemonic desires of Hindu nationalism clashed too violently with the starkness of its discipline. Love had to re-enter the nationalist narrative.

Over the last decade of the century a new organisational principle, a new centre of gravity, was sought beyond conjugality. The axis was eventually located in the loving relationship between mother and son. This time, however, this was no flesh-and-blood woman, all too easily visible within an all-too-accountable household, but the new and supreme deity within the Hindu pantheon—the Motherland, the reified woman.[94] With the reoriented figure of the woman came a crucial shift in the very placing of the patriotic project. It was taken out of the

[92]Cited by Nagendranath Bandyopadhyay, *Balyavivaha* (Calcutta, 1888), p. 31.

[93]Cited in *Hindoo Patriot*, 19 September 1887.

[94]On the composition and control of a dominant cultural symbol and its relationship to a real physical support in society, see Luisa Accati, *The Larceny of Desire: The Madonna in Seventeenth-Century Catholic Europe*, in Obelkevich, Roper and Samuel (eds), *Disciplines of Faith: Studies in Religion, Politics and Patriarchy* (London, 1987).

problematic home space and into the wider, more public arena of the Hindu community—which is an abstraction. The defence of Hindu domesticity, the preservation of the Hindu home, fell away from the nationalist agenda. Vivekananda, who had found the whole age of consent agitation profoundly uncomfortable, proposed to add muscle and sinew to the decadent Hindu through work-oriented asceticism and social service. Bankimchandra, in his last political novels, envisioned salvation through an apocalyptic war with the Muslim.[95] The experience of something approaching a mass upsurge over the age of consent issue generated enabling rhetoric and techniques for political mobilisation and agitation that were, for the moment, found to be more efficacious than the politics of petitions or the annual Congress forums. The very success of the struggle over domestic issues, paradoxically, carved out a political sphere that could now be separated from the domestic arena.

Questions of internal power arrangements were not to be completely resolved. They constituted—as I suspect or hope they still do now—implacable pitfalls, the internal limits within the discourse. Bankim, in the last pages of his last novel, had mocked the grandeur of his own apocalyptic vision through the casual gossip of common people who dismissed the Hindu–Muslim war as supremely irrelevant for themselves. Vivekananda was asked by an American woman missionary in 1898 if he foresaw any hope of eliminating child marriage and cruelty to widows. Sadly, he said, no. The missionary went on with her account: 'Even at the height of his popularity, with the Hindu world at his feet, the Swami shows a strange foreboding of ultimate failure. I cannot give you an adequate impression of the effect, but sitting there at twilight, in the large, half-lighted hall, it seemed like listening to a cry.'[96]

[95]Tanika Sarkar, 'Bankimchandra and the Impossibility of a Nationalist Agenda', chapter four within the present volume.

[96]Lucy E. Guiness, *Across India at the Dawn of the Twentieth Century* (London 1898), p. 147.

CHAPTER TWO

Talking About Scandals

Religion, Law and Love in Late Nineteenth-Century Bengal

I n this chapter I explore the social history of a scandalous event that rocked Bengal in 1873. The stories that circulated around this episode were narrated in farces, in newspaper editorials and reports, and in journals. They were also told through bazaar paintings, woodcut prints, street songs, and on the stages of the new public theatre. They belonged, therefore, to processes that constituted an emerging public sphere where private people argued about their intimate concerns through novel modes of public communication.[1]

Habermas has been criticised for restricting his conception of the public sphere too narrowly to the higher reaches of the European bourgeoisie: the more subordinated classes had parallel exchanges of their own in public.[2] When we look at late-nineteenth-century Bengal through the prism of a scandalous event, we find that our prevailing notion of a middle class—which is perfectly set in the mould of a rich, successful and extremely erudite intelligentsia—begins to curdle and separate. We find a new, more humble rung with its own low life of

---

[1]For an understanding of the formation of a bourgeois public sphere, I have relied extensively on Jürgen Habermas, *The Structural Transformation of the Public Sphere: An Enquiry into a Category of Bourgeois Society*, trans. Burger and Lawrence (Cambridge, Mass, 1989).

[2]See Geoff Eley, 'Nations, Public and Political Cultures: Placing Habermas in the Nineteenth Century', in Craig Calhoun (ed.), *Habermas and the Public Sphere* (Cambridge, Mass, 1993).

literature, in sensational reportage, in obscene farces, and in popular theatre.[3] We find that this level shades further into prostitutes, artisans and minor theatre persons. We see that even the comments of peasants and the songs of street beggars are picked up and woven into more erudite representations of event. It is true that these voices are neither transparent nor authentic: they are mimetically recreated. However, it is important to think about why the representations need to incorporate them, or to refer to them, in public discussions. It is not enough to indicate the existence of multiple levels within a class often assumed to be seamless, and conceptualized on the basis of a few pre-selected themes. It is important to reconnect the levels of the middle class through their mutual arguments and exchanges, and to locate and describe the sites where such exchanges occurred.

Since it is somewhat unusual for Indian historians to look at events that do not directly flow from or into nationalism and nation-making processes, it is necessary to say a few words in defence of this project.[4] In order to locate an occurrence that made a cut into and intermingled social worlds, we need a particular kind of event. Ideally, such an event should be part of the 'ordinary' and the everyday, as well as include dimensions that compel serious, wide-ranging discussions on themes of general interest. In other words, we need the quotidian and the domesticated at the moment of rupture, at the point of their eruption into public affairs. And herein lies the value of a sensational event, a cause

[3]For a discussion on a layered middle class, see Sumit Sarkar, 'Kaliyug, Chakri and Bhakti: Ramakrishna and His Times', *Economic and Political Weekly* (hereafter *EPW*), 18 July 1992.

[4]Notable exceptions obviously exist and the superb study by Ranajit Guha of the abortion and death of a low-caste nineteenth-century widow comes readily to mind. There is also Sumit Sarkar's exploration of a turn-of-the-century murder case involving a religious cult, a Brahmin guru and his low-caste disciples in East Bengal. See Guha, 'Chandra's Death', in Ranajit Guha (ed.), *Subaltern Studies V: Writings on South Asian History and Society* (New Delhi, 1987). Also, Sarkar, 'Kalki Avatar in Bikrampur: A Village Scandal in Early Twentieth Century Bengal', in Ranajit Guha (ed.), *Subaltern Studies VI: Writings on South Asian History and Society* (New Delhi, 1989). As an example of histories of the former category of events connected with mainstream nationalism, see Shahid Amin's study of the Chauri Chaura events in *Event, Metaphor, Memory: Chauri Chaura, 1922–1992* (New Delhi, 1995).

celebré. It straddles the customary as much as the transgressive, it knits up the everyday with the grand themes of a historical period, illuminating interweaving points and mediating elements, revealing unsuspected meanings in known historical developments.

A major archive for reconstituting events in this category is the archive of criminal cases. It is true that the repositories of old case documents are seriously incomplete or kept in unusable conditions, or have simply disappeared for the most part. Unlike the *ancien régime* in France there has been no custom of publishing *memoires judiciares* or trial briefs by lawyers, of *remonstrances* or courts' objections to royal decress.[5] Nonetheless, for the more notorious trials that deal with scandalous themes, we do have reports and representation in other kinds of texts.[6] The examination of a legal offence through a courtroom trial and reports on its public reception[7] immediately bring us closer to legal and judicial processes as well as to the various components of the modern public sphere—the press, the theatre, and popular printed literature—which have always fed avidly on crime. Sometimes we may even find parts of this sphere in the making, as was the case with the new public theatre of Bengal which worked extensively on this scandal. The institutionalisation of the public sphere then takes us into the realm of market forces which condition the representations and their forms. These lead us to the social histories of the creators of such representations.

We need, therefore, a scandalous crime to start with. The coupling of these two words is not fortuitous. Rajeswari Sunder Rajan has drawn our attention to the changing definitions of the word scandal. Whereas in 1582 it denoted a 'moral lapse', and in 1590 a 'damage of reputation' or a 'disgraceful reputation' (1622), by 1814 it also comes to mean 'slander'. By 1838 it means both 'offence to moral feeling or decency'

---

[5]These sources constitute the 'literature of judicial scandal' that Sarah Maza has used in her brilliant study of pre-revolutionary sensational trials. See *Private Lives and Public Affairs: The Causes Célébres of Pre-Revolutionary France* (Berkeley and Los Angeles, 1993), p. 1.

[6]Sumit Sarkar found evidence of the Doyhata case in a newspaper report in a pamphlet. 'Kalki Avatar in Bikrampur'.

[7]For an argument in favour of a connected study of laws, judiciary, the trial process and public responses, see J.M. Bettie, *Crime and the Lawcourts in England: 1661–1800* (Oxford, 1986), Introduction.

and 'injurious report published concerning another which may be the foundation of legal action'.[8] Whereas the older meaning of a violation of norms is carried into early-nineteenth-century usage, a new meaning also develops which moves from slander to legal offence, shifting the onus of definition from the moral community to the law court. It is interesting that the 1838 definition also includes 'published report' as a criterion, indicating both the consolidation of a public sphere and its constitution through the print medium.

The Bengali counterpart to the word is *ketchha*, which is taken from the Persian word *kissa*. While the Persian original referred to stories, mostly of fabulous romances, the Bengali derivation changed its meaning to denote scandalous stories, thus obliquely affirming the potentially transgressive character of romances. In the representations of the scandal that concern us, however, we find the English term frequently in use, even in Bengali texts.

A trial makes scandalous disclosures, publicises intimate transgressions. Its reception has the same function as enlarging the scope of gossip, pulling it out of hidden, intimate, familiar circles into the realm of public concern and argument. An event is something that creates a shared field of discussion and thereby creates an interpretive community which reads the text of the event. An event of the 'gossipable' kind adds a peculiarly intimate twist to it. If gossip flourishes within an intimate group and draws its discussants into a tighter circle of acquaintances and concerns, a scandal performs the same function within an anonymous, abstract public: it draws an unseen community of concerned people closer together by focusing on intimate issues about its constituents. The range of its reception defines the space of the public sphere.

II

In 1873 a sensational murder case came up before the Hoogly Sessions Court at Serampore in south-west Bengal. A powerful mohunt, Madhavchandra Giri of Tarakeswar, the manager-cum-guru of the rich

[8]See her unpublished paper, 'The Scandal of the State: Women and Institutional Protection in Contemporary India'. I am grateful to her for allowing me to use it.

and popular Saivite temple and pilgrimage centre in Hooghly, was accused of first seducing and then raping Elokeshi, the young wife of one Nobinchandra Banerji, who worked as an employee at a military press in Calcutta. The mohunt had established a liaison with Elokeshi with the connivance of Elokeshi's parents, with whom she had been staying while her husband worked in Calcutta. On a visit home to his wife, Nobin came to know of what had been afoot through village gossip, and he angrily confronted his wife. A frightened and repentant Elokeshi confessed all, and Nobin decided to forgive her and take her away from Tarakeswar. The mohunt, however, ordered his musclemen to bar their way. In a fit of blind rage, Nobin severed Elokeshi's throat with a fish knife and then, full of horror at his own deed, turned himself in at the local police station with an unequivocal confession. An Indian jury acquitted him on grounds of insanity but the European judge demurred and the case was sent up to the Calcutta High Court. Nobin was sentenced to life transportation, but in 1875 he received a pardon because of massive public petitions for mercy. The mohunt was sentenced to three years' rigorous imprisonment and a fine of Rs 3000, but Bengali public opinion generally considered this punishment as grossly lenient.[9]

It is evident from the summary above that both the event and the trials were of a sensational nature. The mohunt and his English lawyer were mobbed outside the court and the trial was frequently interrupted by excited crowds of spectators who demanded either clemency for Nobin or a harsher sentence for the mohunt.[10] Calcutta and district town notables got up petitions and subscriptions to help Nobin.[11] A

[9]A history of the scandal and the trials is to be found in citations from the High Court Judicaire at Fort William, Bengal 24/10/7830; Criminal Jurisdiction, Queen *vs* Nobin Chandra Banerjee. Cited in the *Bengalee*, 22 November 1873.

[10]See *The Englishman*, 28 November 1873.

[11]A petition signed by the 'acknowledged leaders of native society' was issued from Calcutta. A second one was signed by 'some gentlemen from Mymensingh' district of East Bengal that had cast some aspersions on the High Court judgement on Nobin, which had allegedly alienated Lt-Governor Campbell and made him turn down appeals for mercy. A third petition came from Maharani Swarnamoyee of the Cossimbazar Raj family, who was renowned for her magnificent charity, and who had received the title of Maharani in 1871. *Hindoo Patriot*, 1 December 1873.

plea for mercy registered more than 10,000 signatures, revealing the involvement of the lower middle class as well.[12]

Six months after the event, the newspaper *Bengalee* commented on its continued publicity:

> No case in our generation has excited such a deep, enduring and widespread interest as the case of Nobinchandra Banerji and the mohunt of Tarakeswar . . . . Groups of peasants who may not have heard of the Road Cess . . . may be seen discussing some subject with great solemnity. Approach them, and you will find the burden of their talk to be Nobin and the Mohunt.[13]

Plays written as late as 1924 referred to the Elokeshi episode in such a way as to assume that it was still public knowledge.[14]

Tarakeswar had been a centre of great scandals, at least from the early nineteenth century. In 1824, Mohunt Shrimanta Giri was executed for murdering the lover of his mistress.[15] In 1912 Nagendrabala Debi accused the mohunt of raping her daughter.[16] In 1924 the Swarajists organized a satyagraha campaign against Mohunt Satish Giri's alleged sexual and financial misconduct and managed to achieve a measure of public control over temple funds.[17] We find that it is from the second decade of the nineteenth century that such scandals become a focus of public attention. Certainly, the focus owes a lot to the new possibilities of publicity—i.e. the new law courts and trial procedures—which, at times, were something of a public spectacle and followed the tropes of a suspense drama. Then there was the press, which repeated the trial events at length and commented on them; and added to this was the

[12]*Sulabh Samachar*, 2 September 1873. *RNP*, 1873; also, *Hindoo Patriot*, 18 August 1873.

[13]*Bengalee*, 1 November 1873.

[14]Pareshchandra Choudhury, *Tarakeswar Mohanto Mahatmya* (Calcutta, 1924).

[15]Amiya Kumar Banerjee (ed.), *West Bengal District Gazetteers, Hooghly*, (Calcutta, 1972), pp. 725–6.

[16]Government of Bengal, Home Political Confidential, FN 111/1912 (1–2): Conduct of the Mohunt of Tarakeswar; Petition by Nagendrabala Devi.

[17]E. Alan Morinis, *Pilgrimage in the Hindu Tradition: A Case Study of West Bengal* (Delhi, 1984), p. 92.

growth of dissident religious sects among Hindus who agitated over the legal redefinition of norms of Hindu conjugality.

Despite its highly sensational nature, the 1824 scandal had not created waves of representations, nor did it have as tenacious a grip on public memory. The 1873 events, in contrast, were vividly remembered and recalled during the 1924 satyagraha. Within the scandal of 1873 I found barely a reference to 1824; whereas the expansion in the range of apparatus that made up the public sphere, and the relative downward reach developing at this time, partly account for the longer lease of life that the 1873 scandal enjoyed.

The talk in relation to the latter ranged over an astonishing variety of subjects.[18] Missionaries speculated on the possible disenchantment of Hindus with their own leadership and institutions. English-owned newspapers debated the morals of native society, British justice, and whether or not the government should embark on a more intrusive course of action *vis-à-vis* Hindu institutions. Bengali newspapers gave elaborate, often verbatim reports of trial proceedings and critically discussed the stance of European judges, Hindu lawyers, the jury, as well as public responses to the events and trials. There were passionate debates about the precise degree of culpability of each of the characters involved in the scandal, as well as about whether the various judgements fairly and correctly interpreted and applied the laws. Finally, as the last level in the spiral, there were arguments about the nature of colonial law and Hindu religious norms.

It is evident, then, that interest in the scandal also spilled into and encompassed the trials, thereby constituting a subsidiary set of events or a subplot which supplemented and interpreted the events of the scandal. It is also clear that a larger Bengali public tribunal organized itself around

[18]Terms such as 'talk' should be used circumspectly, however, since, unlike Habermas' public domain of cafés, salons and literary sessions, I refer to more mediated forms of representations and discussions which were not face-to-face. Also, John Thompson has rightly criticised Habermas for an essentially dialogic conception of the public sphere: 'His way of thinking about print was shaped by a model of communication based on the spoken word.' John Thompson, 'The Theory of the Public Sphere: A Critical Appraisal', in Calhoun, *Habermas and the Public Sphere*, p. 97.

the Hooghly Sessions and Calcutta High Courts that judged the conduct of the trials.

The popular press brought out a series of farces on the rape, the murder and the trials. I have worked on twenty-five of the most major ones,[19] certainly the largest corpus among nineteenth-century farces related to a single contemporary event. At least four of these were reprinted several times; and one had a prolonged run as a play which made the fortunes of a new public theatre company and was enacted by several aspiring theatre companies in Calcutta, Dacca and the district towns.[20] One of these printed plays was the first Bengali publication to display a two-toned, colour woodcut print.[21] Collections of popular songs on the event were compiled and printed.[22] Bazaar painters at Kalighat, another major pilgrimage centre in Calcutta, produced a whole series of paintings (or *pats*) on the theme, and woodcut printers of cheap publishing concerns at Battala, in north Calcutta, duplicated them in large quantities.[23] In the entire corpus of popular painting and print, this was the only event depicted. A brisk market developed over the production and sale of objects commemorating the event—saris and betel-leaf boxes were inscribed with Elokeshi's name, fish knives had it scored into the iron. A balm, claiming to be specially effective for headaches brought on by hard study for examinations,[24] allegedly used the

[19]See also Jayanta Goswami, *Samajchitre Unabingsha Shatabdir Bangla Prahashan* (Calcutta, *c.* 1974), pp. 257–78. Goswami lists twenty-three farces on the topic. Shri Pantha in his *Mohanti Elokeshi Sambad* (Calcutta, 1984) lists a total of thirty-four scandal plays on the event.

[20]Lakshminarayan Das, *Mohanter Ei Ki Kaj!* (Calcutta, 1873 and 1874), pts 1 and 2.

[21]According to Sukumar Sen the farce *Uh! Mohanter Ei Ki Kaj!*, published from the Bentinck Press at Battala, used a two-toned lithograph. Other farces on the scandal also had colour illustrations. See, for instance, *Ajker Bajar Bhau*, anon. (Calcutta, 1873).

[22]Nandalal Ray, *Nutan Mohanta Tappa*, vol. 1 (Calcutta, 1874).

[23]See W.G. Archer, *Bazaar Paintings of Calcutta: The Style of Kalighat* (London, 1953). Also Ashit Paul (ed.), *Woodcut Prints of 19th Century Calcutta* (Calcutta, 1983). See also Jyotindra Jain, *Kalighat Paintings*, op.cit.

[24]We find here the repercussions of a new education system that now increasingly became the source of all middle-class employment and, often, of livelihood as well. The concrete features of the system are rarely taken into account

oil that the mohunt had produced inside the gaol as part of his prison labour.[25] A report on the variety of metal objects in use in Bengal, written in 1894, referred to the sale of these commemorative objects even twenty years after the event. Interestingly, this was the only group of objects that clustered around an event mentioned in the report.[26]

While debates on sexual morality are to be expected from such a scandal—richly spiced as it was with adultery, murder and an exciting trial—it is remarkable how wide-ranging and deeply political the debates were. It was as if the event provided an occasion to all Hindus to ponder upon themes that involved the very constitution of Hindu 'society' or 'public'. These were terms far more in use in contemporary Bengali writings than 'community' or 'nation' and they should be explored independently for this reason, rather than be subsumed under the latter, largely attributed categories.[27] The Bengali equivalent for the word society was *samaj*, a word that had in pre-colonial times referred to a caste or a sub-caste. Now it encompassed the entire Hindu community, at least in Bengal. The new usage probably drew life from early-nineteenth-century discussions about the social and religious reform movements that eventually established distinctions between the Hindu Samaj and the Brahmo Samaj. Interestingly, the word 'public' acquired no Bengali equivalent but was retained as such in Bengali texts,

---

in discussions of modern education: one of them being a regular and rigorous schedule of public examinations of the entire student body at a fixed point. A new pathology takes place as a fresh form of headache comes into being. I would like sometime to explore the presumed relationship between the restorative powers of the product of the penal work of a fallen holy man and the problems of male students, the reasons for the special efficacy of this medicine for this category of patients. *Bangabandhu*, 5 December 1673, *RNP*, Bengal, 1873.

[25]It sold for Rs 9 a seer. *Bangabandhu*, 5 December 1873.

[26]T.N. Mokherjee, *A Monograph on the Brass, Bronze and Copper Manufacture of Bengal* (Calcutta, 1894). I am grateful to Nayanjot Lahiri for the reference.

[27]*Bharat Samskarak* of 26 September 1873 bitterly complained that by not taking stronger steps to clean up the pilgrimages, the government was ignoring Bengali Hindu public opinion: 'The Bengalis are silent, but it does not follow that they have no . . . public opinion', *RNP*, Bengal, 1893. The *Halishahar Patrika* of 21 November 1873 published an appeal by Nobin that was addressed: 'To the People of Bengal', ibid.

where it was commonly used. It came to be used interchangeably with 'people'. It split off from the word *samaj*: while the latter now referred to a religious sect or community, 'public' was a more open, diffused and non-denominational category which constituted itself by openly publicizing its opinions on themes of general, shared interest.[28]

Investigations into the moral health of the Hindu religious leadership had started on a large scale from the early 1860s by reformist journalists which began to report on sexual corruption in the immensely powerful Ballabhacharya sect of western India.[29] *Hutom Penchar Naksha*, the first major Bengali book of satirical fictional prose, made much of the sexual escapades of religious gurus and mendicants.[30] The new education and reform, as well as the development of modern, dissident religious sects scrutinized the power of traditional sacred authorities to rule over Hindu society. They were especially concerned about the ability of traditional sacred norms and institutions to protect the life and the spiritual and intellectual growth of Hindu women. Obviously, the Elokeshi scandal fed powerfully into both reformist and orthodox anxieties since these related directly to the relationship between Hindu norms, leaders and women. At the same time, the scandal went beyond the reformist–orthodoxy lines of debate. As we shall see later, the discussions did not simply reduce the protagonists into a site for contested constructions of tradition, nationhood and community. The intimate sexual-emotional configurations, and the many possible and conflicting lines of their interpretation, remained of crucial and overwhelming significance to the discussants, beyond their symbolic or signifying aspects.

This becomes clearer through a contrast. In 1890, a ten-year-old child, Phulmonee, was killed when her husband raped her. The event

[28] *Hindu Hitaishini* of 29 March 1873 complained that even though many charges had been brought against the mohunt of Sitakundu, the government was ignoring popular opinion and taking no steps against him. This amounted to a violation of 'the rights of people'. *RNP*, Bengal, 1873. Note the justiciary character that is attributed to the people and the claim that the public dictate the legal and judicial authorities.

[29] See Charles H. Heimsath, *Indian Nationalism and Hindu Social Reform* (Princeton, 1964), chap. 3. Also, Amrita Shodhan, 'Caste, Religion and the Law', unpublished Ph.D. thesis, University of Chicago, 1995, chap. 4.

[30] Kaliprasanna Singha, *Hutom Penchar Naksha* (Calcutta, 1862).

forced a rather unwilling colonial government to acquiesce in reformist demands to penalize cohabitation with wives below the age of twelve—the Age of Consent Act of 1891. Bengali revivalist-nationalists, with few exceptions, launched a massive protest campaign against colonial interference with Hindu sacred interiority, while a small and besieged minority of reformers heaped scriptural and medical evidence in support of the new law. In public discussions, Phulmonee and the conditions of her murder practically disappeared. I am told that there is one play on the event, entitled *Phulmonee*,[31] but I have found no evidence that it was performed. There are some farces on the Age of Consent issue; one of them, by the famous playwright-cum-actor Amritalal Basu,[32] satirizes reformism. The incident, however, does not feature in the play at all. The only vivid descriptions of Phulmonee's death are available in the court depositions made by her mothers, grandmother and aunt.[33] Clearly, it was the behaviour of the colonial government that constituted the scandal, not the rape and death of the little girl. In the failure of that case to attain the status of a scandal, and in the displacement of arguments from the core event to the adjacent themes of colonialism and indigenous patriarchy, lies the distance between the more fluid and open interpretive community of the 1870s, and the monolithic nationalist-indigenist interpretive perspective at the turn of the century.

III

What was it that made the 1870s a vantage point for interest in the stories of Nobin, Elokeshi and Madhavgiri before they could be subsumed and obliterated by discussions of Hinduism and colonialism? I shall reflect here on several conditions. The 1870s were, in many ways, an interesting transitional moment in Bengal. Broad, generalized formal political institutions had not yet fully articulated themselves and

[31] I owe this reference to Mrinalini Sinha.

[32] The two plays are *Sammati Sankat* by Amritalal Basu and *Ain Bibhrat* by Harendralal Mitra. See Jayanta Goswami, *Samajchitre Unabingsha Shatabdir Bangla Prahashan*.

[33] See Tanika Sarkar, 'Conjugality'.

the politics of associations and congresses would come into their own only from the next decade. Nor had the limited local self-government arenas and the narrow electoral facilities—that Viceroy Ripon would make available from the 1880s—yet made their appearance. So, certain forms of participatory politics had not entirely taken shape. The exercise of critical reason by private individuals in public was articulated through the new vernacular prose: editorials in mainstream newspapers and journals coming out of Calcutta; the theatre; satirical plays; the new novels and discursive essays whose themes would immediately be translated into simpler polemic in farces; pamphlets and racy news items in the more marginal newspapers. As Habermas shows in relation to Enlightenment Europe, a public domain, in its early phase, is dominantly constituted by intimate matters within a literary mode.[34] A literary mode is eminently hospitable to themes of love, violence and betrayal.

The making of the public sphere in Bengal sees a remarkable downward reach in the 1870s. Theatre escapes the exclusive control of upper-class patrons and their private, amateur shows. The first public companies and stages are formed at the initiative of middle-class young men of north Calcutta. Tickets are priced so as to allow, at least occasionally, the lower middle classes into the new public halls.[35] The great Bengali newspaper, *Amrita Bazaar*, is founded by a district town's middle-class family not renowned for great educational or cultural achivements.[36] In less than a decade, another important newspaper, *Bangabashi*, innovates a novel marketing strategy to target a readership of lower-middle-class commuting clerks from district towns and villages.[37] Farces, pamphlets, tracts and lyrics are written and published by men and

[34]Habermas, *Structural Transformation of the Public Sphere.*

[35]The Calcutta National Theatrical Society advertised its first-class tickets as priced at Re 1, and its second-class tickets at 8 annas, on 10 November 1872. These were expensive, but not prohibitively so. Brajendranath Bandyopadhyaya, *Bangiya Natyashalar Itihas: 1795–1876* (Calcutta, c. 1933), p. 97.

[36]Smarajit Chakrabarti, *The Bengali Press (1818–1868): A Study in the Growth of Public Opinion* (Calcutta, 1976).

[37]Amiya Kumar Sen, *Hindu Revivalism in Bengal, 1872–1905* (Delhi, 1993), p. 239.

even by a few women. These are people with no knowledge of English, Persian or Sanskrit: they now begin to wield their everyday language, the new vernacular prose, as soon as they think they have an interesting story to tell. Stories—whether in newspaper reports or in the great domestic novels of Bankim or in the pulp Battala farces and fiction— are also largely about everyday domestic dramas.[38]

Kalighat paintings and woodcut prints from Battala are no longer the enormous folded scrolls that painters display with songs, dances and narration as part of a composite cultural event; nor are they great art objects commissioned and owned by courtly patrons alone. They are small, portable commodities that can be sold to individuals, piece by piece, at generally affordable prices, and they can be put up on walls in ordinary homes for continuous display. Battala metal-engraved and woodcut prints, often reproducing Kalighat paintings, flooded the market between the 1850s and 1870s. These were much cheaper, being a paisa each when plain, and two paise each when tinted with red, blue and green. Kalighat paintings, on the other hand, cost an anna each. Both kinds were purchased by all sorts of people. Mrs Belnos' painting of a crowded, meagre, single-room family hut of a poor woman, printed in 1832, shows a Kalighat painting against the wall.[39] On the other hand, a rich man's drawing-room is described as decorated with a Battala print.[40] The pictures are biting satires on modern life, sparing neither the traditional holy men nor the new middle class.

The new public theatre was, especially, a space shared between highbrow connoisseurs and a petit bourgeoisie of skilled artisans, clerks and hack writers who patronized the theatre enthusiastically, and who sometimes managed to dictate the terms of its survival and success. The newly formed Bengal Theatre had opened with two erudite plays

[38]In 1873, Bankimchandra's great domestic novel *Bishabriksha* appeared. It talked of conjugal and extramarital love, of polygamy and widow remarriage. See *Bankim Rachanabali*, vol. 1 (Calcutta, 1953). On popular and pulp fiction, see Sukumar Sen, *Battalar Chhapa O Chhabi* (Calcutta, 1984).

[39]On the *pats* and prints, see Archer, *Bazaar Paintings of Calcutta*; Hana Knizkova, *The Drawings of the Kalighat Style: Secular Themes* (Prague, 1975); Paul, *Woodcut Prints*.

[40]Ambicacharan Gupta, *Banger Guptakatha* (Calcutta, 1885).

by the great playwright Michael Madhusudan Datta on classical themes. Both were miserable flops. In despair, the management experimented with a play by an unknown playwright, Lakshminarayan Das. His scandal play, *Mohanter Ei Ki Kaj!* (Is This Worthy of a Mohunt?) seems to be the only thing that he ever wrote that made a name. Nothing else is known about him except that, unlike most authors of Battala pulp, he probably belonged to a low Shudra caste. In fact, quite a few of the authors of these farces were men of relatively low castes.[41] A later play refers to Das' parlour at Panchanantala at Howrah, where street beggars pick up songs on the scandal. For a brief moment, then, he seems to have become a well-known figure in the city, a point of reference, although it seems that his fame did not survive the play.[42]

The play is priced at one anna, which, like the price of a Kalighat painting, was reasonable and likely to command a wide readership.[43] The fortunes of the Bengal Theatre were made from the proceeds of this one play, *Mohanter Ei Ki Kaj!*; its phenomenal theatre run was remembered into the next century by a major playwright-cum-actor of those days;[44] and the play was picked up by a host of other companies and performed outside Calcutta. It also left a trail of scandal plays in its wake, many of which, fondly or enviously, recalled its vast success in their scripts. So 'common' had theatre become that the great men of theatre were already bemoaning the downgrading of a noble art form which would now lower its tone to accommodate the lower orders. Interestingly, Girish Ghose, the giant of the theatre world, wrote a doggerel on this note which focused on the low-caste composition of the new audience as a measure of its corruption.[45]

The early 1870s were a transitional moment in yet another sense.

---

[41]The author is Lakshminarayan Das. Other low-caste authors include Chandrakumar Das, Iswarachandra Das De, Upendranath Das, Tinkari Das Ghosh, Nemaichand Seal, Maheshchandra Das, Jaharilal Seal.

[42]Surendrachandra Bandyopadhyay, *Mohanter Karabash* (Calcutta, 1873).

[43]Harimohan Chattopadhyay, *Mohanto Pakshe Bhutonandi* (Calcutta, 1873).

[44]'Amritalal Basur Smritikatha', included in Brajendranath Bandyopadhyay, *Bangiya Natyashalar Itihas*, p. 237. Incidentally, Basu wonders here whether Lakshminarayan was not a Christian. It seems unlikely, however, for the fact would have attracted attention elsewhere.

[45]Brajendranath Bandyopadhyay, *Bangiya Natyashalar Itihas*, p. 112.

They intervened between the passing of the trauma of post-1857 colonial reprisals and brutality, and the beginning of a new round of repression and racial discrimination under Viceroy Lytton from the late 1870s. Lord Northbrooke's viceregalty constituted a relatively mild interlude, with no costly wars or entanglements with foreign affairs. The trouble over the income tax proposals had died down[46] and there was space to look beyond the doings of the state, though of course these remained important. With the decline of indigo, a major arena of blatant racial outrage was no longer so much in public view. Critical reason and reflection could now turn inwards, within structures of social and religious institutions, towards the family and the intimate domestic domain. This was the time when Bankimchandra wrote his great domestic novels, and when proposals for Hindu marriage reforms by dissident Brahmos constituted the most significant political controversy for Bengali Hindus. It was a moment of relatively frank and open introspection. An appropriate language for the literary discussion of such themes had reached a point of great refinement by that time. The 1870s were the golden age of Bengali satire, as well as of the subtle and delicate combination of tones of irony and romanticism that pervade Bankim's literary essays and novels as much as sections of the Battala farces and scandal plays. The upsurge of white racism, first in Lytton's policies and then during the Ilbert Bill agitation, would soon delegitimize self-criticism, and impulses for change would lead to a fierce status quoism *vis-à-vis* social and religious institutions and norms, grounding an emergent nationalistic spirit squarely in the defence of Hindu patriarchy as the last remaining, autonomous, non-colonized space.

There were other, class- and caste-related reasons for the resonance that such a scandal acquired in the 1870s. A bourgeois public sphere is bound up with the confirmation of its autonomy within civil society. This necessitates the simultaneous existence and acknowledgment of an intimate sphere of domestic affect where the bourgeoisie establishes its claim to an essentially human identity. In colonial Bengal, however,

[46]See Anil Seal, *The Emergence of Indian Nationalism: Competition and Collaboration in the Later Nineteenth Century* (Cambridge University Press, 1968), chapter 4.

the emergence of a bourgeois—or simply a Hindu middle class—public sphere related in a strikingly different way to the intimate sphere. Far from being a bourgeoisie in the established sense of the term, the connections of this middle class with productive forces and relations were markedly passive. The Permanent Settlement had generated a parasitic class of rent-receiving landowners. After the 1840s, most of the major Bengali financial and commercial ventures had collapsed. By the end of the century, trade, manufacturing and industry of any significant scale had come to be controlled by Europeans and non-Bengalis.[47] The classes that had some surplus capital to invest had been traumatized by the fluctuations in business cycles that wiped out their ventures and investments between the 1820s and the 1840s. They had, therefore, turned to land as the most secure field of investment, and a few of the major zamindars were experimenting with improving measures that might turn them into the first generation of capitalist landlords.[48] Large possibilities of profitable investment lay in the untrammelled 'rent offensive' by the gentry, its absolute control over tenants made possible by the Permanent Settlement. Any pro-tenant departures in state policy, therefore, would threaten the last avenues for entrepreneurship as much as make parasitic landlordism a little less comfortable. The highly organized protest movement by Pabna tenants in the early 1870s against the illegal extraction of cess by landlords was, for them, a challenge of a new kind.[49] They also inclined the government a little towards granting a measure of security to an upper category of tenants.[50] From the 1870s, too, there were the beginnings of some official classification of lower castes with the intention of reserving for them some kind of affirmative action in the future. These coincided with a

[47]See Amales Tripathi, *Trade and Finance in the Bengal Presidency, 1793–1833* (Calcutta, 1979), chap. 5.

[48]On this see Nilmoni Mukherjee, *A Bengal Zamindar: Jayakrishna Mukherjee of Uttarpara and His Times* (Calcutta, 1975), chapters 5–12.

[49]See K.K. Sengupta, *Pabna Disturbances and the Politics of Rent: 1873–1885* (Delhi, 1974).

[50]See Benoy Chowdhury, 'Agrarian Economy and Agrarian Relations in Bengal, 1859–1885', in N.K. Sinha (ed.), *The History of Bengal, 1757–1905* (Calcutta, 1967).

widespread self-respect movement among the low-caste Namasudra peasants.[51]

The developments were deeply threatening for the class/caste hegemony of the educated, largely upper-caste, Hindu gentry. These developments also threw into sharp relief the pretensions of its paternalist self-image. In the agitation against white indigo planters during the previous decade, landlords had occasionally confronted planters and supported the peasant's refusal to cultivate indigo.[52] With the Pabna agrarian uprising, the notion of a symbiotic relationship collapsed.[53] The fragility of the paternalist claims of an upper-caste orthodox patriarchy had similarly become evident through reformist agitation and colonial legislation to partially alter gender relations within Hindu conjugality. We find, therefore, the makings of a profound and comprehensive crisis here for an upper-caste, landowning middle class. Colonial rule had entirely deprived the upper-caste gentry of all possibilities of politico/military powers. Activism, whether in rural land relations, or in trade, finance and manufacture, was definitively eroded by the 1870s. Since an autonomous sphere—where the middle class could dictate its terms to production forces and relations—did not develop within civil society, its social privileges, its claims for autonomy and political power in the future could only be legitimized in the realm of human relations and religious belief. And given the problematic reflections of both in the Elokeshi–mohunt cases, at a time when social privileges in civil society had been threatened significantly—the political meaning of the scandal becomes evident. Hindu conjugal sexuality and its Other—adultery and/or rape—became an important register to test the morality of fundamental social and religious institutions.

<hr />

[51]See Sekhar Bandyopadhyay, *Caste, Politics and the Raj: Bengal 1872–1937* (Calcutta, 1990). Also by him, 'Social Mobility in Bengal in the Late Nineteenth and Early Twentieth Centuries', unpublished thesis, Calcutta University, 1985, chap. 5.

[52]See Amiya and B.G. Rao, *The Blue Devil: Indigo and Colonial Bengal* (Delhi, 1992), chap. 5.

[53]See Sengupta, *Pabna Disturbances*. An interesting point to note about the Pabna rising in this connection is how confidently the peasants used the law courts against the landlords.

The very significance, however, would soon turn into a burden. Introspection and self-criticism would appear to be slippery forms of self-indulgence that seemed very inadequately marked off from harsh and racist stereotyping. The scandal therefore marks a point of culmination as well as a point of departure.

IV

The times were therefore right for a major preoccupation with intimate conjugal matters. There had been, from the early decades of the nineteenth century, a number of proposed legal changes pertaining to the Hindu conjugal order. These proposed changes combined to problematize the foundations of Hindu domestic norms. Upper-caste domestic practices had long conditioned the living patterns of most upwardly mobile agrarian, artisanal and trading castes. While Brahmanical norms were widely generalized—for example, the ban on widow remarriage and the custom of infant marriage prevailed among girls from lower castes, whose caste customs did not originally prescribe such things, and even Shudra castes practised sati—there had been a corresponding long-term hardening of gender norms for women. Within Dayabhaga, the neo-Smarta legal school prevalent in Bengal, a progressive whittling away of womens' rights to property had been going on for several centuries. Raghunandan, the influential sixteenth-century authority of the Dayabhaga school of law, had made pre-pubertal marriage obligatory for Brahman girls,[54] and from the eighteenth century the Krishnagar Raj, a seat of Smarta orthodoxy, had tightened up the discipline of austere widowhood.[55] The process was invariably reflected and generalized at aspiring lower-caste levels.[56] Reformist projects therefore threatened not just the upper-caste rigidity from which lower-caste custom was exempt: they also put

[54]See Sureshchandra Bandyopadhyay, *Smritishastre Bangali* (Calcutta, 1961), chap. 4.

[55]See Shibnath Shastri, *Ramtanu Lahiri O Tatkalin Bangasamaj* (Calcutta, c. 1955), chap. 1. Also Rajat Kanta Ray, *Palashir Sharajantra O Sekaler Samaj* (Calcutta, 1994), p. 76.

[56]I have discussed this in 'Conjugality'.

at risk a larger structure of Brahmanical hegemonic domestic practices.

The deep involvement of Hindu public opinion with legal changes and processes indicated a relatively autonomous area of initiative that had been reserved for it within colonial rule. It is important to recognize that colonial law itself had upheld the right of indigenous religious systems to exercise control over the realm of belief and personal relationships. Personal laws were made identical with religious norms, and changes allowed only on the grounds of a more precise procedural interpretation of these. The very legal identity of a person, consequently, created a sharper sense of belonging to a religious community which, in turn, was closely tied to control of the intimate sphere. Such an understanding of Hindu and Muslim personal laws—these could now refer to Hindus and Muslims as monolithic wholes instead of to the customary practices of castes and sub-castes, as in earlier times—even helped to lead on to a notion of homogeneous, sharply bounded, religious community identities.

In the Company period this operation of personal laws had meant a dependence on rulings by pundits. Later, by the 1860s, the services of such pundits in the law courts were dispensed with, since the compilation and codification of a sizeable body of Hindu legal texts had by then been finalized. This displacement of living legal authorities with textual ones remained incomplete, all the same, and the opinion of Hindu lawyers and judges was deferred to up to Privy Council levels.[57] *Amrita Bazaar Patrika* made an interesting case for extending judiciary powers to a Bengali Deputy Magistrate: 'Bengalis are sure to make much better use of the powers . . . than Europeans . . . the fear of society and relatives and friends as well as other considerations will keep them back from doing anything likely to produce lamentations among their own people.'[58] The ideal legal and judicial operation, according to this construction, is the obverse of a universality dispossessed of all particularity. It is expected that the law dispenser is accountable to the opinion of his community and its norms—which override the claims of neutrality.

The institution of a native jury system in seven Bengal districts by the 1860s—including Hooghly, where the Tarakeswar cases were first

[57]For a discussion, see ibid.
[58]*Amrita Bazar Patrika*, 30 January 1873.

lodged—expanded the scope of Hindu public opinion. English judges too deferred to Hindu custom when reaching their verdicts. At the Sessions Court, Judge Field said he was assuming the fact of adultery because Elokeshi had been found 'joking and flirting' with the mohunt, an unrelated male. While this would not count as evidence in the case of Europeans, in Hindu society such behaviour surely signified, in his view, an adulterous connection. Hearing the appeal lodged by the mohunt at the High Court, Judge Markby made a similar point.[59]

In the 1890s the jury was withdrawn from many categories of cases but marriage-related disputes remained within their purview.[60] In fact, in the 1870s there were strident demands for an extension of the jury system. Over the Tarakeswar cases, heated debates followed the decision of the European judge who had overruled the juridical decision that Nobin was insane and hence not culpable.[61] Given the larger context of judicial changes, the Tarakeswar cases tied into a contestation over the European judge's right to rescind an Indian juridical opinion in matters of domestic disputes. They also reinforced middle-class allegations about Lt-Governor Campbell's offensive against the Hindu gentry which manifested itself in the new educational plans, the Road Cess, the arbitrary new Criminal Law Procedure Code, and an antipathy towards Hindu lawyers.[62]

So the crowds that besieged the mohunt and his lawyers as well others who interrupted the court proceedings—the petitioners who asked for a reversal of the court judgement, and the Bengali press who were preoccupied with the course of the trial—stemmed from an awareness of this informal right and function that had been claimed in the name of Hindu public opinion. Kalighat paintings usually depicted scenes from Indian domestic life and mythological events: they made a rare departure in the mohunt case. The courtroom scene in which the European judge sentences the mohunt spawned a series of paintings and

[59]Cited in Goswami, *Samajchitre Unabingsha Shatabdir Banglar Prahashan*, p. 268. Also Shri Pantha, *Mohanto Elokeshi Sambad*, p. 74.

[60]Sharmila Banerji, *Studies in the Administrative History of Bengal* (Calcutta, 1975).

[61]See *Biswadoot*, 3 November 1873, *RNP*, 1873. Also, *Hindoo Patriot*, 18 August 1873 and 1 December 1873. *RNP*, 1873.

[62]See *Hindoo Patriot*, 1/D/1873. Also *Halishahar Patrika*, 28/11/1873.

prints.[63] The specific character of the crime enabled public trials to link up the intimate sphere with the public domain, the everyday with the extraordinary event.

Popular imagination was so saturated with courtroom images that quite a few of the scandal plays were simply a duplication of the trials and of subsequent disciplinary proceedings. The divine world corresponded in many of these to the procedures of earthly justice. Elokeshi and her parents are tried in the courts of the gods where the prison guard and the police constables are Muslim spirits—'Mamdo bhoots'— since, in descriptions of the actual events, the same personnel are shown as Muslim characters.[64] The considerations at the divine trial are no more exalted than they are on earth; Elokeshi is chastised for throwing the Shaivite family name into disgrace by 'tempting' the mohunt. The mohunt is punished for squandering the family properties of Baba Taraknath by his indiscreet lust and for using temple funds for his own defence.[65] The title of one of these farces was a couplet: 'The mohunt is at the end of his tether/ He had developed dysentery, so hard had he to work at the oil press.'[66] The oil press refers to the hard-labour sentence under which the mohunt was supposed to work as a human substitute for the bullock that normally drives the press.

[63]Knizkova, *Drawings of the Kalighat Style;* and Archer, *Bazaar Paintings of Calcutta.* I think that Archer has wrongly identified the temple and the trial scenes as pictures related to a general rather than to a specific theme. He seems to be unaware of the Elokeshi episode and he dates the trial scenes around 1845, going by the style of the headgear of the figures. However, in many of the other paintings and prints the same scenes are firmly attached to this particular scandal. They are also appended in texts of the scandal plays. Their provenance is then decisively to be located within the Elokeshi episode. The paintings that Archer refers to are from the collections of Dr O.M. Samson and J. Lockyard Kipling, both of which were acquired well after the mohunt's trials. See Archer, *Bazaar Paintings of Calcutta,* Plate 7, p. 35, for the courtroom scene which he describes as 'An Englishman Dispensing Justice', *circa* 1845. The picture shows the mohunt in the dock, a Brahman man as also under arrest, and the severed head of a woman. Similarly, Plate 18, p. 46, describes the temple scene and the first meeting between the mohunt and Elokeshi as 'Women at a Shrine'.

[64]Surendrachandra Bandyopadhyay, *Jamalaye Elokeshir Bichar* (Calcutta, 1873).
[65]Ibid.
[66]Tinkari Das Ghosh (Calcutta, 1874).

The inherent suspense associated with an unfolding trial establishes a particularly lively affinity with the nature of drama and lends itself to effective dramatization. In the Elokeshi case, while the drama closely followed and modelled itself on trial scenes, the trial itself was theatrical enough to be consumed as drama. Newspapers remarked on this: 'People flock to the Sessions Court as they would flock to the Lewis Theatre to watch *Othello* being performed.'[67] The Hooghly sessions courts became so overcrowded during the trials that an entrance fee was charged. Only those who followed English were allowed entry since most of the proceedings—the mohunt's English counsel's speeches and the European judge's summing up and verdict—were in English.[68] In a sense, this can explain the popular hunger for Bengali plays that duplicate the court's proceedings. They would render the trials—partly conducted in a foreign language—into a comprehensive vernacular.

How does one explain this popular involvement in scrutinizing the operations of the law? The law was something that was being made and remade in everybody's view for practically the entire century. It was possible to follow from newspapers and published reports not only what laws were passed, but also what people were saying about them. These laws related to the most intimate aspects of life. From the early nineteenth century, along with new laws on sati and widow remarriage, a continuous process of the compilation of customs and the codification of legal texts had been going on. This was accompanied by the printing, translation and popularization of major texts at accessible prices. An informed and wide-ranging public discussion followed these processes of compilation as well as those of the proposed reforms and changes. Law lectures and professorships were instituted by Calcutta notables, newspapers monitored the functioning of Western legal experts, and Hindu lawyers and scholars were prolific with alternative interpretations and rulings.[69]

The most important feature of the process was its visibility, its publicness. The structures governing one's innermost beliefs, closest relationships and everyday practices are necessarily imbricated within

[67] *Bengalee*, 22 August 1873.

[68] *The Englishman*, 28 November 1873.

[69] See *Bengalee*, 8 July 1874, about the institution of the Tagore Law Professorship.

visible and invisible legal processes. These structures were now being dragged out, debated and contested in the public eye. In the process, the ideological basis of prescription and common sense was demystified and made transparent. Simultaneously, legality clashed with religious prescription in unprecedented ways: sati, the universally accepted sign of womanly virtue, was now classified as a crime. Widow remarriage, traditionally an entirely illegitimate desire, was made legal.

Not that the laws inverted the actual pattern of patriarchal practices. They did, however, open up a gap, a tension between what was normatively illicit and what was legally permissible. It produced arguments about what had always been largely unquestioned. That which was used as sacred prescription, as eternal norm, or which had been embedded within an unselfconscious common sense, was now opened up for frontal interrogation. This worried all those who were vested with power within Hindu society. Nobinchandra Sen, upper-caste poet and senior civil servant, opposed Bengali translations of sacred legal texts that the Bangabashi Press had sponsored because he believed they were not meant for low-caste eyes.[70]

V

The 1870s were a great time for other sexual scandals as well. In 1873, there was the Hogg *vs* Hogg case. The director of the postal department, Mr Hogg, suspected a liaison between his wife and Mr Cordery, an official in the department of education. He intercepted their letters and brought charges of adultery. *The Englishman* demanded that, rather than Mr Cordery, Hogg himself be punished for the violation of professional ethic.[71] Bengali newspapers would often turn to this case from the Elokeshi episode with some relief.[72] They would contrast Bengali sympathy for Nobin, who had killed an adulterous wife, with the dry legal sterility of English papers where professional ethic was privileged over true husbandly responsibility.[73]

[70]See Amiya Sen, *Hindu Revivalism in Bengal: 1872–1905*, p. 140.

[71]*The Englishman*, 28 November 1873.

[72]*Bengalee*, 17 May 1873. Also, *Hindu Hitaishini*, 1 November 1873. *RNP*, 1873.

[73]*Bharat Sanskarak*, 27 November 1873, *RNP*, 1873.

In 1875 the widowed daughter of Ishwarchandra Napit, barber to the Lt-Governor of Bengal, was found missing. Since she was known to be having affairs with two police constables, the constables suspected the barber of murdering his daughter. With the connivance of the European police commissioner, the family was tortured and a confession was forced. While the final scene was going on at the Alipore Court and a skull—reportedly that of the dead girl—had been produced to clinch the case, the girl dramatically walked in to announce she had eloped with another lover.[74] The case became a byword for police tyranny and corruption, occasionally also for British misrule and the hollowness of colonial forensic and judicial procedures.

In 1878, the so-called Great Adultery Case reached the Calcutta High Court. Here, Jogen Bose accused Upendranath Bose of adultery with his wife Kshetramoni and of fathering her child. His wife made a spirited rebuttal of the charges in court and accused her husband of being an unworthy partner. The case was further complicated by the fact that Upendranath was an uncle of Kshetramoni. There were especially scurrilous depositions by neighbours and servants reporting graphic bedroom scenes. Both parties were from the upper-caste, educated, and rich-middle class.[75]

Most such cases dealt with a crumbling conjugal order among important people. All the comments evoked dystopic images of a society where conjugal relationships no longer counted for anything. Yet representations of these cases were largely restricted to newspaper reports. The Napit Case produced a single farce of very high quality,[76] and the Great Adultery Case inspired two farces that were nowhere as

---

[74]For an account of the case, see Government of Bengal, Pol. 254—Progs of the Lt-Governor of Bengal, 1873: 'Case of Neemchand' etc.—Howrah Sessions. Also, *Note on the Howrah Murder Case*, No. 1370, Calcutta, 11 March 1873. Also, *Friend of India*, 22 May 1873.

[75]For a brief mention of the case, see Meredith Borthwick, *The Changing Role of Bengali Women, 1849–1905* (Princeton, 1984), p. 141. For a detailed and excellent study, see Pauline Rule, 'Who Owned Khettramoni? The "Great Adultery Case", Calcutta, 1876', unpublished paper. I am grateful to her for allowing me to use this paper.

[76]Anon, *Napiteswar Natak or the Great Barbar Drama* (Calcutta, 1873).

well known: I have no evidence that they were ever performed.[77] A minor farce on the Hogg Case, *The Police of Pig and Sheep*, was enacted on 1 March 1876 at the Great National Theatre. It does not seem to have been repeated elsewhere.[78] Obviously, the Elokeshi–Mohunt Case tapped a more dense and formidable structure of anxieties.

VI

At a time when traditional Hindu sacred authorities were facing a series of defections and challenges from reformers and Christian missionaries, even the orthodox faithful were finding it troublesome to defend or argue in favour of their continued leadership. While the sexual and financial corruption of holy men in control of sacred places had long been common knowledge, the new challenges made their continued acceptance in such locations embarrassing. Around the time that the Tarakeswar cases exploded, there were similar charges of the sexual exploitation of women pilgrims by other mohunts, especially the mohunt of Sitakundu and the mohunt of Chandranath at Chittagong.[79] In 1873 the wealthy mohunt of Begusarai in Monghyr was killed by local peasants for misconduct and oppression of tenants. The Bengali press observed that Madhavchandra Giri had escaped lightly.[80] It is significant that farce after farce appealed to the Sanatan Dharmarakshini Sabha to come to the rescue of Hindu society.[81] This was a new

---

[77]Natabar Das, *Makkelnama* (Calcutta, 1878) and Mahes Chandra De, *Mama Bhagnir Natak* (Calcutta, 1878). See Goswami, *Samajchitre Unabingsha Shatabdir Banglar Prahashan*, p. 253.

[78]Shankar Bhattacharya, *Bangla Rangalayer Itihasher Upadan* (Calcutta: Paschimbanga Rajya Pustak Parishad, 1982), p. 139.

[79]*Dacca Prakash*, 16 March 1873; and *Hindu Hitaishini*, 29 March 1873, *RNP*, 1873.

[80]*Doot*, 22 September 1873, *RNP*, 1873.

[81]See, for instance, Tinkari Mukhopadhyay, *Mohanter Ki Durdasha* (Calcutta, 1873). It is interesting that other ascetics did support the public demand for deposing Madhavchandra from his post as mohunt. One Paribrajak Paramhans, for instance, filed a case against him, asking for his removal. Yet the newspapers and the farces do not ask the ascetic orders to come to the rescue, whereas they appeal to modern revivalistic organizations. See *Sambad Prabhakar*, 14 October 1873, *RNP*, 1873.

and modern organisation that developed as a response to Christian proselytisation and Brahmoism. Traditional hegemonic authorities were obviously in a state of crisis and such disclosures helped to generate clusterings of a new kind of religious leadership that would play a large role in the revivalist movements starting with the decade that followed.

More significant was the doubt over whether the colonial state should not revise the non-interventionist Religious Endowments Act of 1863 and intercede positively in preserving the sanctity of holy places. The doubt hinted at affirming the state as a better guardian of religious life than indigenous authorities. In fact, much of the criticism of colonial authorities was directed at suspected connivance between the mohunt and the government, at too little interference and control.[82]

An interesting fact about the cases was the widespread and immediate consensus that the mohunt was guilty—a conviction that did not wait to be confirmed by court decisions. The trials were celebrated, in farces and in paintings, primarily as great social levellers. Nobin was the poor and helpless Brahmin youth who finally managed with the aid of law and justice to expose the mighty, overpowerful mohunt. He was, incidentally, a purer Kulin Brahmin, more exalted in caste terms than the mohunt, whose precise caste status in his pre-ascetic life was in some doubt. Some thought that the unquestioned public sympathy for Nobin derived from this.[83] The mohunt's prison sentence, his hard labour, his humiliation at the hands of the judges, the prison guard and the police, were the exclusive themes of several farces and many songs. A large number of plays have titles that refer to his woes—that is, they have the punishment as their central theme.[84] I have already referred to the immense popularity of the oil which the mohunt had allegedly

[82]*Sahachar*, 1 December 1873, *RNP*, 1873.

[83]*Bengalee*, 22 July 1873. Also, *Bangabidyaprakashika*, 5 December 1873, *RNP*, 1873.

[84]See Bholanath Mukhopadhyay, *Mohanter Chakrabhraman* (Calcutta, 1874); Tinkari Mukhopadhyay, *Mohanter Ki Durdasha*; Chandrakumar Das, *Mohanter Ki Saja* (Calcutta, 1873); Surendrachandra Bandyopadhyay, *Mohanter Dafarafa*; Jogendrachandra Ghosh, *Mohanter Ei Ki Dasha* (Calcutta, 1874); Surendrachandra Bandyopadhyay, *Mohanter Karabash* (Calcutta, 1873), and several others.

manufactured during his prison sentence. In fact, this form of hard labour was relatively new and its novelty partly explains the ubiquity of this motif in the farces and paintings, as well as in the marketplace.

In 1838 a report was published by a committee appointed from among the principal members and secretary of the law commission. It suggested that the earlier custom of engaging criminals in outdoor labour, such as road building, should be replaced by setting them to do the indoor work of prison manufacture—the products of which would be sold to set up a fund for public works. In 1858 a public exhibition of such items was held in the Calcutta Town Hall and the sale profits amounted to Rs 111,582, accruing from the fifty-five prisons in Lower Bengal in the year 1855–6.[85] There was thus a new and heightened consciousness about the transformed nature of prison labour, much publicized by official sales-promotion techniques: these must have gathered major profits from the mohunt case. The high price of the supposedly mohunt-made oil was also partly a celebration of the demonstrated superiority of the power of law over that of the power of social leadership. Similarly, when the great estate holder Jayakrishna Mukherjee was tried and imprisoned for fraud, *Hutom Penchar Naksha* recorded (or invented) the street songs that celebrated his fall.[86] A scandal play joyfully observes about a case involving the Maharaja of Burdwan: 'Even Maharaja Tejchandra Bahadur is forced to make a daily appearance in the courtroom. English judges do not differentiate between the high and the low.'[87] I found only one play that criticised the humiliation of a holy man by unbelievers and which concluded that Durga had sent the famine of 1873 to Bengal in order to avenge the troubles of her favourite son.[88] Another play depicted the seduction of Elokeshi as a result of the genuine love that the mohunt had conceived for her; in the end, he is deeply repentant.[89] His immoral ways are, otherwise, nowhere in question. The bazaar

[85]John Stuart Mill, *Memorandum on the Improvements in the Administration of India during the Last Thirty Years*. See Robson, Moir and Moir (ed.), *John Stuart Mill: Writings on India* (Routledge, 1990), pp. 116–17.

[86]Kaliprasanna Singha, *Hutom*, p. 45.

[87]Ghosh, *Mohanter Ei Ki Dasha*.

[88]Harimohan Chattopadhyay, *Mohanto Pakshe Bhutonandi*.

[89]Surendrachandra Bandyopadhyay, *Mohanter Dafarafa*.

paintings and the woodcut prints generally show him as a weak, dissolute womanizer, and the temple as a haven for pimps.[90]

The pilgrimage to Tarakeswar had boomed largely because of the fame of its miracle cures for several diseases, especially barrenness.[91] A large number of young women therefore flocked to the place and undertook the prescribed penances within mixed crowds and with no privacy in an extremely congested space. In a number of the scandal plays, Elokeshi visits the mohunt the first time to receive a cure for barrenness and the mohunt, attracted by her, plans the seduction. There were rumours that the mohunt selected his victims from among young pilgrims, and then his musclemen would procure these for him.[92] Afterwards, the women could not return to their families: their only sanctuary lay in the growing brothels of Tarakeswar. Newspapers in 1873 were full of lurid descriptions of the licentiousness of the temple pandas or touts at Puri and Tarakeswar.[93] Much earlier, a satirical verse narrative had depicted Tarakeswar as a place for illicit assignations.[94] There were many reports on the proliferation of brothels at pilgrimages.[95]

The Elokeshi episode was a massive public confirmation of all these fears. The unholy ambience of holy places spilled into wider suspicions about religious occasions and ceremonies in general. These were seen as licensed misconduct in public places—the bathing ghats, for instance, which might also be used by pious women.[96] Missionary criticism of

[90]See Knizkova, *Drawings of the Kalighat Style*; and Paul, *Woodcut Prints*.

[91]Anon, *Ajker Bajar Bhau*.

[92]Maheshchandra Das De, *Madhvgiri Mohanto Elokeshir Panchali* (Calcutta, 1874).

[93]*Halishahar Patrika* report cited in *Sulabh Samachar*, 24 May 1873. Also, *Grambarta Prakashika*, 16 August 1873, *RNP*, 1873; *The Englishman*, 13 December 1873.

[94]Bhabanicharan Bandyopadhyay, *Nababibibilash, circa* 1822. *Rachanasamagra* (Calcutta: Nabapatra Prakashan, 1987).

[95]In Jogendrachandra Ghosh's scandal play, as a sign of ultimate humiliation, Muslim peasants discuss this aspects of Hindu pilgrimages. *Mohanter Ei Ki Dasha*. It is interesting that in another satire, the voice of the Muslim had been used as the supreme criticism of the pretensions of Hindu piety. See *Buro Shaliker Ghare Ron* of Michael Madhusudan Dutt, *Madhusudan Rachanabali* (Calcutta: Sahitya Sansad, 1965), pp. 255–68.

[96]*Amrita Bazaar*, 20 February 1873; *Sulabh Samachar*, 18 March 1873, *RNP*,

Hindu practices was often based on horrified reports of the sexualized nature of Hindu religious beliefs and rites, and such criticism could have shaped the self-critical or self-purificatory mood among worried Hindus. Yet a purely mimetic motivation would be too slight an explanation: we need to seek the roots of a positive reception of this strand of missionary criticism among Bengali Hindus, as criticism which they understood more in relation to their own experiences and problems. The larger reformist critique about the place of women in the Hindu social order was translated at an immediate and palpable level as the vulnerability of women at the hands of their social guardians and superiors. Much of the reporting in vernacular newspapers focused on abduction or attacks on women by zamindars, policemen, upper-caste superiors and holy men.[97] The Elokeshi scandal made the family—natal as well as marital—complicit with the structure of violence. That, perhaps, was the most powerful source of anxiety. All prescriptive texts—religious as well as modern legal—consign the woman to the domestic space under a protectionist ideology. The myth of the domestic sanctuary now stood decisively exposed.

There were other, standard patriarchal worries about pilgrimage journeys by women, especially their enhanced mobility in an age of safer roads and modern transport. The new railways carried a much larger number of women into such ambiguous holy places. The journey exposed 'respectable' women of ordinary means, those who would normally be secluded within the domestic space, to male contact and the male gaze within mixed crowds. Both journey and act of pilgrimage therefore aroused deep male fears about the erosion of boundaries, about women's exposure to men, and to different castes. The railway carriage became the sign of a dangerous modernity, of Kaliyug, of the loss of gender and caste anchorage. A contemporary satirist brilliantly evoked images of socio-sexual chaos in the overcrowded carriage: 'The

---

1873. See also Shastri, *Ramtanu Lahiri O Tatkalin Bangasamaj*, for the same point. Also Jadav Chandra Modak, *Stri Purushe Tirthayatra* (Calcutta, 1870).

[97]See previous notes on the misconduct of 'pandas' and other mohunts. Also, *Sahachar*, 7 July 1873. *Dacca Prakash*, 5 June 1873 and *Bharat Sanskarak*, 30 May 1873, *RNP*, 1873.

"hari" [the lowest of untouchables] on top of the babu, the woman on top of the man, the man on top of the woman, the bum against the mouth, and the mouth behind the bum.'[98]

Reformists argued that the scandal had made pilgrimage redundant because the sacredness of the sites had been disproved by the immorality of its custodians. The orthodox, on the other hand, insisted that the woman's holiest space lay within the family, in devoted service to the household and the family deity. It was only an immoral woman who used a religious pretext to wander outside the home. Scandal plays lectured young women who wanted a son by the grace of Baba Taraknath: while the preservation of the family line was a sacred duty, barrenness could best be cured by pleasing the gods at the domestic shrine. It was deemed more important to be a good woman than to be the mother of sons.[99]

VII

But who is the good woman? Where does her goodness lie, and what destroys it? Up to the 1870s, these questions remained remarkably open and troubled. I think that with these questions we come to the heart of the puzzle, to the waves that the scandals made.

The good woman—whether in reformist or in orthodox rhetoric—would primarily be the good wife, although the terms of description would differ. But how would the laws of the land define the good wife? Here we enter radical uncertainties about legal definitions and their consequences, as well as uncertainties about the more basic question: what precisely *are* the laws for the Hindus?

The nineteenth century was in Bengal the century par excellence for a thorough review of conjugality. The century had more or less started with the sati issue which split Hindu society right down the middle. The agitation in support of widow remarriage had widened cleavages. Around the time of the Elokeshi scandal, huge controversies were going on over the Brahmo Marriage Bill of 1872 which had initially

[98]Kalidas Mukhopadhyay, *Kalir Nabarang: Kalir Mahatmya* (Calcutta, 1873), p. 9. Also, *Bharat Sanskarak*, 29 August 1873, *RNP*, 1873.

[99]Jogendranath Ghosh, *Uh! Mohanter Ei Ki Kaj* (Calcutta, 1874).

proposed a radical package of reformed marriage laws for all Hindus. Since, at this point, Brahmos insisted on classifying themselves as Hindus, the reforms threatened to revolutionize marriage laws for all Hindus. Eventually, Law Member Henry Maine agreed with an enraged Hindu orthodoxy that Brahmos constituted a separate sect and that Manu's prescriptions remained canonical for Hindus. The aborted prospects of a fairly revolutionized conjugality still rolled on towards a thorough review of marriage norms and practices which preoccupied Hindus for the rest of the century.[100]

On trial were the foundational texts of Bengali Hindu conjugality—Manusmriti and the Dayabhaga modifications made by Raghunandan. The core of the system was the notion that the good woman is the chaste wife who remains faithful to the husband even if the marriage is not consummated and even if the husband dies—for marriage is not a contract but a sacrament. Such a wife is alone the true *ardhangini*—half the body of her husband—and it is on this understanding that she is granted a limited usufruct right to the husband's property under Dayabhaga.[101]

Upon this finished structure of an asymmetrical conjugal order, the law allowing widow remarriage dealt a massive blow, the full normative implications of which were being worked out in case after case even beyond the century. Its progenitor Vidyasagar had seen it as a way of saving infant widows. He was bitterly disillusioned by its meagre results.[102] Yet the significance of the act should really be traced in its long-term normative contestation of the fundamental assumptions of Hindu conjugality. Whatever Vidyasagar's intentions, the law itself had not stipulated that only *akshatayoni* or virgin child widows would be covered by it. The act enabled a situation where adult widows, having

[100]See 'Conjugality in this volume'. See also Amiya Kumar Sen, *Hindu Revivalism in Bengal*, chap. 2.

[101]See Lucy Carroll, 'Law, Custom and Statutory Social Reform: The Hindu Widow Remarriage Act of 1856' in J. Krishnamurty (ed.), *Women in Colonial India: Essays on Survival, Work and the State* (Delhi, 1989).

[102]See Sekhar Bandyopadhyay, 'Caste, Widow Remarriage and the Reform of Popular Culture' in Bharati Ray (ed.), *From the Seams of History: Essays on Indian Women* (Delhi, 1995). Also, Asoke Sen, *Ishwarchandra Vidyasagar and His Elusive Milestones* (Calcutta, 1977).

experienced a full-fledged sexual relationship with their husbands, could still remarry and still count as good women—legally, if not under sacred norms. This legal redefinition put enormous strains on the foundational moral concept that the good woman is one who has sexual contact with only one man over her entire lifetime, and if the husband's other marital obligations or death preclude even that, she must still remain untouched.

A legal loophole emerged in the 'Great Unchastity Case' or the Kerry Kolitani *vs* Moniram Kolita case of 1873, which unwittingly further complicated matters. A widow who does not remarry and whose chastity is beyond doubt at the time her widowhood commences is allowed a limited share of the husband's property under Dayabhaga. In 1873, a widow was accused of subsequent 'adultery' (adultery, since the marriage bond continues beyond the husband's death, as long as the wife is his half-body)—a charge proved in court. The High Court decision allowed her continued access to property because she was chaste when she came into property, and because after that the right becomes absolute.[103] This decision tore open the system that had made the woman's property right conditional on her chastity; and it fractured the supreme importance of chastity itself. A bourgeois notion of the absolute nature of property rights, then, clashed with scriptural and customary insistence that without absolute chastity a woman has no right to anything.[104]

The Widow Remarriage Act of 1856 had stipulated that widows about to remarry would forfeit their husbands' property. In the next century, judges and lawyers would perplexedly consider if it was fair to allow an 'adulterous' widow to enjoy full rights to property while a respectable woman, who decently planned to remarry, would have to

[103]See Carroll, 'Law, Custom'. See also *Murshidabad Patrika*, 18 April 1873, *RNP*. Also *Bengalee*, 26 April 1873 and 17 May 1873.

[104]*Dacca Prakash* (20 April 1873) argued that under Dayabhaga, 'when once the widow has come into possession of her husband's property, it is no longer his but hers and no one has any right to deprive her of it.' *Murshidabad Patrika* (18 April 1873), however, indignantly asserted that the High Court decision would encourage unchastity among widows, *RNP*, 1873. *Bengalee* (17 May 1873) used a different argument: 'What we object to is the arbitrary interpretation put by judges on our ancient sacred texts in the face of the opposition of the single native judge who had a seat in the court.'

forfeit the same. Would this be more or less conducive to the moral health of Hindu society?[105]

Completely unforeseen consequences relating to the judicial application of legal provisions combined with a new attitude towards individual property rights and new reformist agitations to loosen up the system of Hindu patriarchy—a patriarchy which had so far exercised absolute control over social mores. Reformist patriarchal norms, on the other hand, never really acquired that hegemonic power. Nor were new laws grounded on any strong or coherent notion about individual right, far less gender justice. Their most significant historical function was not so much the creation of a full-fledged alternative order as to be contestatory, destabilizing, problematizing. They certainly created the conditions for public dialogues, made way for at least the idea of counter-norms. In 1873, the National Theatre staged a highly successful play, *Swarnalata*, which put various aspects of the Hindu conjugal order in the dock. Newspapers provided long reviews of the plot, characters, message and possible social implications of each aspect of the play. They reported at length on audience reactions. The audience was the mirror to public opinion, and public opinion was the de facto jury.[106]

VIII

Other, secondary aspects of Hindu conjugality were taken up energetically in interpretations of the scandals and in the scandal plays. Elokeshi's father was an old man who, apparently, had been cruelly manipulated by the young and greedy stepmother. Unable to satisfy her sexually, he promised to buy her jewellery instead. For this purpose he allegedly sold off his own daughter to the mohunt. This theme dominated nearly all the scandal plays. The helpless lust of old men was a motif in many popular satires and farces, as was the husband's subordination to a young wife—which added a new bite to the popular theme of the henpecked man and domineering woman. More upmarket contemporary satires on the subject were Dinabandhu Mitra's *Biye Pagla Buro* and Michael

---

[105]Carroll, 'Law, Custom'.
[106]*Bengalee*, 9 May 1983.

Madhusudan Dutt's *Buro Shaliker Ghare Ron*.[107] These not only influenced the representation of the motif in the scandal plays, their popularity also shaped the reception and treatment of that aspect of the scandal in the public mind.[108] This inversion of the regular conjugal hierarchy was shown as the cause of familial disorder, of an abdication of the father's sceptre, of a collapse of moral regulations.[109] Characteristically, in the popular, semi-obscene bazaar literature, the more mortal sin was not an old man's possession of a young woman against her will but the latter's power over the man. In the Elokeshi episode, where male guardians within the Hindu family and society emerge as decisively unworthy, and where the culpability of the unchaste woman is somewhat undone via rape and murder, the focus on a greedy and corrupt woman relocates the story to a more familiar and acceptable register of misogyny and restores the trope of a female folk devil who gives a wrong twist to social order.

Another theme very popular in the baazar folk literature—a trend that the Elokeshi scandal confirmed—was fear of a wife's prolonged sojourn at her natal home. Forced transplantation of a very young girl to the totally unfamiliar soil of the patrilocal family was a traumatic process that remained incomplete in most cases; the girl would never entirely identify with the new family and a permanent sense of homelessness would continue to besiege her. A patrilocal patriarchy, therefore, retained deep suspicions about the girl's natal home, about her incomplete emotional integration with her new family. Visits to the parental home were a rare pleasure, dependent upon the whim of the

[107]Dinabandhu Mitra, *Biye Pagla Buro*, first published in 1866. *Dinabandhu Rachanabali* (Calcutta: Sahitya Sansad, 1967), pp. 97–123. It was enacted with huge success by the National Theatre in 1873 with the famous actor/playwright Ardhendushekhar Mustafi playing the main role. See Brajendranath Bandyopadhyaya, *Bangiya Natyashalar Itihas*, p. 120. Michael Madhusudan Dutt's *Buro Shaliker Ghare Ron*, first published in 1859 and first staged in 1866, had a long stage run, well up to the 1870s. *Madhusudan Rachanabali* (Calcutta, 1965), pp. 255–68. See Introduction by Kshetra Gupta, pp. 52–4.

[108]In 1873, the Jorasanko Nabaranga Natyashala sponsored a play on the same theme, entitled *Bridhhyasya Taruni Bharyya* (Calcutta, 1873).

[109]See for instance, Nandalal Ray, *Nobin-Mohanto-Élokeshi Natak* (2nd edn, Calcutta, 1875).

new authorities. They were mostly withheld: the bride soon became the source of the hardest domestic labour within the new household and her absence was intolerable. The wife who spends a large slice of her time with her own parents is a woman who deprives her new masters of valuable labour time. However, control over labour is a concept that needs at least to be masked and mystified, whether in political or in domestic economy. Control over the wife's sexuality on the other hand— the other argument against long absences from the new home—is more familiar, securely grounded in sacred prescription, and therefore possible to articulate more openly. Elokeshi's crisis, in most plays, was explicitly linked to her long stay with her parents, where she escaped the discipline of her husband's home. Sympathetic older relatives advised her that fidelity to her husband was a more urgent and superior need than obedience to her parents, that the married woman has no master other than her husband.[110] In these ways Hindu patriarchy was appropriating certain new turns that colonial laws had given to the structure of disciplinary mechanisms that ruled the woman, transferring the jurisdiction and execution from the hands of a large kin group to those of the husband.[111]

The central problem, however, was what to make of Elokeshi. The plays are dialogic and multiphonal on this point, even though on secondary aspects they give more conventionally patriarchal answers. On the other hand, the bazaar paintings and prints are less ambiguous. In the series on the first meeting between the mohunt and Elokeshi, they all show three figures; a completely captivated mohunt, an older woman go-between who is low-caste (*tili-bou*), and Elokeshi, dressed in a dancing girl's costume and casting an immensely experienced, come-hither look at the mohunt.[112] Clearly she is seducing him. Equally clearly— since in other scenes she is dressed in a sari—the absence of a sari in this one points at her innate unwifeliness, her illicit desires, her status as a public woman at heart.

[110]Ghosh, *Uh! Mohanter Ei Ki Kaj.*

[111]On this see Radhika Singha, 'Making the Domestic More Domestic: Criminal Law and the "Head of the Household"—1772–1843', in *The Indian Economic and Social History Review*, vol. 33, No. 3, 1996.

[112]See Archer, *Bazaar Paintings of Calcutta*; and Paul, *Woodcut Prints.*

Given the condemnation so explicitly made in this group of popular representations, the ambivalence of the scandal plays is striking. Elokeshi was unchaste; she also had a fairly longstanding affair with the mohunt, even if she had been raped in the first instance. She certainly could be no simple victim figure here, despite her rape and murder. That would constitute a total, clear break with Hindu conjugal norms.

The problem of representation is often managed by a double-voicedness. Two sets of women talk about Elokeshi: one the village wives, the other the village prostitutes. On the whole, the wives condemn her, they doubt her love for Nobin, they allege she was only too happy to be raped, they confidently and proudly assert that no one can rape a woman against her will. Elokeshi presents them with sudden access to worth and moral superiority.

In contrast, the prostitutes are compassionate, full of criticism of male lust and weakness. They believe in Elokeshi's innocence since they know how easy it is to be misjudged. Their comments, counterposed to those of the wives, make the boundaries between these two hermetically sealed worlds—of wives and prostitutes—open and porous, the properties of both interpenetrating. Prostitutes bemoan the loss of Elokeshi's wifely status and Elokeshi's fall shows up how fragile the status of the wife is, how narrow the gap between her and her Other. The prostitutes' words, therefore, render ironic the dialogues of the wives. The dialogues also serve to draw prostitutes into the world of drama, as part of the interpretive community.[113]

The inclusion of prostitutes is not accidental or fortuitous; they are a sign of new times within the theatre, a *double entendre*. The Bengal Theatre, which staged the first scandal plays, was also the first to employ prostitutes in female roles, replacing earlier convention where young boys played such parts.[114] It did so in the teeth of both reformist and orthodox opposition, the former objecting to the entry of 'bad' women into a noble cultural form, the exposure of young men to evil influence; and the latter disapproving of the new resources and oppor-

---

[113]See for instance, Chandrakumar Das, *Mohanter Ki Saja*.

[114]Brajendranath Bandyopadhyay, *Bangiya Natyashalar Itihas*, pp. 148–51. The first actresses were Jagattarini, Golap, Sukumari Datta, Elokeshi and Shyama.

tunities that prostitutes would now enjoy as artists, and resenting their elevation.[115] Girish Ghosh would later try to disarm both kinds of opposition by composing plays on sacred themes where actresses enacted holy characters, thereby turning theatre into a moral-pedagogical space and redeeming prostitutes by the aura of the characters they enacted.[116] In Vaishnavite devotion, identification with a holy character leads one closer to God and hence devotion itself is a form of theatre.

The Bengal Theatre also deployed an intensive advertising campaign to make theatre a family entertainment. It did so both by secluding special spaces for respectable women viewers and by focusing on domestic dramas. The scandal plays were among the first such ventures.[117] For the first time, then, the two poles could be contained within the same space and a larger drama unfolded beyond the stage as the respectable female gaze was turned on its erotic Other. Also for the first time, prostitutes played both the wife and the prostitute, as well as the dangerous middle term—the fallen wife. The *double entendre* was extended and enriched. In a very perceptive essay, Sudipta Kaviraj has talked about a spiralling ironic confusion between the wife and the mistress in Bankim's novel *Indira*, leading to a dizzying interpenetration of identities.[118] That kind of ironic comedy of errors belongs perhaps to a perception in the age of theatre: it is also the perception of a time when the basic anchors of conjugality have started to waver.

For wives in the audience, the situation would come to evoke curious responses, creating complicated circuits of desire. There would be the horror of meeting the Other in the flesh; there would also be the sting of seeing her as a successful woman in public. A number of contemporary plays dealt with themes relating to the abandoned wife, with an

---

[115]See *Amrita Bazar*, 16 January 1874. Also, *The Hindoo Patriot*, 18 August 1873.

[116]See Binodini Dasi, *Amar Katha, Nati Binodini Rachana Samagra* (Calcutta: Sahitya Sangstha, c. 1987, 1st edn 1912). It is important to note that this great actress, who enacted sacred roles, and who sent Ramakrishna into a trance, denied at the end of her life that theatre had thereby turned into an act of religion. She insisted that it was pure entertainment and really served no religious purpose. p. 8.

[117]Brajendranath Bandyopadhyay, *Bangiya Natyashalar Itihas*.

[118]Sudipta Kaviraj, *The Unhappy Consciousness: Bankimchandra Chattopadhyay and the Formation of a Nationalist Discourse in India* (Delhi, 1995), chap. 1.

errant husband who pursues an actress/mistress. In fact several of the scandal plays surmised that Elokeshi was left at her father's home for similar reasons. The wife-viewer would be simultaneously exposed to a dramatization of her condition, and to its transcendence by a glamorous rival. The spectacle of her goodness is thus rendered infinitely more problematic by the simultaneous spectacle of a glorious alternative—both transgressively dissolved within the same unchaste woman's body. Visually, therefore, chastity was both problematized and continuously polluted, even while it was formally celebrated.

IX

In 1873 the colonial government was deliberating on new laws for the compulsory registration of Muslim marriages and divorces. In their perception, Muslim men and women walked in and out of marriages far too easily and errant wives returned to husbands they had left as if the marriage was still on.[119] While colonial lawmakers saw in this a sign of Muslim moral immaturity, sections of the Hindu press were more sympathetic, especially towards wives who desired to return to husbands despite an earlier divorce. The *Bengalee* made an immensely significant statement in this connection: 'You say my conduct in taking back my wife is dishonourable: I myself am frail.'[120] Maybe the Hindu middle class found it easier to be more tolerant towards the problems of Muslim women than towards its own, but there were some signs of change, at least in ethical approaches. The limits of the sacred significance of woman's chastity were being probed, and the probings were carried a little beyond the expected limits. A daring assertion is made when the paper says: 'I, myself, am frail.' That is, for the woman, too, fidelity may not be the only test of love. Also that the sexual conduct of men can be judged by the same rules as women.

It is here that the scandal gains its most powerful resonance. All the accounts agreed that Nobin had always been a loving husband—a fact proved when, on coming to know of the scandal, his first impulse was

[119]Government of Bengal, Judicial Department: Registration of Muslim Marriages, No. 373, Dacca, 7 June, 1873, File 506–9/12.
[120]*Bengalee*, 26 April 1873.

not to leave or kill her but to run away with her and retrieve their lost happiness. Yet Elokeshi had lived for some time with the mohunt, most of the time fairly acquiescently. Whether or not she was still loyal to Nobin emotionally, she had certainly decisively surrendered her sexual chastity.

Woman's chastity had become a keyword in the political vocabulary of Hindu nationalism, which had begun to develop at about this time. The Hindu woman's unique steadfastness to the husband in the face of gross double standards, her unconditional, uncompromising monogamy, were celebrated as the sign that marked Hindus off from the rest of the world, and which constituted the Hindu claim to nationhood. The chaste body of the Hindu woman was thus made to carry an unusual political weight since she had maintained this difference in the face of foreign rule. The Hindu man, in contrast, as noted earlier, had allowed himself to be colonized and surrendered his autonomy before the assaults of Western power-knowledge.[121]

It was in this charged political context that the scandal was reviewed. According to newspapers, for a fairly wide segment of middle-class and popular opinion Nobin was morally wrong in taking back his guilty wife. Such love conceals a lapse from the moral duties of the husband and of the Hindu man's dharma. Abandoning her would have been both morally right and prudent; even killing her for such a crime was not excessive. However, for the murder to be justifiable it should have preceded the escape attempt. Less judgemental and more sympathetic songs still criticise Nobin for trying to rescue an unworthy wife and thereby putting his own life in danger.[122]

At the same time, Nobin's passionate love for an unfaithful wife powerfully captured the popular imagination. According to police reports, he had rushed to the police station after the murder with these words on his lips: 'Hang me quick. This world is a wilderness to me. I am impatient to join my wife in the next.'[123]

The words were reported verbatim in all the newspapers, and plays

[121]See chapter one in this volume.

[122]See for instance, *Bangadarshan*, 13 September 1873; *Bharat Samskarak*, 6 September 1873; *Hindu Hitaishini*, 1 November 1873.

[123]Reported in *Friend of India*, 5 June 1873.

and songs were woven round them.[124] There was no single manner in which the words were related. People confident of the Hindu husband's dharma still responded to their emotional pull and wondered about the sources of such love. We have already noted the reference to the Lewis Theatre, where *Othello* was being played. The popularity of the play was enormous. Perhaps the theme of tragic sexual jealousy at least partly structured the reception of the event by the theatre-going and reading public, lifting it above the domain of unconditional assent to the domain of murder. Conversely, a growing unwillingness to live by prescriptive gender judgements alone, an ability to see love as an unresolved social problem, conditioned the reception of *Othello* as well as of the scandal plays.

On the whole, however, a fairly moderate version of conjugal duties prevailed. Nobin's words were celebrated not as the sign of unreason and weakness but of noble and strong love.[125] The incorporation of this love within the given boundaries of Hindu conjugality was attempted through a narrative move. In most of the plays, Elokeshi is first drugged and then raped.[126] The interval between the first rape and the confession—that is, the time when Elokeshi had lived with the mohunt—is telescoped and practically erased so as to reduce her moral culpability and to legitimize Nobin's forgiveness.

A few of the plays go a little further. If all the scriptures, including the great Manu, insist that the woman should be obedient to her male guardians, that she must not act or think or judge for herself, then did Elokeshi have an option beyond obeying her father and the holy man in her husband's absence? If she lived within a structure of prescriptions that left her with no option, had she transgressed at all? If she had not, should not the prescriptions be on trial rather than the woman's conduct? A number of plays make this point by focusing on the scene where Elokeshi helplessly gives in to her parents, rather than on scenes of rape and seduction. Lack of will and helplessness are identified as the source of her ruin rather than an incurably immoral female nature. Passivity,

---

[124]See, for instance, De, *Madhavgiri Mohanto Elokeshir Panchali.*
[125]Ghosh, *Uh! Mohanter Ei Ki Kaj!*
[126]Bholanath Mukhopadhyay, *Mohanter Chakrabhraman* (Calcutta, 1874).

meekness, gentle obedience—that is, precisely the prescribed wifely norms—are not only portrayed as dangerous but also as repulsive traits in order to reduce the entrenched aesthetic charge and emotional appeal of their figuration.[127] Soon, strong counter-images were evolved of independent, assertive and active figurations of female virtue as alternative inspirational models. Interestingly, this figuration takes place not within the domestic space so much as within an emerging space of anti-colonial activism.[128]

A few reformist voices carry the interrogations even further. If social norms and prescriptions rather than an innately weak feminine disposition had caused the predicament, then was the woman for killing? However strong his love and bitter his temporary rage, was Nobin not a murderer, and hence deserving of punishment? Was then the European judge not more correct than the Indian jury and public opinion? The petitioners who pleaded for Nobin's release had admitted that Elokeshi was more sinned against than sinning; however, given the choice of leaving her with the mohunt and killing her, Nobin, they said, had acted as a true husband, since a life of dishonour is worse for a woman than death. Plays and songs and most newspapers did not go beyond this. *Bengalee*, the reformist newspaper, raised a lone voice to articulate an unexpected argument: 'In sympathising with the unfortunate Nobin people forget that the victim was not the man that he and all Bengal believe to be a vile seducer, nor the still worse scoundrel who bartered his daughter's virtue . . . but a tender girl of 16 years . . . . What had she done to forfeit her young life?'[129]

She had been unchaste, but that no longer seems to suffice as an adequate reason. For, 'I myself am frail'. Here we have—even for reformers who usually moved within patriarchal parameters of womanly purity and companionate marriage—an unusually powerful articulation of male guilt. Rammohun Roy had expressed it when he described

[127]De, *Madhavgiri Mohanto Elokeshi Panchali.*

[128]See for instance, Upendranath Das, *Surendra Binodini* (Calcutta, 1876), where a woman outwits a tyrannical sahib. The play was a contributory factor behind the passage of the Dramatic Performance Act.

[129]*Bengalee*, 1 November 1873.

how men ensure that ignorance remains the lot of women and then describe it as her natural condition.[130] Vidyasagar expressed it in a lament: 'Alas, the wretched women of India . . . for what sins in your past lives are you born as women of this country?'[131] Couched in protectionist terms, this nonetheless goes beyond the parameters of naturalizing gender differences and stipulating a protective ambience towards the 'weaker sex'.[132] It grounds the weakness of women in male prescriptions, demands, and the disciplinary order. Hindu nationalists of subsequent decades would displace this male self-division with guilt about surrender to Western and colonial cultural domination.

The new public sphere surely did not promise anything like a coherent challenge to the divisions: male—public/female—private. Nonetheless, that division does not act as a central, unambiguous structuring principle either. It radically questions its own presuppositions, which falter even while they are being recast. I think that for a limited historical moment the faltering was more significant, and a simple or flat notion of recasting does not capture much of what was really involved.

It is within this sense of guilt that the deepest resonances of the scandal need to be located. And the real transition to Hindu cultural nationalism lay through a suppression and displacement of this guilt. Soon, public debates would decisively shift their ground and there would be little room left for looking at women like Elokeshi—a girl whose father sold her off, whose guru raped her, and whose husband killed her.

---

[130]Cited in Prabhatmohan Gangopadhyay, *Banglar Nari Andolan* (Calcutta, c. 1945), p. 15.

[131]Ishwarchandra Vidyasagar, *Bidhababibaha: Dwitiya Pustak in Vidyasagar Rachana Sangraha* (Calcutta, 1872), p. 165.

[132]For an elaboration of the notion of protectionism, see Kapur and Cossman, *Subversive Sites: Feminist Engagements with Law in India* (New Delhi, 1996), pp. 22–3.

CHAPTER THREE

A Book of Her Own,
A Life of Her Own
The Autobiography of a Nineteenth-
Century Woman

(On getting married) 'I went straight into my mother's arms, crying, "Mother, why did you give me away to a stranger?"'

(After marriage) 'My day would begin at dawn and I worked till two at night . . . I was fourteen years old . . . I longed to read books . . . But I was unlucky, those days women were not allowed to read.'

(Learning to read at twenty-five) 'It was as if the Great Lord himself taught me how to read. If I didn't know even that much, I would have had to depend on others . . .'

(Looking back on her youth) 'In the meantime the Great Lord had decked my body out just the way a boat is fitted out . . . How strange it was: So many things came out of my body, yet I knew nothing of their causes.'[1]

These are some important words and themes from *Amar Jiban*, the first autobiography written by a Bengali woman, and very probably the first full-scale autobiography in the Bengali language. Her writing and her life stand in a peculiarly significant relationship to each other, since the author, Rashsundari Debi, a housewife from an upper-caste landed family in East Bengal, seemed to possess none of the things that presumably make a woman's life noteworthy.

[1]Rashsundari Debi, *Amar Jiban* [*AJ*], pp. 18, 22, 31, 44. Reprint of 1897 edition in *Atmakatha, Ananya* publications (Calcutta, 1981). *AJ* was first published in 1876. A second, enlarged version came out in 1897, a third one in 1906, and a fourth edition appeared in 1956.

It was an uneventful, unremarkable life. Rashsundari was born around 1809 in Potajiya village in Pabna district, in a landowning family. When she was twelve, she was married off to Sitanath Ray, a prosperous landlord from Ramdiya village at Faridpur. From the age of fourteen, she looked after the entire household and brought up twelve children. When she was twenty-five, however, Rashsundari made a daring departure. She secretly taught herself to read and studied all the religious texts that her home possessed. Later, she also learnt to write. At fifty-nine she became a widow, and her autobiography was finished in the same year, in 1868. She revised and enlarged it when she was eighty-eight.

Only one event of an exceptional kind had interrupted the even, quiet rhythms of a pious housewifely existence. Orthodox Hindus of those times believed that a literate woman was destined to be a widow. In Rashsundari's own family there was so much talk against women's education that she would not even look at a piece of paper lest she was suspected of reading.[2] The first tentative experiments among liberal Indian reformers and Christian missionaries to educate women from reform-minded families had produced a sort of orthodox backlash and had hardened Hindu opinion against it. The meek and submissive housewife had no doubt at all that she was going against the grain of familial and social expectations. This one act of disobedience, then, partially deconstructs the 'good wife' role she played all her life.

Why did she, on her own, and in great trepidation, make this deeply transgressive departure? And what bearing does this desire and this achievement have on the fact that Rashsundari was the first Bengali person to write out her own life, to recreate, even invent it through the autobiographical act, and thereby gather it closer to herself and possess it more fully? What were the resources available to her that could have produced this desire and what are the new possibilities that we can read into women's lives and women's writing from the presence of this desire?

In the book Rashsundari explains that it was an irrepressible urge to read a particular sacred text that made her struggle to read.[3] The

---

[2]*AJ*, p. 23.
[3]Ibid., p. 21

book was *Chaitanya Bhagavat* [*CB*], the first Bengali biography of Chaitanya, the Krishna-maddened saint of medieval Bengal who had promised salvation to the poor, the low-caste, the woman—categories excluded by the Brahmanical orthodoxy from higher spiritual learning.[4] She went on to read other lives of Chaitanya and of Krishna.[5] Her reading, then, had a lot to do with lives divine and saintly. With a covert design that hid behind a seeming unintentionality, Rashsundari was audaciously structuring her mundane life story on that sacred pattern. Each detail of a thoroughly commonplace and homebound life was arranged to exemplify a godly intervention, the crowning proof of which was her apparently miraculous access to the written word. Her life was meant to be read as if it was enclosed within a divine purpose, as almost an extension of God's own life. It was as if the two lives—God's and the devotee's—were intertwined within a single narrative frame, interanimating each other. In fact, the last sections of the autobiography describe, without any apparent sense of incongruity,

---

[4]Vrindaban Das, *Sri Chaitanyacharitamrita*, ed. Kanchan Basu (Calcutta, 1986), p. 143. Vishnu is the preserver of Creation who has taken on different incarnations in different ages to save and protect the world. From early medieval times, major devotional traditions developed around the incarnation of Krishna who spent his youth among the low-caste cowherds of Vrindaban, which devotees associate with the important pilgrimage centre located at modern Uttar Pradesh. Later, he became the king of Dwarka and played a major role in the battles which the epic *Mahabharata* narrates. Chaitanya, who founded a massive, popular devotional movement in Bengal, was born in 1486 in a Brahmin Vaishnav family at Nabadwip, the major centre of Brahmanical scholarship in medieval Bengal. A noted scholar himself, he later became an ascetic, and preached an extremely emotional form of bhakti that was accessible to all castes and which required public congregational singing and dancing in Krishna's name. His acolytes started a vast proselytisation campaign in all parts of Bengal. A group of disciples went to Vrindaban and prepared a theological canon for Bengali Vaishnavs. Chaitanya was deified in his lifetime and became a central figure of adoration. He died around 1533. *CB* was composed about fifteen years after his death. Interestingly, the Chaitanya movement generated the first (and a very rich) corpus of biographical literature in the Bengali language. Studies of the Vaishnav movement in Bengal are vast and highly interesting. I have particularly used S.K. De, *Early History of the Vaisnava Faith and Movement in Bengal* (Calcutta, 1961); Ramakanta Chakrabarti, *Vaisnavism in Bengal, 1486–1900* (Calcutta, 1985); Hitesranjan Sanyal, *Bangla Kirtaner Itihas* (Calcutta, 1989).

[5]*AJ*, p. 41.

not events from her own life, but from the various lives (incarnations) of Vishnu himself.[6]

Rashsundari read from a fairly wide spectrum of late medieval devotional (bhakti) texts and her reflections drew largely upon terms that have long and multiple lineages within Hindu religious discourses. Unless we refer often and in some detail to this thick web of intertextuality, *Amar Jiban* will make only a limited and emasculated sense—as a mere string of random effusion and exhortation held together by a few sparse facts from a commonplace life.

Again, even though the history of her own times and place seems remarkably absent within the text itself, the book, as a material product created by a woman and printed for a nineteenth-century readership with an assured interest in a woman's writing, belonged crucially to her century. We need to explore the insertion of historical processes into the life as well as into the text, even though Rashsundari herself showed no overt preoccupation with them.

II

Vaishnav bhakti in Bengal (devotional discourses and practices that established a direct emotional connection between Vishnu in his incarnation as Krishna,[7] and the devotee), seemed to grant an unprecedentedly large and free space to the woman. The great body of bhakti lyrics glorified the illicit love between Krishna and the cowherd maidens (*gopinis*) of Vrindaban, of whom Radha was of paramount importance. A popular trope within devotional expression was to borrow the woman's voice and emotions. Esoteric cults loosely affiliated to Vaishnavism placed a powerful emphasis on the practice of sexual rites between a man and a woman who were not married to each other. Though all these traditions seemed to privilege the woman's experience and emotions in multiple and prominent ways, they delineated, at the same time, a fundamentally problematic space for her by largely containing the libertarian impulses and possibilities within devotional

[6]Ibid., part II.
[7]Ramakanta Chakrabarti, chapters 4 and 5.

meditation and sexo-yogic practices. Ultimately, their combined effect was to heighten the sheer instrumentality of the woman's body and emotions within devotion itself. Again, even though post-Chaitanya bhakti had generated an immense body of religious writing in Bengali, and had stimulated reading habits among sections of Vaishnav women and low-caste rural households, Vaishnavism had tense and paradoxical perspectives on the matter of scriptural and textual knowledge. Rashsundari's devotion and writing as a woman, therefore, related in complex ways to traditions which were partly enabling but partly so constricting that she needed to make crucial departures and breaks of her own within bhakti.

Rashsundari made a major innovation in religious as well as in literary conventions by articulating a devotional statement through the autobiographical mode. There were at least two distinct Bengali language resources available to her for writing about divine intervention in human lives, although none was autobiographical. One was the genre of medieval and late medieval *mangalkavyas* or verse narratives about the exploits of a deity who establishes his/her worship on earth by working through a human agency.[8] These would generally be sung or recited by professional expounders of sacred texts (*kathaks*) with explanations and commentaries. Shorter versions would be orally transmitted by women during women's rites.

Initially these cults had low-caste, folk origins and were shunned by the Brahmanical orthodoxy. Several centuries of rule by Muslim dynasties in Bengal, however, saw a decline in the socio-political hegemony of Brahmins. They sought to retrieve it by appropriating some of these deities within the mainstream Hindu pantheon. A number of upper-caste poets composed *kavyas* or long sacred ballads about them and Brahmin kathaks read them out to village gatherings. This partially—though only very partially—closed the cultural gap between upper and lower castes and gave Brahmins a larger entry and control within what used to be autonomous subaltern beliefs and practices.

As an upper-caste Vaishnav woman in an orthodox family, Rashsundari would have listened to readings and practised rites connected

[8]Sukumar Sen, *Bangla Sahityer Itihas* (Calcutta, 1965).

with these cults and texts. She, however, never mentioned them. It seems that in her remembered and self-constructed life, Rashsundari chose to opt out of the world of women's culture, piety and collective rites with their songs, ritual, colour and bustle. The choice has wider connotations which we shall explore later.

The other tradition available to her and one which did inspire her devotion, was that of Vaishnav hagiography. She herself had read at least two of them—*Chaitanya Bhagavat* [*CB*], and *Chaitanya Charitamrita* [*CC*]. *CB*, written by a disciple of a close acolyte of Chaitanya, and within fifteen years of Chaitanya's death, has a captivating narrative flow and combines quotidian, intimate details with an effusive, hyperbolic mode of devotional expression.[9] *CC* was composed later by Krishnadas Kaviraj under the inspiration of a theologian who belonged to a group of scholars whom Chaitanya had sent to Vrindaban to prepare a Vaishnavite canon for Bengal. These theologians (Goswamis), had worked out a consensus in the mid sixteenth century with the various Vaishnav sects in Bengal which gave their texts canonical status among Bengali Vaishnavs. The *CC*, unlike the Sanskrit Goswami texts, was written in Bengali.[10] It could, therefore, have a far wider reach and popularise the theological concepts of the Goswamis among non-learned *bhakts*. It also provided a model for the theological discussion in the vernacular that was built around the unfolding of a life-story.

Rashsundari drew much from both texts. She divided her writing into small sections, dealing with specific themes, and organised the sections into broad parts, covering whole phases of her life. She also had access to a chaste, literary vocabulary, and a fast-flowing, vivid style. Yet these hagiographies would not adequately serve her purposes. She needed a sustained, autobiographical mode to deal with the life events of an ordinary woman devotee, not holy chronicles about the wives and mothers of saints. She, therefore, needed to improvise.

There was yet a third alternative available to her, an oral model for

---

[9]It was particularly detailed about Chaitanya's early years. Although its accessibility made it immensely popular, its scholarship was not very highly thought of.

[10]Sukumr Sen, Introduction to Krishnadas Kaviraj, *Chaitanyacharitamrita* (New Delhi, 1963).

recording the popular miracle lore connected with the lives and activities of ascetics and holy men and women. Their sacred status was confirmed through tales of ecstatic trances and of miraculous manifestations. Rashsundari, however, was secure in her status as a successful housewife. She had neither renounced her mundane life nor aspired for extraordinary powers and competences. Her closeness to God could only be proved by her own writing. It was at once a miracle in its scope of achievement as well as a record of God's intervention in her life. Yet, it was a miracle that she alone had witnessed and her self-written life alone could testify to it. Unlike all these other modes of recording divine intervention in human lives, the autobiographical mode was indispensable for her. Her religion, her life, and her writing thus connected with one another to form an unbroken circuit.

III

By making her autobiography and her piety dependent on each other, Rashsundari tried to make two statements. The very act of writing established that her relations with God were more nuanced and more intimate than those that exist between most human beings and divinity. She also needed to problematise her own relationship to her household or *sansar*, since, on the surface, this sansar seemed to exhaust the entirety of her lived experiences. We need to explore the different meanings of this term in Hindu discourses and locate the forms of excesses beyond it that had been worked out in devotional and philosophical traditions. We would then find the ways in which *Amar Jiban* drew upon as well as departed from them.

Sansar is the domain of the householder, the stage of *garhasthya*, a vital phase within the prescribed four-stage life-cycle of a pious Hindu. Only an ascetic may renounce this realm of worldly responsibilities. The observance of prescribed ritual, caste and gender norms that had been spelt out by the Vedas and subsequent sacred law-codes would constitute the essence of a pious life or dharma. The woman enters sansar through the sacrament of marriage, the only sacrament that is available to her. For her, sansar is the unending flow of domestic work and responsibilities, primarily connected with cooking, serving, and child-rearing. Ideally, the woman should have no other religious activity, except for some prescribed ritual observances.

In a broader, theological sense, sansar, as governed by the scriptural prescriptions and injunctions (*vidhi nishedha*), is sustained by the rule of karma. This is the conviction that actions performed in one life bear results through successive rebirths and that only a strict obedience to the prescribed rules of sansar would eventually wear out the fruits of past action and deliver a human being from the karmic order of rebirth which is fundamentally painful. Sansar is thus the site of dharma as well as a site of trials. Some of the later philosophical schools sought to mark out a domain which would confirm yet also transcend the rule of sansar.[11] For our purposes, we may, perhaps, rather schematically identify three such sites.

Parts of the Upanishads had postulated an ultimate and fundamental identity between Brahman or Absolute Reality and Atman or the individual self and also among individual selves.[12] According to Shankaracharyya, a 'beginningless ignorance', stemming from Brahman's illusion-bearing power of maya, makes the individual self erroneously identify itself with a particular and finite body-mind, in a state of separation from and opposition to other selves. Only a few seers can, in this life, realise the deeper reality and achieve liberation from the bonds of karma. The rest are trapped within maya and are condemned to a strict observance of vidhi nishedha or prescriptions-injunctions.[13] It is interesting that while the source of human sorrow is located indirectly in a stratified and self-divided human order, a transcendence is sought within metaphysical knowledge alone. At the same time, the more the hierarchical order of the empirical world is left intact, the more intense is the emphasis on the essential oneness of all selves. While Shankar's monistic philosophy belongs to the realm of erudite specula-

[11]Accounts of holy women in June McDaniel, *Madness of the Saints: Ecstatic Religion in Bengal* (Chicago, 1989), Swami Gambhiranand, *Shri Ramkrishna Bhaktamalika* (Calcutta, 1952).

[12]R.C. Zaehner, *Hindu Scriptures* (Calcutta, 1992).

[13]Satish Chandra Chatterjee, 'Hindu Religious Thought', in K.W. Morgan, ed., *The Religion of the Hindus* (Delhi, 1987); U. Bhattacharyya, *Bharatdarshanshar* (Calcutta, 1949).

tion, the dichotomy between an apparent reality and a deeper truth obscured by maya became a part of universally accessible religious common-sense. We shall find resonances of this in *Amar Jiban*.

A second form of excess was constituted by body-centred philosophies. Certain lower-caste, esoteric, popular religious sects, some of which were loosely affiliated to Vaishnavism, aspired to trap divine energies, even divinity itself, within the human body through ritualised violations of purity-pollution taboos and secret sexual rites. They proclaimed a body-centred philosophy, stressing the primacy of bodily sense-perceptions over scriptural knowledge. Propagated largely through songs that encoded their rites and theories, their philosophy of *dehavad* had become familiar to nineteenth-century villagers, even though upper-castes, on the whole, considered them deviant and contemptible. *Amar Jiban* uses fragments from dehavad but the influence is limited. Even though the body-centred philosophy with its defiance of caste and pollution taboos seems an attractive and liberating form of excess over sansar, a lot of the texts reveal that the female body and emotions were supposed to be used in an instrumental capacity, for filling the male body with extraordinary powers which would eventually liberate it from all desire for the woman. Nor were they unmarked by the deep-seated conviction in the innate depravity of the woman which characterised upper-caste codes.[14]

For Rashsundari herself, it was the tradition of Krishna-centred devotion (which, in Bengal, also included Chaitanya as an object of adoration) that was of paramount importance. From the thirteenth century onwards, Bengali Vaishnavism had developed a rich stream of devotional literature, both in Sanskrit and in the vernacular.[15] The core of it dwelt on Krishna's early sport (*leela*) in the holy land of Vrindaban. An aesthetic code, derived originally from classical literature, provided the pattern for devotion. The devotee vicariously entered the leela by identifying himself/herself with one or other of Krishna's associates at Vrindaban. While most devotees were supposed to internalise

[14]Sudhir Chakrabarti, *Sahebdhani Sampradaya O Tader Gan* (Calcutta, 1985); Manindra Mohan Bose, *The Post Chaitanya Sahajiya Cults of Bengal* (nd, Calcutta reprint, 1986).

[15]S.K. De, *Early History*.

the mood of the lesser companions, the love between Krishna and his most cherished lover Radha was the supreme object of contemplation for all Bengali Vaishnavas.

The *Bhagavat Puran*, a medieval devotional text on Krishna's erotic leela, was acknowledged as the primary source of religious knowledge within Bengali Vaishnavism. The leela acquires a distinctive configuration here. Krishna sports with thousands of cowherd boys and girls (gopas and gopinis) of humble caste who are dearer to him than the arrogant higher castes.[16] He asks married gopinis to seek pleasure with him and fills all of them with infinite bliss. It is a pastoral idyll of endless love and ecstatic pleasure, of eternal music and fragrant flowers, where sansar and its unbending vidhi-nishedhas stand suspended. The devotee, through mere contemplation of such bliss, finds access to an image of surfeit. Yet the laws of sansar are not entirely inverted or cancelled out. What the image of surfeit promises is, rather, a dream of the values of sansar, taken to the limits of their possibilities.

The Krishna of *BP* is a male figure who fills thousands of gopinis with equal bliss. Radha, as a separate figure, has not yet made an appearance in this text. We have a god who brings nothing but pleasure to his many devotees in equal measure, a king who plays with shepherds. Here power dreams of an absolute condition of hegemony where it may translate itself as love and fulfilment for the powerful—the human devotee, the low-caste, the woman.

Religious imagination, however, could not indefinitely sustain this state of infinite bliss. Inexorable existential and social problems of pain and inequality re-enter the narrative and fracture it at different points. A polygamous patriarchy had imagined itself as capable of satisfying endless women equally. Later devotional texts introduced the figure of Radha who breaks up the undifferentiated mass of loving womanhood. She loves Krishna with an angry, resentful love, straining against the basic asymmetry within the relationship, since Krishna must love others and must eventually leave her to eternal *viraha* (pain of separation). Her

---

[16]Thomas J. Hopkins, *The Social Teaching of Bhagavat Purana*; J.A.B. van Buitenen, 'On The Archaism of the Bhagavat Purana', in Milton Singer (ed), *Krishna: Myths, Rites and Attitudes* (University of Hawaii, 1966).

resentment forms a language through which the devotee articulates the arbitrariness of God's power over the world and a human condition marked by inequality. A Sanskrit couplet, ascribed to Chaitanya, expresses a passionate yet resentful longing for Krishna in a language of unusual violence: 'Let that immoral faithless one come and ravish me.'[17]

The Vrindavan of *BP* had been a condition of uninhibited, unbounded fulfilment. In other Vaishnav works, problems of a patriarchal order clash with the articulation of devotion in an erotic mode. If an endless love-play becomes the ideal repository for the most perfect relationship with the most desired being—that is, with God—then to be adequately demanding and challenging, to be worthy of a lifetime of yearning, that desire cannot be confined to conjugal boundaries where the love object is already attained. Most of post-Chaitanya devotion agreed on the illicit nature (*parakiya*) of Radha–Krishna love.

Here sansar acquires yet another meaning. It is the ensemble of licit relationships that bars Radha's way to Krishna. A paradox is set up: the world of patriarchal injunctions, insisting on the woman's unconditional monogamy, is her dharma, yet desire for Krishna is a call coming from God himself. The erotic situation corresponds to a spiritual problem. Karma enjoins submission to the rules of sansar, yet sansar, with its unending demands and rigid prescriptions, is an obstacle that thwarts a complete surrender to God. God calls out to the devotee and goes back empty-handed. Sansar is divinely-ordained and also an impediment. The paradox makes both God and the devotee weep.

There was, then, within bhakti, a problem of reconciling faith with a painful world order. When they reflected on Hinduism, Christian missionaries were traumatised over the absence in it of a Manichaean division of the world between God and the Devil, by the ascription of an obviously skewed earthly scheme to a divine and not a diabolical agency.[18] For the Vaishnav, faith begins with an acceptance of God's work while arguing about its disorders. This was often conveyed through yet another devotional trope that shocked missionaries; abuse of God.[19]

---

[17]Kaviraj, *Chaitanyacharitamrita*, p. 616.
[18]W. Ward, *A View Of The History, Literature And Religion Of The Hindoos*, vol. 2 (Serampore, 1815).
[19]Ibid.

Since submission to divine will is founded on an already-given (and, hence, already-transcended) critique of the world order, faith involves a critique of the way faith must be.

To these ways of negotiating with God and sansar, Chaitanya had added another possibility—a congregation of devotees who could be assured of equal access to salvation by the existence of a new scheme of devotional activity that was available to all: not caste status or scriptural learning but simple faith expressed through ecstatic singing and chanting of God's name. Salvation was to be easier for the socially dispossessed since their hearts had not been hardened by pride. The promise of spiritual equality empowered Chaitanya (himself a Brahmin) and his largely upper-caste acolytes to undertake a massive proselytisation campaign among low-caste yet socially and politically significant groups—artisans, traders, manufacturers, tribal chieftains.[20] Possibly, the success of Islamic proselytisation was judged to lie in its congregational practice and its conviction in an unstratified spiritual order. Even though some post-Chaitanya sects and groups did violate Brahmanical injunctions about caste and gender, on the whole Chaitanya's bhakti was not meant to transform broader social relations. Rashsundari's Brahmin family was devoutly Vaishnav, but deeply orthodox.

IV

These, then, very crudely, are the shapes of sansar, and the ways in which an excess is created beyond them. How much of this would have been available to an unlearned housewife like Rashsundari? Although Vaishnavism had generated reading habits and sacred vernacular texts in abundance for subordinate groups, and although women in the mendicant orders were often literate,[21] all the women in Rashsundari's family were insulated from literacy.[22] Even in the freer atmosphere of her mother's home, where the village school was taught, and where

[20]Ramakanta Chakravarti, *Vaisnavism In Bengal*. Also Hitesranjan Sanyal, *Bangla Kirtaner Itihas* (Calcutta, 1989).

[21]Hitesranjan Sanyal, *Bangla Kirtaner Itihas*; ibid.; Asit Kumar Bandopadhyaya, *Bangla Sahityer Itibritta*, vol. 5 (Calcutta, 1985).

[22]*Amar Jiban*.

Rashsundari as a child was told to spend her days since her friends were unkind to her, she was not expected to learn anything. She did pick up the letters from the work that the boys were doing, but she told nobody about it.[23] Not only did Brahmanical custom continue to reign in upper-caste homes, Vaishnavism itself was ambiguous on the matter of scriptural learning, counterposing simple faith to the path of knowledge. Since the unlearned was privileged over the arrogant Brahmin scholar, by the same token learning would remain restricted.[24]

Yet much of Vaishnav doctrines could be orally transmitted at a fairly high level of conceptualisation. Ritual occasions within households or local congregations organised recitations and commentaries (*katha* and *path*) as well as devotional music (*kirtan*) which was interspersed with an expounding of texts. Texts were, therefore, quite ubiquitous, penetrating into even oral performances. The *BP*, for instance, would be read out over a month at a time. Morning sessions would be devoted to recitations from the Sanskrit original and, in the evening sessions, their meaning would be expounded in Bengali.[25] This way, an unlearned listener gained what has been termed phonetic competence—that is, an overall understanding over whole blocs of Sanskrit terms. At the same time, she would also acquire 'linguistic competence' over each word that was read out and explained from the Bengali texts.[26] I would suggest that this notion of dual competence may be extended from the realm of words to that of concepts. The simultaneous exposure to recitations from the erudite Sanskrit, as well as from the more accessible Bengali texts, created a 'phonetic' grasp over complex conceptual problems in Sanskrit works and a literal, 'linguistic' competence over each idea in vernacular theological expositions. Popular religious songs and literature move with effortless ease into knotted theological problems.

[23]Ibid., p. 8.

[24]See Vrindabandass, *Chaitanya Bhagavat*, for a forceful attack on the empty arrogance of Brahmin scholars.

[25]W.J. Wilkins, *Modern Hinduism: Being An Account Of The Religion And Life Of The Hindoos In North India* [1887] (New Delhi, 1987).

[26]Paul Singer, 'Book Of The Hours And The Reading Habits Of The Later Middle Ages', in Roger Chartier (ed), *The Culture Of Print—Power and the Uses of Print in Early Modern Europe* (Cambridge 1989).

Yet the notion of a shared culture cannot be pressed too far. Ordinary labouring people and women were excluded from a systematic culti-vation of interest and understanding by a lack of leisure and by rules of seclusion. Women's religious life was confined to routinised and elabo-rate worship of the family idol and a range of women's rites. Rashsundari wrote that she and her kinswomen were excluded from these recitations which were held in the outer male quarters.[27]

There was, then, a ubiquity of sacred texts which established a vis-ible, powerful bond between reading and piety. Snatches of recitations would penetrate into women' quarters. At the same time, women inter-ested in a more complete and autonomous understanding were simulta-neously stimulated and frustrated by imperfect access. The fact that Vaishnav mendicant women read fluently would aggravate their sense of deprivation. The nineteenth-century premium on women's educa-tion and orthodoxy's criticism of reformism added a new twist to the situation. Vociferous abuse of women's education would frighten the woman aching to read. It would also make her realise that very close to her women like herself were being helped to read.

Excited by such fears and such desires, Rashsundari worked out a double-edged position *vis-à-vis* her sansar. She underlined her obedient surrender and unqualified success here. At the same time she took care to indicate that a deeper truth lay veiled behind this apparent reality, this partial truth, this maya that was her sansar.

By evoking this contrast, Rashsundari reserved an interior space for herself which was her faith. She prised open both sansar and faith to accommodate a new figure: the serious yet domesticated woman bhakti who has created her own autonomous and individual life of devotion within the household. The striking thing about her faith was the way she insulated it from all that sansar had to offer to her piety: temples, religious festivals, domestic rites and rituals, the family idol, initiation by the family guru or religious preceptor. Even though she would have participated in all of this, she simply did not write about it. Her auto-biography, therefore, resisted her lived life more than it reflected it.

Rashsundari chose to ground her faith in something that her sansar

[27] *Amar Jiban*, p. 37.

withheld from her—reading and writing about sacred matters. By refusing the resources that prescribed religion gave her as a woman, Rashsundari, in effect, laid claim to an ungendered religious activity, to spiritual equality with men. Within her writing, she chose to withdraw from all collected and shared acts of devotion into an entirely interior activity. In pre-print days, reading, especially of sacred texts, used to be loud or at least mumbled. Since her reading, for a long time, was a deep secret, Rashsundari had to engage in the unusual mode of silent reading. The enforced silence underlined the privacy of the act. This was a space, a room of her own in a household where she had brought nothing of her own, not even her own name: 'The name that I had brought from my father's home has been lost. Here I am just the mother.'[28]

The claim to a non-feminine, individualistic religious practice went against the grain of orthodox prescriptions. It also went beyond nineteenth-century reformism. Reformers did not see women's education as a self-absorbed, self-centred activity. It was meant to be the basis of a companionate marriage, it was to train the woman into a family-oriented piety.[29]

Yet the boldness of Rashsundari's claim went largely unnoticed, in her own world, as well as among later readers. Jyotirindranath Tagore, a leading avant-garde literary figure, wrote an admiring preface to her book. He found her sound housewifely qualities wholly admirable and a fitting rebuttal of orthodox fears about educating the woman.[30] Later on, the nationalist scholar Dinesh Chandra Sen saw in her the self-effacing image of feminine nurture, an icon cast in the image of the Motherland herself.[31]

Partha Chatterjee uses her writing as an example of the appropriation of a woman by a male rationalist enterprise, shaped, in its turn, by Western power–knowledge.[32] Each of these readings unproblematically annexed a complex, highly individual endeavour by a woman to

[28]Ibid., p. 56.
[29]Ghulam Murshid, *Reluctant Debutante: Responses Of Bengali Women To Modernisation* (Rajshahi, 1983). Also *Bamabodhini Patrika* (Calcutta, 1863).
[30]Preface to *Amar Jiban*, 1897 edition.
[31]Preface to *Amar Jiban*, 1957 edition.
[32]Partha Chatterjee, *The Nation and Its Fragments*, op.cit., chs. 6 and 7.

a different agenda and narrative, and considered her story as concluded, exhausted of any other possibility after that. I would suggest that these linear readings could only be enabled by missing out on the various writing devices with which Rashsundari complicated her agenda.

V

There are difficulties in reading the text since Rashsundari simultaneously occupied two very different sites: that of a conformist housewife in an orthodox family and of an early woman author engaged in the highly public, audacious act of writing about her life. The two compulsions could be fitted together only by devising a novel mix of rhetorical modes that would mask a public unveiling of her life and recast it as an expression of prescribed Vaishnavite self-abnegation and humility as well as of proper womanly modesty and obedience. What emerged out of such constraints was a sustained, skilful and delicate double-speak, enabling her to announce her problems and her triumphs without letting go of her Vaishnav humility or her feminine modesty. It also insidiously portrayed her own gender-marked experiences as highly problematic ones, without using the mode of overt critique.

A multi-intentioned, polysemic content lay blandly enfolded within seemingly innocent statements. In the very first colophon, she described herself as 'lowly, ignorant that I am, and a woman, moreover.'[33] While colophons are conventionally self-deprecating, Rashsundari stretched hers to evoke other possibilities. She bracketed herself within the same categories that Chaitanya had promised to save—the low-caste, the ignorant, the woman. By using near-identical terms she obliquely invoked the promised inversion of status, the assurance that lowliness is a condition of salvation. In the same sentence she also subtly reminded us about the remarkable feat that a person as deprived as herself has accomplished by writing the book. And she did all of that without recourse to open self-praise or self-aggrandisement.

She let us know how pretty she was by simply repeating what others had said about her. In fact, she even composed a little verse about her

[33]*Amar Jiban*, p.2.

looks: 'Everyone called me a little golden doll.' Her neighbours used to comment on her attractiveness: 'Whoever marries her will be truly blessed.' She would not say that she was a domestic success. She simply said that all her in-laws were extremely kind and no one ever had a word of criticism about her all these years.[34] Indirect statement or reported speech could convey what she could not directly say about herself.

Rashsundari attained a level of sheer mastery in signifying something very different from what she was saying overtly. She did it by a careful framing of her direct statements. She would conclude an episode with pious sentiments, resigning herself to divine will. At the same time, she surrounded it with vivid details that described very painful consequences flowing from her obedience. As a result, the surface message got scrambled and confused so that she appeared compliant, and, also, a victim-figure precisely as a result of that compliance. She had been extremely eager to please others as a child. She began to help out an old and infirm relative with domestic chores without letting others know about it. When her family learnt about it, they praised her so much that she volunteered to do all the housework. All good, womanly instincts, that pleased her family and, later, her readers. She, however, concluded the episode with a surprise sequel that can wrench our thinking on to very different tracks. 'That was the end of my days of playing. Now I worked all the time.'[35] She made only a factual statement about herself, but the words are packed with resonances. Popular folk verses have often repeated the same problem: 'Let us have a lst quick game together, for the son of a stranger (i.e. the husband) is coming to take me away and I shall never play again.'[36]

The strategy was deployed with meticulous long-term planning, spread over three chapters, in the course of which she gradually introduced the theme of her secret reading. She prefaced the event with long, vivid and richly-detailed accounts of the gruelling household labour that she regularly performed. There is a moving description of how she had found no time for a single meal for two whole days. She saved the narration from the taint of self-pity or resentment by frequently inserting phrases

[34]Ibid., p.19, p.7.
[35]Ibid., p.14.
[36]Bhabataran Datta, *Bangladesher Chhara* (Calcutta, n.d.).

like: 'Why should I talk of such matters? .... It is shameful to even think
of these things.' She finished up with: 'Thinking over the ways of the
Lord, I began to laugh. I never mentioned it to anyone.'[37] She had it
both ways. She proclaimed her predicament to the whole world through
print and she reserved the image of the self-effacing Hindu wife who
suffers her deprivations with smiling forbearance.

She conveyed powerfully how a little girl was brutally uprooted
from her home and grafted abruptly on an unknown family. It seemed
to her that God had given her a life-sentence. 'I have been incarcerated
within the prison-house of this sansar. There will be no release for me
till the end of my days.' She immediately followed it up with a song of
praise. 'The mind is overwhelmed when I ponder over your mercy.
You have been kind to your subjected daughter.'[38] Mercy here referred
to the fact that her healthy body stood up to this strain. Yet, obviously,
it was the strength of a slave that God had blessed her with. Again, her
use of the somewhat strange word 'subjected' robs God's mercy of some
of its content even though her intention had been to indicate that the
painful experience bore happy results. Words, intentions, and effects are
conjoined in a curious syntax to produce multiple meanings, all at odds
with one another. The long-range effect was to build a strong sympathy-
base for her act of disobedience, her reading. The final impression is
one of insidious, delicate, masked expressions of pain that complicate
gestures of compliance but that also always stop short of criticism.

At only one place does the dialectic between the submissive devotee
and the self-aware victim figure break down, or, rather, Rashsundari
chose to snap out of the endless transaction between the two. Towards
the end of the third chapter she expanded the prison-house metaphor
quite meticulously. Her new home would not relieve her from work to
visit her natal home. The few occasions that she did get permission, she
was let out for a few days like a prisoner out on parole. Servants would
surround her like so many prison-guards. Even when her mother was
dying, she was not allowed to pay her last visit. She ended her chapter
with a reproach, a cry: 'Dear God, why did you ever make me a part of

[37]*Amar Jiban*, p. 26.
[38]Ibid., p. 17.

humanity!'[39] This is one chapter, one statement that ends without a single recuperating word of praise.

Wherever she referred to the social order, she referred to it as a part of God's design.[40] God, thereby, is held responsible for patriarchal oppression, for her own searing experiences. She had an alternative which she chose not to use—that of describing her oppression as a violation of God's will. Her choice indicates something about her relationship with her God. The more smilingly and patiently she offered her devotion the more she underlined the tyranny of his rule. The devotee's surrender accentuates divine despotism rather than absolves it.

Rashsundari's devotion, then, had a more complex design than either willed surrender or critique. That ambiguity and tension inform her manipulation of the *yatra* or folk-theatre metaphor. These theatres, with their travelling companies, their elaborate stage props and musical accompaniment, had acquired tremendous popularity in nineteenth-century villages.[41] The director-cum-manager was called *adhikari*. Rashsundari described God as the adhikari of a play unrolled before her eyes. The play is presumably about her own life, but she is alternately an actor and a spectator while God has scripted and directed it: and he is watching it too, since the whole purpose of the play is to amuse him. The subject of the play has no clue at all as to the direction of the script, nor does she have any control over it. She allows herself to be blindly manipulated.[42]

Interestingly, the only role that she seems to be playing is as the mother of a son.[43] Probably this was so because it is the only empowering role a woman could play. At the end of the act God comes and takes the son away. She copes with the pain by telling herself that it had been only a play, his leela.

God also enacts his many lives (incarnations) before her eyes. There is a crucial difference between her life as theatre and God's lives as

[39]Ibid., p. 27.

[40]Ibid., p. 26.

[41]Subir Raychoudhury (ed.), *Bilati Yatra Theke Swadeshi Theatre* (Jadavpur University, 1971).

[42]*Amar Jiban*, p. 70.

[43]Ibid., p. 71.

yatra. She is helpless before her own life while God scripts his own. He changes roles—as Ram, as Krishna, as Chaitanya—and begins a new play the moment the old one begins to weary him.[44] The metaphor ties up with philosophical speculations on the origins of creation: that creation itself is maya, an illusion conjured up by God to amuse himself, It has personal resonances as well. It expresses not just the spiritual helplessness of the devotee but also the specific social helplessness of the woman whose passivity and fatalism are deeply scored with gender inequalities. A woman's life is lived out in a permanent condition of homelessness—in a literal sense.

A feeling of marginalisation had probably accompanied the spread of this immensely popular art form in the nineteenth century, marking out within the spectacle the boundaries between the director/author and the actors: between the play on stage and the passive spectators. A mid-twentieth-century novel tried to describe the first destructive impact of this new art form upon a local community. It completely disrupted the older, more collective performances of devotional music where everybody sang about their own bhakti. This gave way to a spectacle, alienated and distant, which could only be passively consumed.[45]

Rashsundari's self-alienated life was a thing of endless surprise, wonder and marvel. The devotee gains a purchase on the divine spectacle of leela at the cost of learning not to identify with her own life.

VI

A possibly exaggerated account of childhood fears creates the space to let God into the narrative. The problems could have been overemphasised since, in a number of ways, Rashsundari was luckier than most girls of her time. Even though she was fatherless, her relatives loved her, and she was brought up by a wise, serene and adoring mother. Since the family was affluent, and the girl pretty, fixing a match was not a problem. In fact, she was kept at home well beyond the usual age of marriage since her mother would not let her go. Even in her new home, the in-laws loved the bride. Her first experiences contrast sharply

[44]Ibid., pp. 73–5.
[45]Advaita Mallabarman, *Titash Ekti Nadir Nam* (Calcutta, 1956).

with the more typical feelings of another girl-bride: 'Every time my mother-in-law looked at me a pint of blood would dry up in my body.'[46]

These facts emerged only incidentally while Rashsundari dwelt on her many fears and anxieties. More childish and sheltered than her companions, she was a butt of their teasing. She also had a morbid fear of kidnappers. In a world filled with troubled apprehensions, the first words about God came from her mother, who tried to remove her fears. This, incidentally, also marks the first appearance of the mother in the narrative, bearing the words of God. It is the only purpose she serves in the autobiography. She tells Rashsundari: 'Why should you fear anything, we have Dayamadhav [the name of the family idol] at home.'[47] It was as if the mother gave birth to the idea of God.

She continued to nurture and develop the idea and to remove other fears. Rashsundari had another bout of terror when she first discovered that she was the daughter of a dead man. 'All these years I had thought that I was just my mother's child.' She wept at the new discovery because the notion of a dead father aroused the dread of ghosts. Her mother consoled her again with the name of Dayamadhav.[48]

The third time that God's name was invoked, and developed at some length, was when a fire broke out at home and the frightened children ran away and lost their way. Their cries of distress brought out some villagers who took them home. Rashsundari thought that Dayamadhav had heard her cries and come to her rescue. The mother then explained the different grades within divinity which were interconnected as sedimented layers within one single truth. Human agency had been used by Dayamadhav to rescue children who had appealed to him. Yet, while Dayamadhav was the specific name and shape in which God was contained within their particular family, the Great Lord who rules over the whole world was Parameshwara. 'He belongs to everybody. He has created everything in this world, he loves everyone, he is the Lord God of us all.'[49]

[46]Saradasundari Debi, *Atmakatha*, first published Dacca, 1913. Reprinted in *Atmakatha* (Calcutta, 1981), p. 7.

[47]*Amar Jiban*, p. 8.

[48]Ibid., p. 9.

[49]Ibid., p. 12.

Although the first mention of God was as a family idol which seemed to affirm a polytheistic divinity, eventually a monotheistic God is established. From the third section till nearly the end of the book God is called Parameshwara. The designation is curious since this is an appellation rarely attached to Krishna. On the other hand, Christian missionaries and monotheistic religious reformers like the Brahmos called their God by this name. Rashsundari seems to have extrapolated a non-Vaishnav designation to her God. He is also, for much of the book, a curiously faceless, abstract figure without any of the lush and vivid mythological attributes of Krishna. The family idol, a central figure within a devout Vaishnav household, is never once described in the book.

When Rashsundari came to know about God, 'on that very day my mind sprouted the first seeds of intelligence.'[50] Her way to God was thus through thought. It was the cerebral way, not the pietistic, emotive, ecstatic or ritualistic ways that are commonly associated with women's devotion. This way would be along an intellectual trajectory of reading and writing.

God came to Rashsundari not as an icon nor as myth and ritual, but as words spoken by the mother. The mother came into the text only to bear the words of God. The two were linked within a single structure to remove a nervous child's constant fears. The structure broke down when, at twelve, Rashsundari heard that she was about to be married off. Terrified, she rushed to her mother to ask: 'Mother, will you give me away to a stranger?' Her mother tried to rise to the occasion with a denial. But this time her words rang false and she was crying.[51]

Rashsundari's world—held together by her mother's reassurances—crashed around her as she realised that her mother was lying and that her mother was, after all, as helpless and vulnerable as Rashsundari herself. She was a woman. In utter terror, her words choking her, Rashsundari tried to retrieve something of the early structure of reassurance. 'Would Parameshwara come with me?' Her mother replied that he would go with her wherever she went. Bereft of the precious, living, human mediation of the mother, a male God was left to Rashsundari

[50]Ibid.
[51]Ibid., p. 14.

as the memory of her mother's speech, as the promise of reassurance. He was, therefore, both a residue and an extension of her mother. A male divinity had to be imagined who was free from the limits and vulnerabilities of a mother. At the same time he was entirely a creation of that mother.

When the terrible, unbelievable ordeal of parting arrived, and the little girl lost her home, her birthplace, her mother and every face she had known all her life, Parameshwara was the only bit of her old identity that she carried with her from her old life. In a new place, filled with total strangers, where even the spoken dialect would be different, she went over his name again and again within her terrified heart: 'I admit it was only out of fear that I called out to you'.[52] She made clear what location and function she had allotted to God in her life—deliverance from fear and pain. What she is silent about, yet what comes through from her subsequent experiences, is how inadequate God was to the task. By the end of the book the early expectation had gone. God was now a powerful, whimsical figure who played with her life. She could only hope that he would show pity for her. 'Even if you are cruel to me, I shall call you the Merciful One.'[53]

Her mother had been, above all, her teacher, her guru. Rashsundari took great care to establish that she had none other. Even though in Vaishnav households the family guru is a powerful figure who ritually purifies the body and the mind, Rashsundari did not mention hers. Nor did she refer to her other prescribed religious activities. She made the narrative bare of all influences that would have gone into the making of her religious life. Both Pabna and Faridpur had old and strong Vaishnav associations,[54] but *Amar Jiban* is silent about them. What is most striking is that she did not discuss what the sacred texts, the ones she had mastered against such odds, had to teach her.

By making her mother bear the entire weight of a complete religious instruction that must have actually been acquired piecemeal through her entire life, Rashsundari endowed her mother with a specifically

[52]Ibid., p. 18.
[53]Ibid., p. 72.
[54]Ramakanta Chakravarti, *Vaisnavism in Bengal.*

nineteenth-century role. In Vaishnav hagiographies, the mother is a source of nurture but not of instruction. For the nineteenth-century Hindu revivalist-nationalist, on the other hand, the Hindu woman, being untainted by Western pedagogy and values, being ruled by Hindu scriptures alone, had escaped colonisation—in contrast to the Hindu man. As the sole bearer of a lost freedom and as the site of a new nation, she was the purest influence and source of instruction within the Hindu home.[55] Liberal reformers, on the other hand, believed in the modern pedagogical principle that an enlightened mother was the best early guide for education as well as for morals. In fact, they based their arguments for educating women on this conviction.[56]

Obliquely, this move of Rashsundari made a larger point. The mother's teaching, however potent, had ceased in her life from the age of twelve. From a very early age, then, Rashsundari's spiritual growth would have been self-made. As we shall see, *Amar Jiban* is a jealously individualistic narrative, shaping the material of her life around the lonely efforts of a heroic individual. In this sense, too, it is a typically nineteenth-century product, with something of the *bildungsroman* about it. Debendranath Tagore's *Atmacharit* was an autobiography similarly patterned on a lonely spiritual quest where he gathered the ingredients of his religion all by himself. The difference lies in the organisational, mobilisational, institutionalising imperatives that structure the later part of his book.[57] Rashsundari's gender-constrained religious activism, in contrast, had to be confined to reading and writing.

VII

Rashsundari wrote out her life as a series of trials that she survived with God's grace. We have referred to her childhood fears. The real ordeal, however, was married life. Marriage began with a forced parting from everything she loved. The event was synonymous with great grief, with copious weeping. Bengali girls were generally married off very early, for ritual compulsions demanded that they should be in their husband's

[55]See chapter one.
[56]Ghulam Murshid, *Reluctant Debutante*.
[57]Debendranath Tagore, *Atmacharit* (Calcutta, 1898). Reprinted in *Atmakatha*.

home when puberty set in. The loss of the natal home at childhood has been described in all nineteenth-century women's writings as a traumatic experience, uprooting a child from the security of her own home and exiling her forever to the mercy and control of total strangers.[58] Other women recorded excruciating memories—how a mother went blind with continuous tears after losing her daughter this way.[59] A genre of devotional songs described the annual three-day visit of the goddess Durga to her parent's home. They were immensely popular all over Bengal in the eighteenth and nineteenth centuries—at a time of growing affluence among some upwardly mobile agricultural and commercial castes and the spread of Brahmanical patriarchal customs among them.[60] Already, sixteenth-century law codes had hardened Brahmanical gender injunctions—including the propagation of infant marriage for girls—to shore up the declining socio-political hegemony of Brahmins after centuries of Muslim rule in Bengal, large-scale conversions to Islam, and the spread of syncretic practices.[61] The powerful estate of Krishnagore had in the eighteenth century reinforced Brahmanical orthodoxy.[62] The *agamani* songs about Durga's mother and her searing pain as the time of parting draws near, would, then, have a double resonance for Bengali women. Women, by their late twenties, could well be daughters aching for their mothers as well as young mothers pining for their married daughters.[63]

Rashsundari described the ways which regulated her movements as a new bride as the rules of old times or *sekal*. Hers was a pious, deeply orthodox Hindu family, governed by Brahmanical injunctions and untouched by Westernised, reformist values. This was precisely the authentic Hindu space that militant Hindu revivalist-nationalists of the nineteenth century valorised as the domain of residual freedom,

[58] Kailashbashini Debi, *Hindu Mahilaganer Durabastha* (Calcutta, 1863), would be a particularly good example.

[59] Gnanadanandini Debi, 'Smritikatha', in Indira Debi (ed), *Puratani* (Calcutta, 1957).

[60] Tanika Sarkar, chapter one in this volume.

[61] S.K. De, *Vaisnava Faith and Movement in Bengal*.

[62] *Diwan Kartikeyachandra Rayer Atmajibancharit* (Calcutta reprint, 1956).

[63] Tanika Sarkar, chapter one in this volume.

an abode of happiness that constrasted with the deprivations and humiliations of colonial rule. An icon was constructed of the true patriotic subject, the good Hindu woman with her simple dress, her ritually pure conchshell bangles and red vermilion mark, her happy surrender and self-immersion in the sansar, and her endless bounty and nurture expressed by cooking and feeding. She was charged with an immense aesthetic, cultural and religious load in nationalist writings, as Annapurna, the goddess of food, as the bounteous Motherland.

Apart from reformist contestations of this image of Hindu female virtue, women's own writing from the 1860s seriously interrogated its foundations.[64] These shared two major planks of criticism—the withholding of education from women, and the trauma of early patrilocality and forced planting of little girls in new families. Rashsundari, who was a pious Hindu housewife herself, occupying the concrete social space marked out by the icon, and who otherwise was careful to surround her statements with sentiments of obedience, was nevertheless quite outspoken in her assessment of the system. 'I am filled with loathing when I look back on all that . . . the coarse clothes, the heavy cumbrous jewellery, the conchshell bangles, the vermilion mark . . .' She used images of blindness, of dumbness and of paralysis, of the blindfolded bullock moving mindlessly round the oil-press, to describe the gamut of injunctions that governed the bride.[65] She was condemned to strict silence, to limited, awkward movements, to the absence of all contact with most older and male relatives. Since the boundaries of permitted movement varied in each family, no bride was quite sure of the exact scope of restrictions. As a much older wife with several children of her own, Rashsundari had thought it might be forbidden for her to appear before her husband's horse. Throughout her text she enviously compared her fate with that of 'modern' girls who were blessed with education 'these days'. In her day, everyone believed that 'women were fit for nothing except domestic drudgery.'[66]

She herself was obedient and her in-laws affectionate. Yet, grafting remained a pain-filled process. Incarceration was the recurrent image

[64]Kailashbhashini Debi, *Narishiksha* (Calcutta, 1884).
[65]*Amar Jiban*, p. 21 and p. 31.
[66]Ibid., p. 33.

for this stage. 'I was caged for life, in this life there will be no escape for me . . . I was snatched away from my own people . . . and given a life sentence . . . I would shed tears in secret but since I had to spend my life with these people, I eventually became a tamed bird . . .'[67] The love she gave her in-laws was not spontaneous affection but the result of training and necessity, the habit of the caged bird.

At fourteen Rashsundari was looking after the entire household without any help. Her world was the kitchen, and her 'cage' had distinct spatial connotations. She was in charge of the many ritual requirements of the family idol, she nursed her mother-in-law, looked after a stream of unexpected guests and cooked two meals every day for at least twenty-five people.[68] Her account of her daily work deconstructed the iconic figure of the contented female in two crucial ways: she listed her service to the family idol as work and not as the emotional release and aesthetic gratification that it is meant to be for women. She also went into a very full account of the gruelling work-schedule, although all the time thanking God for her strong body which could take the strain. She thus rid the image of womanly nurture of its association with emotional fulfilment and remade it in the image of a slave. She made a similar reconstruction with the image of mothering. The hard, unassisted, continuous work involved in nursing a series of twelve babies in quick succession was conventionally read as the cherished devotional or patriotic icon of happy, self-effacing motherhood. Rashsundari restored the feel of slog to the image. All night a stream of children would keep her up. 'One would say, Mother, I want to piddle, another would say, Mother, I am hungry, the other one would say, Mother, take me in your arms.'[69]

She extended the same idea with brilliant success to the theme of food—on cooking, feeding, eating and fasting. She literally spent her entire youth cooking and feeding others. In the prosperous East Bengal countryside, among affluent families, the preparation of excellent meals of immense variety and skill was a constant preoccupation. Women were graded, and family memory organised, according to the meals that had been brilliantly prepared and lovingly served by women. On

[67]Ibid., p. 19.
[68]Ibid., p. 24.
[69]Ibid., p. 29.

the other hand, ritual fasting and even starving as a matter of preference among women was valorised in a whole range of prescriptive texts and literature.[70] Her eating was a peculiarly non-structured, uncertain activity. Nineteenth-century behavioural manuals that taught women proper deportment in their new homes confessed their helplessness on the matter. 'My child, I can give you no good advice on this. If you serve yourself, you will be called shameless. If you wait for others to serve you, you may have to go without food.'[71] Even in far more 'modern' families, women faced the same problem.[72] In fact, femininity was crucially tied up with a professed indifference to food, to the habitual neglect of eating. Interestingly, the same prescriptive authorities that had relegated women to a lifetime of not-eating in the middle of endless feeding, and had fixed this role in the image of Annapurna, the goddess of food, had also imagined the terrifying counter-image of Kali, the primal female force that devours Creation itself. Female saints would often exercise their saintly privilege with bouts of voracious eating and with demands of being physically fed.[73]

Rashsundari described her acts of cooking and feeding as hard work. She made no reference to the possibility of excitement in cooking, the gratification of feeding loved ones, the aroma and taste of memorable dishes that she would have prepared as a successful housewife. She frankly and humorously talked about her senile greed for good food in old age, as if age had somehow defeminised her and released her from prescribed inhibitions.[74] She emptied out the act of cooking from associations of creativity and filled it with hard labour, with deprivation. She refused the iconic privilege of Annapurna.

[70]Nandalal Seal, *Vratakatha* (Calcutta reprint, 1930). A whole host of behavioural manual for women, written in the late nineteenth century, advised a cultivated disregard for food.

[71]Saudamini Gupta, *Kanyar Prati Upadesh* (Dacca, third edition, 1918).

[72]Even in the highly enlightened Tagore family, married women faced a disconcerting uncertainty in relation to a regular flow of meals. See Gnanadanandini Debi, *Smritikatha*.

[73]See lives of Lakshmididi and Gopaler Ma in Swami Gambhirananda, *Shri Ramakrishna Bhaktamalika* (Calcutta, 1952). Also June McDaniel, *Madness of the Saints*.

[74]*Amar Jiban*, p. 70.

She was quite clear about the deprivational aspect. 'Forget about being cared for in other ways, most days I did not even get to eat two proper meals.'[75] She once went without a meal for two days since guests arrived without notice and the high standards of family hospitality had to be maintained by the wife, who offered up her own meals. At night, children would get up and interrupt her meals and she had to stop eating to tend them since their bawling disturbed her husband's sleep.[76] It was not possible to share the problem with him. Rashsundari chose to refer to Krishna as a father, although in sacred myths Krishna played a number of familial roles, but never that of the father. She refused the more conventional feminine approaches to him—as his mother or his lover. As a Bengali woman, both those roles would have involved her in the act of providing nurture. She was tired of being the source of nurture. In the realm of religious imagination, she needed to create a source of stable nurture for herself.

If the kitchen was a cage, so was the sexual body of the young woman. Rashsundari's first child was born when she was eighteen. Till the age of forty-one, she gave birth, as roughly two-yearly intervals, to eleven more children. Lying-in rooms were notoriously insanitary and childbirth was surrounded with a range of extremely exacting rituals.[77] Vaishnav households had somewhat more lenient ritual expectations, and that, along with the mild and healthy climate of her birthplace, probably accounts for her unimpaired good health.[78] Childbirth would still have been a dangerous moment in her life. Census figures show that in the nineteenth century the highest incidence of mortality among Bengali women occurred in their most fertile years.

Rashsundari summed up these years in her life in a few terse words: 'The Lord only knows what I went through all these years.'[79] We find little about her husband in *Amar Jiban*. We are told that he would be impatient when babies cried at night, that, bound as he was by strong ties of custom, he was of no help to her in her desire to read. He cried

[75]Ibid., p. 24.
[76]Ibid., p. 25.
[77]W.J. Wilkins, *Modern Hinduism*, p. 9.
[78]Ibid., p. 10.
[79]*Amar Jiban*, p. 24.

when she was seriously ill and given up for dead, but he also said stoically: 'Is she gone? So let it be then.'[80] There are no memories in the book about the time when they were young together. His own death was described as a social catastrophe, making her ritually inauspicious. She said that she had lost her 'crown of gold', not that she had lost a limb—which would have signified the loss of something far greater than social status. She followed it up with an extraordinarily strange statement: 'I do not regret what God had willed.'[81] If convention demanded that she did not speak openly about her sexual relations with him, it certainly would not recommend such fatalistic stoicism in reporting her husband's death. Other widows had left long, loving accounts of their husbands' last moments.[82] She also departed from the norms of a widow's speech in a small but significant way: whereas widows are expected to see their prolonged life as a curse, Rashsundari thanked God for her long life.[83] There was no effort at preserving the memory of her sexually active years, except as a bind. The husband, as a partner in that life, is equally absent. Was that entirely the effect of inhibition?

The Hindu marriage system, which revivalist–nationalists valorised as a domain of affect, compensating for a miserable colonised existence in the public sphere—a domain which they were committed to save from all colonial intervention—initiated the conjugal relationship with a traumatic separation from the childhood home and an abrupt termination of childhood. Cohabitation was ritually obligatory from the onset of puberty, often when the girl's body was not mature enough to sustain sexual penetration.[84] There was no question of choice, of consent, of cancelling the tie and shifting to another partner, however incompatible the marriage or whatever the problems with the husband. The husband's polygamy or even his death would not dissolve the

[80]Ibid., p. 55.

[81]Ibid., p. 45.

[82]See Saradasundari Debi, *Atmakatha*. Also Kailashbashini Debi, '*Atmakatha*', in *Atmakatha*, vol. 2 (Calcutta, 1982).

[83]*Amar Jiban*, p. 78.

[84]There was a detailed discussion of the brutal, even fatal effects of sexual penetration into immature female organs during the Age of Consent debates in 1890–91. Prior to 1891, there was no legal bar to cohabiting with wives above the age of ten. See Bengal Government Judicial, FN J C/17.1, Proceedings 104–117, June 1893.

marriage bond. The sexually most active years in a woman's life would coincide with the years of most exacting labour. It would also lead to dangerous and draining childbirths. In this situation it is, perhaps, necessary to read her silence about her sexual experiences not as inhibition, as repressed speech, but as a turning away from her own sexuality which would appear as little more than a trap for her.

Rashsundari was forty when her first son was married. She did not conceive after that.[85] It was customary for parents to terminate regular sexual relations at that point, and we may assume that this was what happened to her, since forty-one was too early for an onset of the infertile phase. Rashsundari described her middle age, which was presumably free from sexual activity, with affection and nostalgia. It was a time of relative power and privilege, a point where she emerged as a figure of considerable authority within the household. She was the mother of grown-up sons, a mother-in-law. For the first time, she used the words 'My sansar'.[86] It was a time of integration.

The new experiences of her life coincided with a new view of religion. At the very end of the book she gave conventional and familiar names, forms and myths to God. For the first time, too, she addressed him by the name of the family idol. A self-created God, wrested and saved from her mother's home, was merged into a shared, collective devotional knowledge. She ascribed to herself the usual range of religious practices permitted to a Vaishnav woman of means: endowing the family idol, providing for an annual congregational feast. Her religion now expressed a family of property and status, and no longer the lonely struggles of the bhakti. Yet something new remained in her endeavour. The money she endowed came not out of family inheritance but from the proceeds of her own publication.[87]

VIII

In Vaishnavite hagiographies, closeness to divinity is established through trances or through miracle-making abilities. Rashsundari had no claims to extraordinary powers since they were incompatible with her secure

[85]*Amar Jiban*, p. 36.
[86]Ibid., p. 32.
[87]Ibid., p. 80.

housewife status. Yet her own signs had to be in some ways within the realm of the marvellous, the unusual, to establish the seriousness of her bhakti. She formulated a series of what we may call tamed, domesticated, everyday miracles, non-supernatural in manifestation, yet sufficiently wondrous to be ascribed to divine inspiration. They were located in changes within her own body, in her ability to dream strange dreams, and, finally, in her ability to read.

Certain normal, expected bodily changes were interpreted as signs of a wonderful and persistent care with which God had altered her body for the different stages of life. Her youthful body had been healthy, pretty and fertile. In middle age the strength remained but fecundity dried up, as befitted the respected seniormost woman in a large household. As the house filled up with a younger generation, and her responsibilities dwindled, her strong body began to age and decay, shedding its old capabilities. She now awaited her last journey across life with a lightened load. With this account Rashsundari defamiliarised a normal female life-cycle by imparting a sense of wonder at the perfect fit between the body and its changing functions. The familiar body was made strange, exotic and holy, the sign and site of God's handiwork. 'Plain eyes can see it quite clearly.'[88]

The supremacy of sense-perceptions as the primary source of religious knowledge, and of the human body as the object of this knowledge, tie up with strands within body-centred popular esoteric cults. Yet, unlike them, Rashsundari did not seek to manipulate and stretch the limits of the ordinary body. To her, the normal changes themselves were infinitely wondrous. The cultic practices involved a relationship with a male body and the object was to impart great powers to that. In a way, then, it was a replication of the patriarchal order on a different register. Rashsundari's religious project, however, was autonomous and self-centred.

Her dreams were occasionally anticipations of events that were about to happen. She dreamed, for instance, that she was reading the *CB* before she had learned to read. The next day, accidentally, she managed to identify the book. It had, therefore, been a message from God. Similarly, she had a vision of a shower of golden flowers, symbolising the

[88]Ibid., p. 44.

birth of a male grandchild. She also dreamt of things that had happened without her conscious knowledge—for instance, the death of a son. She even saw a ghost once.[89] These experiences were close to abilities that a whole range of otherwise ordinary women might possess, powers of a rather low grade that singled them out as curiosities rather than as people touched by the divine. Rashsundari, however, linked them up with a superior spiritual competence by pointing out the parallels with dreams seen by fathers of Ram or Chaitanya.[90] Dreams, therefore, became a privileged access to a superior reality.

The unexpected retrieval of a long-lost object in an unchanged, unblemished condition, was interpreted as yet another sign from God.[91] Some essence of herself had remained in his safe custody, retaining its old lustre even though her mortal body had gone into decay. The retrieval of lost objects, we must remember, was also an essential part of miracle tales.

Her reading was the fourth and most important miracle in Rashsundari's life. She first read a sacred book in manuscript form.

Vaishnav manuscripts were profusely produced from the seventeenth century onwards, and manuscripts remained much in use till the mid-nineteenth century. These were, however, awkward to handle since the stained paper was too fragile to be sewn together. Leaves were pressed between illumined wooden covers. Each page had to be detached while being read.[92] Reading was, therefore, a delicate, time-consuming process, involving careful movement. It acquired the aura of an act of worship. Books were also extremely expensive. Rashsundari's family possessed quite a few, indicating an unusual degree of investment in reading.

Rashsundari had longed to read since she was fourteen. When she was twenty-five, she dreamt that she was reading the *CB*. The very next day, her husband told a son in her presence to replace it among other manuscripts. She identified the manuscript by its illumination, and later she detached a page and hid it. She also surreptitiously acquired a palm-leaf on which her son was practising letters. Then, over a very long time,

[89]Ibid., pp. 50–1, p. 56, p. 60.
[90]Ibid., p. 50.
[91]Ibid., pp. 63–4.
[92]J.C. Ghosh, *Bengali Literature* (1848), p. 20.

and in deepest secrecy, she matched the letters on the leaf with those on the page. With great efforts of memory she also recalled the letters that she had learnt as a little girl and identified them. Eventually, she became *jitakshara*, master of the word, a magnificent term which she coined herself.[93] Much later, she learned to write and read printed books with support from her grown-up sons who had received the new education. 'I discovered that printed letters are the best.'[94]

For a long time, her reading ability remained unsuspected. Only a few maidservants were later trusted with the secret. Much later, her widowed sisters-in-law were told, and, contrary to her apprehensions, they were delighted and eager to learn from her.[95] But for quite some time reading was a forbidden pleasure. It was not an act of rebellion since it was a secret and she did not let it interfere with her other duties and obligations. On the surface, nothing had changed. In reality, a miracle had taken place.

It was a transgression of the deepest kind. She was now a woman with a double-life. As a Vaishnav, Rashsundari used the pattern of transgression that was most familiar to her to describe her condition. She structured it on the mode of the illicit love of Radha for Krishna, the conflict between the woman's religion within sansar and a higher religious urge turning her against it. She used expressions very familiar to the literature of divine illicit love. Her household was against her desire, there was no one to help her, she had to time for it. It split up her very self, yet she acknowledged its divine inspiration. It had taken hold of her entire being. 'I was forever yearning.'[96] It is interesting that orthodox critics of women's education were convinced of an equation between the woman's intellectual desires and her sexual immorality. One kind of transgression was conflated with another kind. When girls' schools were first started in Calcutta, the editor of a Bengali newspaper sarcastically offered his services to teach girls at night.[97] The reformist

[93]*Amar Jiban*, p. 21.
[94]Ibid., p. 42.
[95]Ibid., p. 38.
[96]Ibid., p. 23, p. 28.
[97]*Samachar Chandrika* (1831), in Brajendra Nath Bandopadhyaya (ed), *Sambadpatre Sekaler Katha*, vol. 2 (Calcutta, 1941).

leader Sibnath Shastri's mother was an educated woman. When his schoolteacher discovered this, he immediately sent her a letter through the little boy, asking her for a secret assignation. If a woman was educated, she must be immoral.[98]

If this was the kind of attitude that Rashsundari expected from her milieu, what were the resources that could have given her hope? Rashsundari said that in her youth she would hear her elders fret about the new-fangled interest in women's education. 'Now, of course, we are ruled by a female sovereign. . . . This is the age of Kali.'[99] Victoria's rule was coupled with Kaliyug, the last and most degenerate period within the Hindu time-cycle of four ages. For Rashsundari, the terms would carry very different resonances. If Victoria's rule heralded a modernity that promised education for women, then it was a resource and not a burden for her. Possibly, a Vaishnav notion of time reinforced her choice. Post-Chaitanya bhakti had welcomed Kaliyug, when the saviour Chaitanya had been born. In this age, women, low-castes, and the ignorant were blessed with a larger possibility for salvation. If this was an age of decline, it was also a time for more generous hopes. Interestingly, this trope within Vaishnav piety found a resonance among the liberal rationalists of the nineteenth century who hoped for a deliverance from social malaise through reform and education. Rashsundari knitted the two kinds of hope together: Kaliyug was a time of love and salvation for all, it was a time when girls were taught to read. 'Blessed, blessed be this Kaliyug.'[100] A Vaishnavite and a gendered construction of time met to contest a dark perspective on modernity that was shared by a traditional Brahmanical orthodoxy and the Hindu revivalist/nationalist alike.[101]

By claiming that God had taught her to read, Rashsundari took her place within the new domain of the great secular miracle-tales of nineteenth-century Bengal. For colonised Bengalis, excluded from most of

---

[98]Shibnath Shastri, *Atmacharit* (Calcutta, 1952), p. 22.

[99]*Amar Jiban*, p. 28.

[100]Ibid., p. 77.

[101]On the representation of Kaliyug in the nineteenth century, see Sumit Sarkar, 'Kaliyuga, Chakri and Bhakti: Ramakrishna And His Times', in *Economic and Political Weekly*, 18 July 1922.

the exalted public stations of life where their transformative abilities would have registered themselves, a mastery over the new education was the only way of proving individual greatness. A new realm of secular miracle literature had shaped itself around marvellous accounts of such mastery. Rashsundari's book was read as a sign of traditional womanly virtues. Yet its very production places it within the new genre. The appropriation of a radical departure as a traditional virtue was something more than a misreading. It was a process that enabled an absorption of the new into commonsense.

X

I was interested in *Amar Jiban* not only because it initiates the autobiographical genre in Bengali and because it is one of the earliest examples of women's writing in the language. Nor was it entirely because *Amar Jiban* is a rare and early example of an individual woman's devotional quest, articulated in her own words. My interest was sharpened as I came to realise how different the text had turned out to be from what I had expected of a woman's autobiography, a woman's writing, a woman's bhakti.

The erotic mode had been singularly privileged within Vaishnavism and among popular, esoteric cults. For a lot of women, bounded by an unbending patriarchy, it carried access to an imagined erotic relationship of immense richness. Krishna could also be appropriated as one's child, framing the absorbing female experience of mothering within a more perfect world of meanings. Rashsundari's Parameshwara, however, was a very different God. He had an ambiguous and problematic role in her life.

There were other departures as well. It would be simple-minded to posit a straight connection between female subjectivity and female writing, to assume that the latter reflects the former in a direct, unmediated way. In fact, for the writing woman, the act of writing itself reconstitutes her subjectivity in radically new ways. Yet, a woman's writing is far too easily related to the cultural world it came out of. In *Amar Jiban*, on the other hand, there is very little by way of the direct speech of women, or speech-effects specifically associated with the woman's world—no proverbs, riddles, tales, pungent and earthy idioms. Her prose is far removed from everyday, colloquial forms. The language is definitely not gender-marked.

In sharp contrast to expectations from women's writings, the book is astonishingly bare of visual or sensuous content. There are no descriptions of exterior landscapes, nor of domestic scenes. There is no impression of taste, sound or smell. The objects she handled, the spaces she passed through, the faces she saw bear no features in her narrative. The great rivers and waterways of Pabna and Faridpur—Padma, Brahmaputra, Ariyal Khan—are condensed into the single image of a boat-journey through the rivers of life. They also shape a dream-sequence where her dead son comes to meet her on a tiny boat, across the great, melancholy expanses of a river. Events that took place around her are similarly condensed. There is a brief poem on an epidemic fever at her Faridpur village.[102] But there is very little about anything else. At the time the book was being revised, her birthplace Pabna had became the seat of a highly-organised peasant agitation against the arbitrary cesses and rent-enhancements that a group of landlords had imposed on tenants. Around the same time, untouchable cultivator castes of Faridpur had gone on strike to improve their low ritual status, and had refused to work for the upper-caste gentry.[103] Rashsundari was a landlord's daughter and a landlord's wife. She, however, made no mention of these events even though they must have made a considerable stir in her milieu.

Amar Jiban is a curiously self-absorbed narrative. Other people appear simply to make a very specific point about her and then they disappear. They do not have an independent life of their own within her text, nor do they live out relationships with one another. It is uncompromisingly non-dialogic. The husband, who had been given a few perfunctory references in the main body of the text, was granted a separate, brief section towards the end of the first part of the book because, she felt, people would want to know about him. A curiously impersonal obituary was therefore appended, for narrative requirements, not because she wanted to talk about him.[104]

She turned the narrative focus intensely and exclusively upon herself,

---

[102]*Amar Jiban*, p. 60. On Pabna and Faridpur, see W.W. Hunter, *The Imperial Gazetteer Of India*, vol. 7, 1883.

[103]Ibid.

[104]*Amar Jiban*, p. 57.

first of all by abstracting herself from her concrete world. 'I came to Bharatvarsha (India), and spent a long time here. This body of mine, this mind, this life itself have taken different forms.'[105] She lived out her life in two villages. They are, however, absent, except as mere names. Nor are there more intimate, familiar locales—the sub-division, the district or even the province. Her time-scale is oddly precise, very different from CB, CC. She departed from popular, rural ways of patterning time and memory: pinning down a human event by referring to a natural one like a flood or a famine, or by referring to an event of local importance. There is no local time, village time, family time. She gives herself nothing less than a whole sub-continent and almost an entire century to live in.

In their larger historical–geographical dimensions these landmarks were remote to her lived life. Yet, evidently, they were meaningful to the design of her self-created, narrated life. At the time she was writing, a united Indian empire had emerged, renewed and revamped after a sub-continental uprising.[106] Bharatvarsha, then, was an effect of a new political reality. The name also occurs in the CB.[107] The Vaishnavite pilgrimage circuit, spreading from Nabadwip in Bengal to the Puri temple in Orissa (which was a gateway to South Indian temples), to Mathura-Vrindavan in North India and Dwarka in Western India, gave Vaishnavas a vivid sense of a large, sacred geography. Again, when the book was being written, the nineteenth century had already self-consciously separated itself out from an undifferentiated mass of time, a recurrent replay of identical historical cycles. It had come to see itself as the site of a new and unique history, which gave time a direction, a teleology.[108]

Rashsundari needed this large context to abstract herself from her actual lived life. She transcended its narrow limits and its inability to intersect with grand historical narratives by giving herself the largest possible temporal and spatial frames that she could relate to. Her life could now become an adequate site for the play of a grand divine purpose.

[105]Ibid., p. 2.

[106]An earlier reference to *Meyerajar rajatwa* (rule of a female monarch) by the village people shows that Victoria's rule was a widely-known political fact. *Amar Jiban*, p. 23.

[107]Vrindabandass, *Chaitanya Bhagavat*.

[108]See Sumit Sarkar, 'Kaliyuga'.

Autobiography, as a genre, most obviously confuses the boundaries between the word and the world, deluding us that it is a life we are reading and not a text. I found that *Amar Jiban* thwarted these expectations persistently. In very many ways, its textuality is underlined by the distance it sets up between Rashsundari's lived experiences and her narrative preoccupations. It was through writing a book that the life she wanted to express could live.

XI

In its textuality and conditions of being, *Amar Jiban* was a nineteenth-century production, although Rashsundari seldom reflected upon her times.[109] They gave her a publisher, a printer, a market for her writing. They created a modern readership that would want to read about an ordinary woman. They also gave her a language that she could write in—a vernacular prose which was accessible to a neo-literate person with no training in the classical languages or in English. It was a prose that could express the life-events of a housewife as well as the devotional exhortations of a devotee.[110]

If nineteenth-century processes had enabled the writing of *Amar Jiban*, they remained incomplete, even botched-up. And here I have a personal debt to recount. A hundred years after Rashsundari, in the early decades of this century, a grand-aunt of mine was seized with the desire to read. Her affluent, educated, upper-caste family was uncooperative and she had to keep her desire a secret. The only reading matter that would come her way were paper packets carrying groceries from shops into her kitchen. The paper came out of torn pages from schoolboys' exercise books, scored over with sums and spelling lessons. While cooking the evening meal, she would pore over them in the flickering light from her hearth-fire.

Rashsundari's life and writing stood at the confluence of two orders

---

[109]Apart from a reference to Victoria's rule, there is no other mention of any political event of her times. About social developments, she approvingly referred to the growth of women's education and to the spread of print culture.

[110]Bengali prose had existed from at least the sixteenth century, but a prose literature came into its own from the early nineteenth century, along with the spread of print.

of patriarchy, and of women's desires. On the one hand, there was her relationship with the bhakti tradition. It allowed the woman, seeking an excess beyond a homebound existence, a certain ambiguous space. On the other hand, there were her own times, when a new system of liberal pedagogy came to include women as its target. This, however, was riven with doubts about its own agenda. If a liberal pedagogy was a weapon of the coloniser, it asked itself, would the education of the woman not indicate a possible surrender to colonisation? In any case, liberal reformism operated within severely narrow margins, even inside its middle-class boundaries.[111] For other women, seized with the hunger for the written word, it had little to offer beyond stray pages torn out of school exercise books.

[111]Schools for girls remained largely restricted to Calcutta in the nineteenth century and their numbers were extremely limited. Despite Rashsundari's enthusiastic anticipations, only women from families influenced by liberal reform would enjoy access to education. See Usha Chakrabarti, *Condition Of Bengali Women Around The Second Half Of The Nineteenth Century* (Calcutta, 1963). The tradition of employing Vaishnav mendicant women to educate upper-caste Hindu women remained largely restricted to families with considerable property rights, possibly because of the necessity to train them in property management, if the need arose. See B.C. Pal, *Memories Of My Life And Times*, vol. 1 (Calcutta, 1932).

CHAPTER FOUR

Bankimchandra and the Impossibility of a Political Agenda

Recent cultural studies of nineteenth-century Bengal have been preoccupied with Bankimchandra Chattopadhyaya more than with any other literary or polemical figure.[1] And, despite the much-proclaimed 'death of the author', Bankim's real intentions and political agenda continue to haunt scholarship. The reasons are not very difficult to gauge. For Bankim was, acknowledgedly, the real maker of the Bengali novel, of mature and serious Bengali prose, and the founder of literary journalism and literary criticism. His writings, therefore, may be taken to express, more decisively than those by others of his period, the processes by which intellectual opinions are made. Bankim was also a wonderfully inventive political and social satirist-cum-polemicist who was often bafflingly inconsistent in his convictions and his targets.

Recent studies on Bankim have recognized such shifts but have hastened to attribute them to his initial composition and subsequent

---

[1]There is a rich corpus of Bengali works on Bankim. In English, the better-known works include Ashis Nandy, *The Intimate Enemy: Loss and Recovery of Self under Colonialism* (Delhi: Oxford University Press, 1983); Tapan Raychaudhuri, *Europe Reconsidered: Perceptions of the West in Nineteenth-century Bengal* (Delhi: Oxford University Press, 1988); Ranajit Guha, *An Indian Historiography of India: A Nineteenth-century Agenda* (Calcutta: K.P. Bagchi, 1988); Sudipta Kaviraj, 'Signs of Madness: A Reading of the Figure of Kamalakanta in the Work of Bankimchandra Chattopadhyaya', *Journal of Arts and Ideas* (June 1989); Partha Chatterjee, *Nationalist Thought and the Colonial World: A Derivative Discourse?* (Delhi: Oxford University Press, 1986).

revision of substantive, identifiable and clearly defined agendas. Most of all, there is a tendency to read in them a thwarted desire to escape from the prison-house of derived meanings imposed by a European Enlightenment epistemology.[2] This prison-house, it is believed, either made a non-colonized epistemology impossible even within a nationalist framework, or suppressed the very desire to transgress the chains of reason and rationalism and made it possible only to express such desire in the broken utterances of an assumed madness.[3] There does not seem to be sufficient inclination among such analyses to reckon with a corpus of writing that was notoriously elusive and that continued not only to raise very different questions and offer contradictory resolutions at different places, but also to satirize and laugh at whatever seemed closest to an agenda. The propensity to read Bankim's convictions as obvious and given partly stems, I feel, out of isolating his political and novelistic prose from each other, or out of ignoring his novels as decisive components of his political writings.

A persistent and somewhat repetitive preoccupation with assessing the exact degree of his affiliation to the Enlightenment also tends to dismiss the political questions and problems which Bankim negotiated. This then introduces a degree of staleness in our conclusions, since all of the nineteenth-century colonial intelligentsia was irrevocably 'contaminated' by Enlightenment discourses. As a result we do not sufficiently reckon with the ways in which this intelligentsia processed and negotiated with, revived and reanimated, Hindu philosophical, religious and aesthetic currents. Nor do we conceptualize the possibility of a unique mix and productive interrogation of all epistemologies, Enlightenment and Hindu-revivalist. The questions that the nineteenth-century polemicists asked themselves, and the precise manner in which they handled them, seem bypassed. In this chapter I therefore focus on Bankim's early writings and try to show how their dominant concerns are muted as well as insidiously reinserted by narrative and discursive devices. I shall briefly dwell on the implications of this movement within and between

[2]The most original and powerful articulation of this position was first developed by Ashis Nandy in *The Intimate Enemy*. Subsequent studies of colonial discourse have, I feel, repeated his insights without his subtleties and flexibilities.

[3]This is the thrust of Kaviraj's work on Bankim's satire in 'Signs of Madness'.

his prose forms, and indicate how the movement persists even in his later writings—when he seemed to be speaking in a recognizably dogmatic, authoritarian voice.

I

Bankimchandra Chattopadhyaya (1838–1894) was born in a well-to-do Brahmin family connected with the medium rungs of colonial administration.[4] He reached the highest levels of the new Western education available to Indians of his day, passing through a modern school, Presidency College, Calcutta University, and a law course. He worked as deputy collector and deputy magistrate in several western, northern and central districts of Bengal for thirty-three years, achieving a reputation as a courageous administrator who stood up to the oppressions of Indians by British misrule several times over his distinguished career. Bankim was also exposed to the company of wandering ascetics early in his life: his father cultivated such men. As a young student in a school that dispensed English education he decided, on his own, to simultaneously study the entire syllabus of Brahminical learning, and attended a traditional institution or *tol* at the renowned centre of Bhatpara. Here he studied classical literature, grammar and philosophy. He maintained a lively contact with the pandits of Bhatpara throughout his life.[5]

He was first married at the age of eleven but his child-wife died when he was fifteen. He seems to have started looking for a new wife soon afterwards and had a hand in selecting his second wife, who, for those times, was relatively grown-up. All his life Bankim made fun of contemporaneous romanticizations of child marriage and wrote longingly about the self-aware love of strong, mature women.[6] Even at the height of his 'revivalist' phase, he said nothing in support of the agitation against the Age of Consent Bill and cast aspersions on the

[4]For an excellent short biographical sketch, see Jogesh Bagal, 'Introduction', *Bankim Rachanabali* (Calcutta: Sahitya Samsad, 1953), I, pp. 9–26.

[5]For a study of Bankim's relationship with the Bhatpara pandits, see Shyamali, 'Bankimchandra O Bhatparar Panditsamaj', *Baromas* (Autumn 1988).

[6]'Shakuntala, Miranda Ebong Desdemona', *Vividha Prabandha, Bankim Rachanabali*, I, p. 209.

learning of Pandit Sasadhar Tarkachuramani, the greatest proponent
of the anti-Bill camp.[7] He greatly admired Shakespeare's heroines and
compared Kalidas's coy women lovers unfavourably with the bold and
passionate words of love uttered by Desdemona and Miranda.[8] One
of Bankim's favourite daughters was unhappily married to a husband
who loved another and committed suicide. Soon after this Bankim wrote
his powerful novel *Bishabriksha,* where he probed various problems arising
from asymmetrical love relations, and their specific configurations
within Hindu marriages. The different social and emotional traumas of
conjugality constitute a prominent vein through most of his essays and
novels up to the 1880s. These were then abandoned as a central concern
of his discursive prose, though they retained a prominent space in his
novelistic writings.

Perhaps more intensively than most of his celebrated Bengali contem-
poraries, Bankim explored and employed various currents of Comtean
Positivism, Benthamite Utilitarianism, the social and gender philosophy of John Stuart Mill, and several strands of French Socialism.[9] At
the same time, he wrote commentaries on Hindu philosophies and
made original and acute reflections on the Nyaya, Sankhya, Vedantic
and Bhakti schools. This interlinked exploration was combined with
his personal knowledge of peasant, caste and gender problems, and a
satirical attitude towards English-educated babus like himself. This
culminated—in the essay 'Samya' (Egalitarianism)—in a profound critique of the contemporary system of Brahminical, male and landlord
oppression which he considered, on the whole, to be even worse then
the generalized deprivation of Indians under colonialism.[10]

In 1882, Reverend Hastie, Bishop of the General Assembly, severely
attacked the fundamentals of Hinduism. Bankim replied with an angry

[7]Hindu nationalists opposed the reformist proposal to raise the age of consent
for married and unmarried girls from ten to twelve in 1891. For a discussion of the
centrality of this debate to agitational nationalism, see chapter six. See also *Debatattva
O Hindudharma, Bankim Rachanabali,* II, pp. 776–822.

[8]See 'Shakuntala, Desdemona Ebong Miranda', I, p. 204.

[9]See Bagal, 'Introduction', II, pp. 11–28.

[10]Published in 1879, on the eve of his debate with Reverend Hastie. *Bankim
Rachanabali,* II, pp. 381–406.

and spirited defence of Hinduism and, subsequently, wrote a series of monographs reinterpreting Hindu doctrines to prove that they held their own among, and even surpassed, all other varieties of religious and social thought. He also repudiated 'Samya' and refused to republish it in his lifetime. At the same time, he composed readings of Indian history that looked for and denied the existence of any nation-making spirit among historical Hindus.[11] He sought a political model within Hindu mythological and devotional texts and constructed a completely redefined hagiography of the sacred figure of Krishna, the incarnation of Lord Vishnu.[12] In his writings of this time he tried to reorient the location of patriotism from his earlier vision of freedom for the woman, the low caste and the peasant, and he now sought it within a disciplined regime of the Hindu sacred order, which needed to prove it had an earlier glorious history than the Muslims.[13] Yet something of his earlier social critiques persisted in his novels of this time. In these the imagined Hindu nation falters and damages itself more fatally than his political and religious essays had allowed for. Conversely, Bankim's earlier, 'liberal-rationalist' vision faltered as he explored the themes of sacred glory and patriotic discipline.

II

Bankimchandra inherited and drew upon three sets of critical energies which appear to be mutually exclusive, or non-accommodating. There was first the inheritance of liberal reformism premised on the concept of a Hindu social pathology that reformers saw as cruel and constrictive in relation to women. Reformers saw Hinduism as choking their lives, their normal desires, their intellectual possibilities. Bankim's historical

[11]'Bangalir Bahubol, Bharat Kalanka, Bharatbarsher Swadhinata Ebong Paradhinata' (1879), *Bankim Rachanabali*, II, pp. 209–13, 234–41, 241–5.

[12]*Krishnacharitra* (1886); *Dharmatattva* (first published as *Anushilan* in 1888); 'Shrimadbhagabat Gita' (1886–1888); *Debatattva O Hindudharma* (posthumously published), *Bankim Rachanabali*, II, pp. 407–583; 584–679; 680–775; 776–822.

[13]This position was developed in his two late novels, *Anandamath* (1882; fifth and revised version in 1892); and *Sitaram* (1887), *Bankim Rachanabali*, I, pp. 715–88; 873–958.

understanding as well as his concern with human relations show that he shared many features of this reformist analysis. They also show that he ruled out a full-throated celebration of the non-Westernized Hindu way of life that had inspired contemporaneous positions of Hindu revivalist-nationalism in Bengal.[14]

Yet Bankim also shared the specifically Bengali guilt about 'loyalism', about having accommodated and colluded with foreign rule. This anguish grew powerfully in the self-critical, self-reflective years after the Great Revolt of 1857, when Bengali Hindus opted for loyalty to the British throne. This guilt, and the shame of submission to foreign rule, would both stimulate and limit Bankim's critique of Hinduism, as it would inhibit an agreement with the categories of critical analysis associated with an alien system of power-knowledge. Bankim always made much fun of and caricatured the researches of contemporary Indologists like Max Müller; so also the ridiculous ignorance of the white administrator and the alienated English-educated babu.[15] In fact, his mockery of the latter was excruciatingly sharp, being also a mockery of himself. This self-irony added a particularly vicious bite to writings that occasionally resounded with colonialist abuse of Bengal' increasingly critical and disloyal educated middle class, whose unrepresentative, alienated location was exaggerated to reduce the political charge of its

[14]Hindu revivalism, as the reform of Hindu society from within and as combining with a hard antipathy towards other religions and a fundamentalist commitment to selected sacred texts, has been exhaustively discussed in the context of Bengal by Amales Tripathi, *The Extremist Challenge: India between 1890 and 1910* (Calcutta: Longman, 1967) and Amiya Sen, *Hindu Revivalism in Bengal* (Delhi: Oxford University Press, 1993). By Hindu revivalist-nationalist I refer to a political formation in the last three decades of the century, a formation which defended unreformed Hindu custom as perfect and inviolable and portrayed this defence as a struggle against colonial encroachments into Hindu domestic practices. This group was particularly influential during the agitation against the Age of Consent Bill in 1891.

[15]See *Lokrahasya* (1874); *Kamalakanter Daptar* (1875); *Muchiram Gurer Jibancharit* (1880), *Bankim Rachanabali*, II, pp. 1–48; 49–90; 113–28. All these were written in a phase when he was drawing openly from Western Utilitarian and Socialist traditions. In fact, there is somewhat less of this self-irony in his later, Hindu-chauvinist phase. Irony, therefore, was something of a safeguard against a close identification with reformism.

anti-colonial criticism. After the debate with Hastie, Bankim's satire transformed itself into a congealed objection to all criticism that emanated from outside Hindu society.[16]

Finally, there was the politics of revivalist-nationalism: this involved fiercely opposing liberal-reformist schemes on the grounds that they would fatally disrupt the very existence of Hinduism. In the late nineteenth century, such nationalists even resisted the idea of internal reform and occasionally adopted a status-quoist position on the entire question of contemporary Hindu domestic norms—since they conceived of the traces of the vanquished Hindu nation as located exclusively in these arrangements. If the autonomy of this space was compromised, they argued, then the triumph of colonization would be complete.[17]

If internal reform was ruled out by early Hindu nationalists as a way of self-redemption—since it seemed to confirm alien critiques of Hinduism—then the Hindu could redeem and prove himself through acts of militant heroism against an external enemy who had been victorious over the Hindu in the past. This adversary was no longer invulnerable and, in that respect, quite unlike contemporary British power, which was ensconced in invincible material progress. Bankim was the first Hindu nationalist to create a powerful image of an apocalyptic war against Muslims and project it as a redemptive mission, an achievement intended to endow the Hindu with political energies that he had, all along, enviously associated with Islam.[18] Yet in Bankim's understanding nothing about the Hindu of the past or the Hindu of the present suggested his ability to convincingly bring such a project to fruition.

Bankim therefore shared important positions with revivalist-nationalist suspicions of the reformist project as well as of the reformist persona: a refusal to accommodate criticism from outside, and a concern with nation-making that acquired an exclusive hold on him in his later years. At the same time, unlike Hindu nationalists, he did not think of British rule as entirely destructive. In fact Bankim even invested British

[16]See *Dharmatattva* and *Krishnacharitra*, *Bankim Rachanabali*, II, pp. 584–679; 407–583.

[17]See 'Conjugality and Hindu Nationalism' herein.

[18]See *Sitaram*, *Bankim Rachanabali*, I, pp. 873–958.

rule with certain regenerative possibilities because he believed that Indians needed a period of apprenticeship to learn modern technology, without which they were doomed to a state of permanent powerlessness.[19] This was a belief that cut across his two phases and unified some of his concerns. Also, he never came to see the Hindu social system as already perfect, although his grounds for criticism of it altered somewhat in the directly polemical prose of his later years. Rather, he proposed a new, comprehensive disciplining of the system through a syllabus designed to recover 'real' Hindu values.[20]

Bankim's liberal project was premised on a basic self-criticism more acutely sensitive to the oppression of the upper-caste Hindu woman than to the oppression of the lower castes and classes. Hindu fundamentalist nationalism, too, would often be bitterly, pungently self-critical: yet it located its primary fault in surrender to an alien civilization. Here, a continuing and prominent sense of victimhood at the hands of foreign power overlaid feelings of guilt for having accepted British rule. At the same time, any concrete sense of guilt in relation to flesh-and-blood women was displaced and concentrated into an abstract, feminine shape—the shape of the enslaved Motherland.

The rhetoric of Hindu nationalism gradually came into its own in the decades after 1857. As the panic of the revolt receded and colonial repression began to be cast in unmistakably racist and authoritarian terms, the loyalist Bengali intelligentsia was faced with the moral implications of its own complicity with alien rule, and beset with doubts about the progressive potential of such complicity. It is perhaps no accident, then, that the economic critiques of colonial rule in terms of drain-of-wealth, deindustrialization and immiserization began to be worked out only by the post-1860s generations. Similarly, literary self-representation by these new generations became overwhelmingly satirical, marked by a mordant and black humour.

Irony directed towards the self became the dominant trope across a wide cross-section of representational modes—in satirical novels, in

---

[19]See *Anandamath* and *Dharmatattva, Bankim Rachanabali,* I, pp. 715–88; II, pp. 584–679.

[20]See *Debi Choudhurani* (1884), and *Dharmatattva, Bankim Rachanabali,* I, pp. 789–872; II, pp. 584–679.

bazaar art, in farces and the theatre, and in journalistic prose.[21] The object of criticism was no longer the unreformed Hindu man who exploits women, but the reformed westernized man whose very body is taken over, marked and maimed by a regimen of colonial discipline— the alien discipline exercised through clock time, office space and Western education. While such an auto-critique was the starting point of a militantly anti-foreign rhetoric and the search for a redemptive, heroic mission, the fact that it was posed in these terms problematized the existence of the accompanying agenda. Who was going to be subject of the redemptive exercise if Bengali manhood had so irrevocably compromised itself?

Even for the self-flagellating Hindu nationalist of the later decades of the century, there fortunately remained a locus of unconquered purity: the body of the Hindu woman. This body was disciplined by the Shastras alone and proved its capacity for pain and suffering, and herein lay the redemptive hopes of the whole community. The Hindu woman's body was moulded from infancy by a shastric regimen of non-consensual, indissoluble, infant marriage, and by iron laws of absolute chastity, austere widowhood and a supposedly proven capacity for self-immolation. The obvious asymmetry of conjugal relations— the wife was to remain scrupulously loyal to her husband and even die when he did, while he was not even obliged to be monogamous—was taken as the sign of the world's only divine system—the shastric—which had created the most perfect form of womanly chastity and love. Thus, the Hindu woman was fitting subject to embody the redemptive mission of forming the future nation.

For Hindu nationalists, woman's subjectivity and agency were rendered complete by this act of embodiment. Her entire being, conditioned by scriptural commands, was adequate to sustain an embryonic nation that lay hidden and protected within her chaste womb. She was perfect as she was, her glory lay in the discipline that formed her. Any modification in that disciplinary regime would fatally injure that perfection and lead to a fall from grace. Thus, any suggestions that

[21]See Tanika Sarkar, 'The Hindu Wife and the Hindu Nation: Domesticity and Nationalism in Nineteenth-century Bengal', originally published in *Studies in History*, VI: 2 (1992): reproduced herein as chapter one.

social and religious reformers made to change the conditions of her conjugal discipline, to educate her and make her a conscious subject, would not only spell the ruin of the Hindu faith, but also of the Hindu nation, for there was no one else fit enough to be its future subject. This figure of the Hindu woman produced the most complicated series of negotiations between Bankim and revivalist-nationalists, and between Bankim and reformers. It is therefore useful as a point of entry into the larger social perspectives and contested political resolutions which Bankim grappled with in many different ways in his writings.

III

In 1865 Bankimchandra began his literary career by writing a novel.[22] In the next two decades—his relatively 'liberal' phase—he composed a dense and contorted cluster of novels, satires, essays on religion, philosophy and social-historical issues on literary and aesthetic themes.[23] The plots of his novels often developed in historical terms and grew through patriotic and heroic motifs, yet they also provided a concentrated focus on sexual and emotional tangles within domestic arrangements. War, history and patriotism were the richly textured backdrop that heightened the dramatic tones of human relationships in his work. At the heart of his explorations through times historical and contemporary lay the vexed questions that liberal-reformist critiques of Hindu conjugality had foregrounded. Bankim posed them with a clarity and pushed them with an audacity that took them well beyond the modest and respectable confines of the companionate-marriage framework which had been as much as the reformers had hoped for. His concern was to counterpose different patterns of female sexuality and ways of loving to one another, to flesh them out within contrasting domestic and extra-domestic conventions, to question the limits of accepted codes

[22]This was *Durgeshnandini*, a historical novel. *Bankim Rachanabali*, I, pp. 53–136.

[23]This included ten novels, from *Durgeshnandini* to *Krishnakanter Will* (1877), and ten collections of essays. It also included his founding of the path-setting journal *Bangadarshan* in 1872, which he edited for the next four years and with which he remained closely associated later.

and transgressive behaviour, and to test given models of male sexuality and love as well as suggest alternative possibilities. He probed these ideas as these were manifest within the structures of widowhood and polygamous male sexuality; he examined the woman's anguish within these structures, as also the man's conflict between on the one hand his strong love and willed commitment, and on the other his polygamous license and inclination.[24] He articulated wide-ranging configurations of female transgressions within extra-marital relationships and contrasted the woman's moral-emotional dilemmas with socially sanctioned codes.[25]

Bankim also compared female sexuality and love at different stages of life, and within familial and extra-familial contexts: the childlike, angelic, innocent love of a very young girl who is coy and inarticulate in love and who is born to be the doting wife (a romantic model derived largely from the aesthetic conventions of classical Sanskrit drama), as against that of the older, passionate, strong-willed woman who finds herself in unconventional, even amoral roles and situations.[26] In doing all this he was critical, as liberals were, of the Hindu woman's condition.

Yet the basis of his criticism was different. To the fully domesticated child-wife he counterposed not the formally educated wife or the child widow who remarries, but, instead, the adult, mature and passionate woman who could hold her own in public spaces and political intrigues, who could take a man's place in a crisis, and who could provide a strong model of intellectual and moral behaviour. This woman might even transgress Hindu gender codes and find herself in complex emotional and social crises where she had to make her own decisions. In his later, more Hindu-supremacist phase, such women would be carefully trained under an ethical/intellectual/physical/religious pedagogic system that Bankim had sketched in his contemporary discursive prose as the way

[24]See especially *Bishabriksha*; also *Krishnakanter Will* and *Chandrashekhar* (1875), *Bankim Rachanabali*, I, pp. 261–342; 539–606; 399–476.

[25]See *Chandrashekhar* and *Rajani* (1877).

[26]This is most evident in the contrast between the young and innocent Tilottama and the powerful figure of Bimala in *Durgeshnandini*. This is also evident in the contrast between the shy, inarticulate Kunda and the older and assertive Suryamukhi in *Bishabriksha*.

to the recovery of Hindu greatness and nationhood.[27] The woman, even in his nationalist phase, is given not only a transgressively activist role, even her education is non-gendered. Such an idea went beyond both reformist and revivalist-nationalist conceptions.

In his second novel, *Kapalakundala*, Bankim tried to articulate a fairly unique kind of woman whose possibility he was fond of imagining and arguing about—the a-social woman who is entirely undomesticated, even after she experiences the most perfect form of domestic and sexual love.[28] Kapalakundala remains the freest and most self-sufficient human being and embodies an ideal that Bankim was to develop later with great emphasis—the ideal of a non-attached person who encompasses wisdom, kindness, concern and selflessness but finds fulfilment entirely within herself or himself and is totally independent. But whereas in his later writings Bankim would link such self-sufficiency with some broader politico-religious goal—thereby making it a contingent state that emerges out of a rigorous regime of self-discipline—here it remains an aesthetic exercise which detached itself from ulterior religious or social purposes.[29] The unfettered woman is a radical imagining, and is in no way linked to the more familiar woman who longs to rid herself of earthly encumbrances in order to wrap herself up within a divine attachment. Kapalakundala, whom the quirks of fortune caused to be abandoned on wild seashores in her infancy, experiences, yet is unmoved by, ties of love, household, property, and even spiritual calling: 'I would be happy, perhaps, if I could go back to the sea, if I could wander by myself among the groves on the beach . . .'.[30]

Bankim's notion of modern individualism, portrayed by this un-cluttered and solitary spirit, had to be embodied as a woman since it

[27] See *Debi Chaudhurani* and *Anandamath*, *Bankim Rachanabali*, I, pp. 399–476; 715–88.

[28] Published in 1866. *Bankim Rachanabali*, I, pp. 137–88. He used to argue with his brother Sanjivchandra about whether such a woman was at all within the realms of possibility. *Kapalakundala* was written to prove and actualize such a concept. See Bagal's 'Introduction', *Bankim Rachanabali*, I, pp. 30–1.

[29] See, for instance, *Anandamath*, *Debi Chaudhurani* and *Sitaram* among novels, and 'Dharmatattva' for an elaboration of the concept of non-attachment. *Bankim Rachanabali*, I, pp. 715–88; 789–872; 873–958; II, pp. 584–679.

[30] *Kapalakundala*, *Bankim Rachanabali*, I, p. 126.

grew out of his profound dissatisfaction with the social burdens of domesticity. In the oppressive view of domesticity which Bankim was critiquing, domesticity is, for a woman, an existential condition—so much so that the deeper her satisfactions and rewards within it, the more she loses her core of individuality—herself. This is why an aesthetic realization of perfect and moral human freedom (moral because it acknowledges and fulfills moral obligations with perfect non-attachment) inevitably implies a radical social critique inasmuch as it is embodied in a woman, the most unfree of human beings: 'Had I known that marriage means enslavement, I would never have married', says Kapalakundala; and to her sister in law Shyama: 'Let us assume that I'll put up my hair, wear a nice dress, put on all manner of jewellery . . . and even hold a little golden doll of a baby in my arms . . . Let us assume the whole lot. . . . But . . . where is happiness in all this for me?' To which Shyama replies: 'Isn't it a happy occasion when the flower blooms?' And back comes Kapalakundala's chillingly transgressive reply, implying rebellion against religious and reformist norms about women's place and purpose: 'The people who watch the flower bloom, feel happy to see it bloom. But where is happiness for the flower in this?'[31] Understandably, Bankim chooses to place his most powerful and compelling, his most activist women characters, in non-domestic situations and vocations.

The specifically liberal form of self-criticism of this phase in Bankim's novels informs a typical situation recreated within very different kinds of relationships. In these situations a woman accuses a man, in supercharged words, of bringing about her ruin, and the man admits his responsibility. There is a remarkable range among such fictional prosecutors and great variations in their transgressive locations. In *Bishabriksha* it is a low-caste servant woman of dubious morals who flings her accusation at a debauched, modern babu and says he has sinned in taking advantage of her genuine love for him when he really felt no tenderness for her.[32] In *Chandrasekhar* a married woman who has long nurtured her childhood love for another man is made to undergo a severe penance which dissolves her sanity into a state of induced delirium. When her husband discovers she has remained physically faithful

[31]Ibid.
[32]*Bishabriksha, Bankim Rachanabali*, I, p. 341.

to him, he considers her chaste, only to have her insist on calling herself unfaithful because, in her mind, she has loved another. Instead of repenting, however, she accuses him: 'We were as two flowers growing on the same stem. Why did you tear us apart?'[33] In *Krishnakanter Will* the man leaves his blameless and loving wife for a widow. He kills the widow on suspicion of unfaithfulness and the wife dies out of years of neglect. The spirits of both women return to haunt the man for both had loved him and he had 'killed' both.[34]

A mad maidservant, an adulterous wife, a chaste wife, an adulterous mistress who had been a widow in the first place—all are equally wronged and all accuse their men with the same force of conviction. In the maidservant's case the fact that she is socially subordinated to the man who ruins her is not explicitly mentioned, yet so deeply is the class dimension embedded into the structure of the plot that it adds a subtext of fresh guilt with its own separate weight. In allowing such women the role of angry prosecutors, Bankim moves beyond the codes of accepted practice and belief that derive either from Hindu prescriptive texts and their adherents among the orthodox, or from reformist and dominant strands of colonial law-making—all of which were deeply convinced about the duties of the married woman and their culpability in the event of transgression. Bankim's impatience with the effects of domesticity on the woman's inner being, and his representation of the powerful, assertive and self-sufficient woman, are more radical than most reformist agendas of his time.

Similar scenes haunted his later novels just as powerfully, even when he had stopped discussing the Brahminical ideological underpinning of human relationships. In *Debi Chaudhurani*, Hindu filial obligations thwart the love between a man and a woman.[35] In *Sitaram* there is a poignant inversion of the trial of Sita (the final event in the *Ramayana*). In the *Ramayana* the king stages a public trial of a queen even when he knows she is innocent, simply because there is gossip about her having been unfaithful to him. Bankim's novel expresses its criticism of this

---

[33]*Chandrashekhar, Bankim Rachanabali*, I, pp. 468–70.
[34]*Krishnakanter Will, Bankim Rachanabali*, I, p. 605.
[35]*Debi Chaudhurani, Bankim Rachanabali*, I, p. 816.

epic event via the public words of condemnation and protest, uttered by another woman, who forces the trial to close down. In such scenes we see the operations of a powerful sense of guilt towards women, but a guilt that did not result in Bankim arguing for structural changes in women's immediate social position, such as the reformists advocated. The guilt is both created as well as exhausted at the level of the emotional situation, and is not problematized in his discursive prose directly, except fleetingly, in 'Samya'. In the novels, too, it is unfocussed, not located in particular, reformable aspects of the woman's social existence or in concrete dimensions of normal human relations. It is encountered instead in individual, tragic situations which dissolve ultimately into the extremes of madness, hysteria, delirium and death—in psychotic situations, that is, rather than in social ones. Ultimately, the social implications and aspects of these tragic situations are subsumed and submerged within profoundly unresolvable and asymmetrical emotional crises which then disappear from the social realm altogether.

The social interrogation inherent in these melodramatic moments of accusation is never pushed towards a final resolution or an authoritative summing-up of the situation. Nor does it emerge as *the* climatic moment in the plot; questions are in fact reinserted within a larger array of opinions and possibilities that make up the internal logic of the plot. What, then, is the purpose of this somewhat static and determinedly open-ended arrangement of conflicting points of view, made with great force but not really argued through? One is led to ask: even though some of these statements seem to work against explicit social and moral codes, do they justify a reading of the entire text as heretical? Given the fact that we are dealing here with fiction, which poses special difficulties in arriving at clear-cut conclusions, I feel that these scenes, while they do interrogate and destabilize the first-order meaning of the narrative, cannot be necessarily privileged as representing authorial intention, and as subverting the obvious narrative and social codes. They represent the inclusion of alternative, even transgressive, *possibilities* within the narrated world; and this world as a whole reveals a range of unrealized possibilities that throws a particular form of existence into sharper relief through a series of comparisons and contrasts. The limits of this existence, as well as its possibilities, are thereby indicated with more confidence and clarity, even if Bankim's purpose is not so immediately political as much as indicative, subjunctive, hypothetical. Only once—in his polemical prose—did Bankim unambiguously proclaim a feminist agenda, and that one piece he was soon at pains to disclaim.[36] His hesitation to push his interrogation to the point of statement is itself indicative of a historical and political predicament, and we reduce its proportions when we seek within it some hidden but clear conviction. Even in his relatively eclectic, liberal phase, Bankim was no reformer. Nor was he a convinced radical. His radicalism consists in opening out several worlds in which radical possibilities flicker, exist, and are extinguished.

IV

Bankim's discomfort in his novels with Hindu social codes and with the aesthetic conventions of Sanskrit drama—which powerfully regulated the literary representation of female sexuality—went considerably beyond the limits of both reformist and orthodox thought.[37] Since Hindu womanhood was central for much nineteenth-century thinking about social and national matters, Bankim's accounts were comments upon the Hindu way of life and the Hindu nation. At the same time, as we have seen, he refused, even in this phase, to formulate a fully developed social critique or advance anything like a coherent gender ideology. There is a straightforward argument in defence of this: Bankim was too good a novelist to turn his novels into thinly disguised ideological exercises, and human and emotional problems justifiably dominate his novels. But to assess his thinking further, let us turn now to the considerable corpus of non-fictional work, that Bankim produced in these years.

This was a phase in which he experimented with marvellously diverse

[36]This was 'Samya', *Bankim Rachanabali*, II, pp. 381–406.

[37]See Subha Chakraborty Dasgupta, 'Structural Forces in the Emergence of a Genre: The Novel in Bengal', in *Jadavpur Journal of Comparative Literature* (1991).

forms and concerns and with different genres of prose, stretching the existing boundaries of discursive writing to include literary criticism, philosophical commentaries, short popular essays on science, politics, religion, history and the Bengali language, essays also on land relations and caste and gender issues. Plus he wrote prose that expressed the most glorious fun, cocking a snook at all the powers that be—pandits, both Brahmanical and Orientalist, the Babu, the Sahib, the rationalist and the orthodox thinker. This satirical work also demystified and ridiculed prominent social and literary archetypes—the chaste child-wife, the romantic heroine of classic literature, the modern woman, and, above all, the Bengali Hindu man in all ages, forms and shapes. The richest vein in Bengali satire was tapped in such work and was expressed in brilliant caricatures of most social types and modes of thought.

The versatility of his themes, the sheer abundance of subjects, indeed the very comprehensiveness of his concerns, taken collectively success-fully refuse a fixed agenda and disperse the possibility of a stable, identi-fiable social critique: the sheer versatility makes the range of targets too wide. Too many issues were made fun of, as was his own writing self, the subject that producted the satires.

Let us take up one piece which makes substantive political criticism of a far-reaching feminist kind. In 'Prachina O Nabina' (The Old Fashioned and the Modern Woman) he says that men who want to improve the condition of women actually scheme to improve their own lives by making women fit-in better with their own changed views and expectations. Reformist plans of the companionate marriage, he suggests, use women in a purely instrumental manner. The target of such bold feminism is not so much the orthodox Hindu who resists any enlargement of the woman's sphere, but the reformer who sees the need for change. At the same time, Bankim directly questions the need for a woman's absolute chastity on the grounds that it probably does nothing to add to her life, but only helps the man feel secure. We must remember that, at this time, the transcendent moral value of a woman's monogamous love was accepted by reformers, nationalists and colonialists alike, and they all projected it as a condition and source of womanly goodness. However, the radical edge of Bankim's statements is blunted because the overarching format is non-serious and the criticism concludes with farcical suggestions and fun.[38] Satire makes critique readable, but here, as elsewhere, Bankim constantly blurs and disperses the thrust of his criticism by destabilizing its form and changing polemic into humour, always scrambling the serious with the non-serious. I am not arguing for solemnity or for hard political messages, but I am suggesting that Bankim did not seek to express serious criticism through an unambiguous vehicle. Though he articulated powerful social criticism, he stopped short of formulating a political or social agenda in this period and about these issues.

There are, all the same, several entirely serious polemical pieces which relate to themes of nation and freedom, to the non-existence of both the love of freedom and the sense of nationhood in the entire span of Hindu/Bengali history, of the resources of history for nation-building. These discuss European philosophical systems and Hindu religious and philosophical traditions, and the possibilities each offers for a communitarian life, for consciously instilled social bonding.[39] Bankim refuses to differentiate in any absolute way between freedom and foreign rule since an indigenous ruler might just as surely curb personal freedom, while a foreign ruler might ensure a larger slice of it by keeping internal oppression under control. He applies the Utilitarian standard of the largest happiness for the largest numbers: 'for most people, both [foreign rule and self-government] have the same effects'. He talks of caste oppression in pre-colonial India and argues that, under British rule, 'the Shudra, or the common subject has slightly improved himself.'[40] The easy cause–effect equation that nationalists tended to make between alien domination and generalized unhappiness is thereby problematized. He forcefully foregrounds fundamental divisions within Indian civil society and pre-colonial contradictions, suggesting in fact that the appearance of an external power might even loosen the bonds

[38]'Prachina O Nabina', *Vividha Prabandha*, Part 1 (1887), *Bankim Rachanabali*, II, pp. 249–56.

[39]*Vividha Prabandha*, Part 1 and Part 2 (1892). *Bankim Rachanabali*, II, pp. 159–256; 257–380.

[40]'Bharatbarshe Swadhinata Ebong Pradhinata', *Vividha Prabandha*, *Bankim Rachanabali*, II, pp. 244–5.

of internal hierarchies and controls. Above all, even as he searches for the possibilities of nationhood and social bonding Bankim refuses to see Hindu society as a seamless whole which can all be emancipated with nationhood. He resists most of the closures of nationalist thought that simplistically located all operations of power within foreign rule. Bankim does the same with religious systems, both Hindu and Christian. His polemic with Christianity, in fact, pre-dates his exchange with Reverend Hastie. He explores the resources Christianity offered to universal brotherhood and egalitarianism but complains that it dimmed these possibilities by constant evocations of evil, by a morbid self-monitoring.[41] At this time he wrote about Hindu philosophical systems with the same critical impartiality, judging doctrines by the criterion of social usefulness.[42] Only in one essay does he begin to construct an ideal Hinduism which is both pristine and authentic as well as capable of ensuring social cohesion and nation-building.[43]

The sensitivity to internal power operations is articulated most powerfully in 'Bangadesher Krishak' and in 'Samya'. In the first, Bankim comes nearest to a critique of the notion of progress under colonial auspices. Using the Utilitarian criterion he argues that the modernization of technology and the expansion in the country's wealth must be set against the fact that the producers of wealth—the low-caste Hindu and the poor Muslim peasant—are impoverished and left without security: 'We admit that the country as a whole has progressed but peasants do not share in that progress'.[44] Progress is hollow when producers and the largest masses are excluded. While here his critique is focused on the Permanent Settlement, which equipped the landlord with absolute power, in 'Samya' the critique is broadened and deepened into a fundamental observation not just about a particular arrangement or even a regional system but about Indian society as a whole.

'Samya' was a relentless exploration of the *Homo hierarchicus* within

[41]'Dharma Ebong Sahitya', *Bankim Rachanabali*, II, p. 258.

[42]'Gyan, Sankhya Darshan, Trideb Sambandhe Vijnanshastra Ki Boley', *Vividha Prabandha, Bankim Rachanabali*, II, pp. 217–21; 221–34; 273–80.

[43]'Gourdas Babaji Bhikshar Jhuli', *Vividha Prabandha, Bankim Rachanabali*, II, pp. 263–71.

[44]'Bangadesher Krishak', *Vividha Prabandha, Bankim Rachanabali*, II, p. 289.

Hindu society and the interlocked and extreme character of class, caste and gender oppression that, in this society, went beyond hierarchical divisions in other societies. 'Our country is a land of inequalities, all kinds of inequalities sprout and begin to bloom on this fertile soil as soon as they are sown', he wrote.[45] While class divisions, as well as differences between ruler and ruled, and between the learned and the unlearned, exist in all societies, India he says contributed uniquely to the corpus by adding caste and by keeping a whole people without dignity, rights and adequate means of livelihood through its operations. Bankim then substantiates the related nature of caste and class rule by returning to the theme of the poverty of the low-caste Hindu and the Muslim peasant. He shows that the vulnerability of these groups in land relations is specifically related to the power of upper castes. At this time Bengali landowners were faced with a revision of their hitherto untrammelled power over tenants through new, contested rent regulations. They were simultaneously faced with peasant protest and organized resistance to illegal cesses.[46] Bankim's class, in other words, was squeezed by both the state and the subordinated tenants, and very few erstwhile liberals were in a mood for introspection and self-criticism. In any case, liberal reformers were somewhat less concerned with the fate of peasants and low castes than about women of their own class and families. This context adds a sharp edge to Bankim's social criticism which was, in this case, unusually comprehensive and radical.

He uses gender oppression to clinch his case on the extremes of inequality in Hindu society, since sexual double standards here are most blatant, allowing male polygamy while demanding strict female chastity, seclusion and an ascetic widowhood, and prohibiting widow remarriage: 'The extent to which women are enslaved to men here cannot be seen anywhere else'. He refuses the argument that unequal rights are grounded in unequal capabilities, since capabilities are not naturally unequal but have been made so by unequal conditions. But, more importantly, he argues, 'we do not recognize that even if capabilities differ,

---

[45]'Samya', *Bankim Rachanabali,* II, p. 400.

[46]Benoy Chowdhury, 'Agrarian Economy and Agrarian Relations in Bengal, 1859–1885', in N.K. Sinha (ed.), *The History of Bengal* (Calcutta: Calcutta University, 1967).

that should lead to unequal rights.' With a somewhat wild eclecticism he evokes John Stuart Mill and Rousseau together to make a plea for the absolute value of liberal rights. He not only makes the customary reformist appeal for education and for an end to women's seclusion, he also admits that women should be economically independent of men, both by winning larger property inheritance rights and by earning their own living. This can only happen if the sexual division of labour is scrapped at both ends and men share the housework. The demand for absolute and unconditional chastity from women is unreasonable, he suggests, since men are not expected to conform to those standards. Even if most women accept the terms of their oppression, that is no argument for letting oppression continue. Centuries of social conditioning have produced an unacceptable brainwashed consent.[47]

In all this Bankim goes far, indeed very far beyond the liberal reform agenda, and suggests changes that startled and alarmed them. His programme is all the more astonishing because he never publicly defended a single item of reformist agitation on far more moderate issues and, in fact, weakened reformist positions by ridiculing their dependence on foreign legislation—even though he himself had no compunction about appealing to the same foreign government to reform land relations through legislation.[48] One may wickedly suggest that Bankim, whose antipathy to reformers was evident even while he himself made proposals for radical change, was actually issuing a warning to them about the ultimate consequences of their proposed changes by highlighting their logical direction with great force and clarity. Or, that he was attempting to undercut their agenda for change by extending it to what would be, for those times, their *reductio ad absurdum*. More seriously speaking, however, we need to recognize precisely what Bankim set forth as an agenda in his most liberal and rationalist phase. Further, we must understand exactly what he repudiated and excised from his political imagination when he desired to break away from this phase.

[47]'Samya', *Bankim Rachanabali*, II, pp. 385–405.

[48]'Bahuvivaha', *Vividha Prabandha*, Part 2, *Bankim Rachanabali*, II, pp. 314–19. 'Bangadesher Krishak', *Vividha Prabandha*, *Bankim Rachanabali*, II, pp. 287–314.

V

In 'Samya', Bankim came closest to an agenda and voice that promised
to be the most far-reaching, the most radically humanitarian that had
emerged until then among the Bengali intelligentsia. Such an agenda
was produced, moreover, without any reference to Hindu philosophical
resources. The three great 'incarnations of egalitarianism' (*samyavatar*)
that he invokes were Christ, Buddha and the proponents of the French
Revolution.[49] He made no secret of his rationalist affiliation and unambiguously proclaimed his lineage within Enlightenment universalism.
Unfortunately, given our recent critical certainty about the derivative
and emasculating nature of such affiliation, we do not reflect adequately
upon the social radicalism and relevance of Bankim's voice.

Bankim gave up these positions, never to return to them, after his
debate with Reverend Hastie. The themes of class, caste and gender
abruptly disappear from his writing, their absence filled by reflections
on all that constitutes authentic and fully historicized Hinduism, on
the culpability of the Muslim in Indian history, and on how the Hindu
nation may be imagined and constructed. For Bankim now the resolution of social and national malaise seemed to lie in imagining an
apocalyptic war with Muslims through which Hindus would ingest
their valour and prove their ability to make a nation.[50] For all these new
aspirations, a rigorous schedule and a severe disciplinary regimen are
planned, a regimen which will eventually transpose discipline from an
external religious-pedagogic authority to the self-monitoring ethical
agent. This agent will in turn build the nation through the right knowledge and practice of authentic devotion (*bhakti* and *anushilan*).[51] It would
seem, then, that the compulsions of Hindu nationalism overrode and
displaced earlier liberal concerns. In the process, Bankim's self-critical,
radical sensibility was transformed to an authoritarian, totalitarian, and
intolerant voice.

Yet even 'Samya' had not raised the issue of certain specific kinds of
freedom. British rule and the notion of progress are seriously questioned

---

[49]'Samya', *Bankim Rachanabali*, II, pp. 383–8.
[50]See 'Imagining Hindu Rashtra' in this volume.
[51]*Bankim Rachanabali*, II, pp. 584–679.

in relation to peasant poverty, but the whole issue of political freedom was rendered somewhat irrelevant by counterposing to it the theme of internal oppression and power relations. The peasant, according to Bankim, is the object of enlightened social engineering and cannot take the political initiative. Nor can such initiative lie with the educated middle class which is complicit with a system of class, caste and gender privileges. Bankim articulates freedom and welfare for the victims of social oppression powerfully, but this agenda is left without an agent. Therefore, ironically, it is the state which is asked to assume a socially-informed agency.[52] In this, Bankim the civil servant seems unable to escape from himself. This plea for state intervention sits oddly with his claim that reformers are wrong in expecting domestic change to come through state legislation, and that change should wait till agency is internally generated within the people who most need change.

In fact, the creation of a will for social change is invoked only in relation to liberal demands for government legislation in the sphere of domestic reform. Otherwise, Bankim does not take this up in the 1880s; the whole problematic had changed, and he now looks for an ethico-religious site for the new nation, which he identifies with collective self-discipline and not with freedom.[53] What is obvious in the earlier stage, however, is that he does not believe in the agency of the intelligentsia because of their vested interests as well as their moral flaws and historical inability to even comprehend the value of freedom and nationhood. Since this is a class that is doomed, he refuses its demands for political rights. Bankim made himself extremely unpopular by supporting British moves to muzzle the vernacular press—moves that were condemned by reformers and Hindu nationalists alike. He emphasized the irresponsibility and ill-informed nature of the press to suggest that it needed to be controlled.[54] He had nothing to say about the nature of the controlling agency. Similarly, he used satire and caricature formidably against the politics of associations and organizations, of the

[52]This is particularly evident in *Bangadesher Krishak*, *Vividha Prabandha*, *Bankim Rachanabali*, II, pp. 287–314.

[53]See *Krishnacharitra* and *Dharmatattva*, *Bankim Rachanabali*, II, pp. 407–583; 584–679.

[54]See Bagal, 'Introduction', *Bankim Rachanabali*, I, pp. 20–1.

mimicry of imported political models that these involved, and of the ridiculous misadventures of those who formed them.[55] He undercuts precisely the struggle for specifically democratic and public spaces where Indians could grow through discussion and the experience of organization.

His compassion for the state of Hindu women paradoxically also included the idea of 'willed' self-immolation, an idea which was kept insulated from any notion that such consent may be normatively engendered. Bankim invoked the figure of the woman happily embracing death as a unique political resource. In fact, such self-immolation in his work always occurs at the point of political catastrophe, when the Hindu male has irretrievably compromised himself and Hindu greatness is preserved in the woman's act of self-destruction, which flows from love and strength. In *Mrinalini*, for instance, Nabadwip, the capital and last bastion of Bengali Hindu power, is taken over by a handful of Turks. The king and queen flee ignominiously through a back door, the subjects tremble inside locked houses, the Hindu general betrays his king. At the edge of the devastated city, a girl lights a pyre and smilingly places herself there at the feet of her dead husband and becomes a sati.[56] This is the sole act of courage, love and commitment in a city and country about to succumb to a 'foreign rule' that is destined to last seven hundred years. In 'Kamalakanter Daptar', the great satire that laughs at everything, a moment of deep solemnity occurs when Kamalakanta ponders on the old glory of his ruined country and thinks of her as the icon of a goddess that is going to be immersed. Will the regenerative Mother ever return again? Kamalakanta is about to despair when he reminds himself of the other woman in whom the sacred fire still burns:

> I can see the funeral pyre alight, the chaste wife sitting at the heart of the blazing flames, clasping the feet of her husband lovingly to her breasts. Slowly the fire spreads, destroying one part of the body and entering another . . . her face is joyful . . . life departs and the body is reduced to ashes . . . when I remember that only some time ago . . . our women could die like that, then new hope arises in me and I have faith that we,

[55]See the satirical pieces in *Lokrahasya, Bankim Rachanabali*, II, pp. 1–48.
[56]*Mrinalini* (1869), *Bankim Rachanabali*, I, pp. 189–260.

too, have the seeds of greatness within us. . . . Women of Bengal! You are the true jewels of this country.[57]

Bankim is one with the Hindu nationalist in locating redemption via the immolation of the woman's body, in identifying her greatness as her willed acceptance of those scriptural commands which stand for love and courage. What is new in Bankim is an eroticization of this spectacle of violent death. The blazing flames are made to stand in for the fire of desire that moves from one part of the body to another and that slowly consumes and finally annihilates her in the moment of a longed-for, ultimate climax which is both death and love.

Here is the paradox of on the one hand a sharp and impatient social concern combined with a rationalist commitment that is at a vast distance from Hindu nationalism, and on the other a vision which not only shares some basic ground with such a nationalism but even contributes crucially to its arguments and imagination. The nation is identified with and rejuvenated by the most extreme form of violence that the woman can exercise upon herself, in conformity with her religion. Further, as the search for nationhood begins in history and religion, any faith in rationalism is made immobile by being denied an effective agency within Indian society, and nationhood is severed from democratic organization and collective protest. In many ways, the ground is already cleared for authoritarian and exclusivist definitions of the Hindu nation which search for an absolute and disciplined faith in Hindu resources alone, disregarding self-critical reflections on their own social tyranny. The emphasis is on an individual self-discipline leading towards collective improvement of the nation. The question of individual rights and self-improvement are submerged within a denial of the individual and an exclusive identification of personal happiness with national greatness.

This compulsion towards a totalitarian community and an authoritarian regimen caricatures Bankim's own earlier, more egalitarian, concerns over its glorification of the pedagogical values of hierarchical divisions. The subject needs to defer to the monarch, because that imparts training in obedience. Similarly, family norms must be preserved:

[57] *Kamalakanter Daptar, Bankim Rachanabali,* II, pp. 73.

the 'husband used to be the god, and now he is treated like an old pal.'[58] Deference keeps alive the urge in social superiors to strive to deserve it, to aim at excellence. In this period Bankim wrote weighty polemical and pedagogical tracts, and not even one satirical piece. Self-irony and multivalence also disappear.

Critics have pointed out that Bankim remained confined within rationalist knowledge, that even his turn to Hinduism and Hindu knowledge was mediated through rationalist categories. His muscular and warlike definition of bhakti—a devotional system based on a personal relationship with a personalized divinity—relied on a unique and original recasting of the Krishna myth according to a Western model of historicist construction and aimed to incorporate the values of nation-building and statesmanship which he envied in other religions. As 'a result of my Western education', Bankim writes, 'I am now fully convinced about that [the perfection and divinity of the mythological hero Krishna]'.[59] Bankim himself never denied his Enlightenment, rationalist affiliations. He reaffirmed his loyalty to his old Utilitarian masters, although he was now at pains to assert that a more perfect form of the same aspirations was available in Hindu traditions and in the pedagogical armoury that he had culled from these in his *anushilandharma* (religion of self-discipline). Hinduism, for him, was the best edition of universal truth, not a departure from those standards. He reiterated the need to learn certain things from the West and continued to lash out at certain aspects of Hindu traditions—Vaishnavite sensualism, blind faith in the infallibility of the Vedas, even the concept of *adhikar-bheda* (unequal access to truth). While he no longer commented on the social implications of this basic hierarchical concept, he still aspired to a universal application of his anushilandharma. The putative Hindu nation could not afford to waste human resources.

Woman, however, remained for him the locus of the nation in a far more activist way than she was for Hindu nationalists. The pedagogy of anushilandharma was imparted to a woman and a woman embodied its actualization and glory. The only approximation of the saviour Krishna is a woman to whom Bankim significantly addresses the words that

[58] *Dharmatattva, Bankim Rachanabali,* II, p. 620.
[59] *Krishnacharitra, Bankim Rachanabali,* II, p. 407.

invoke Krishna in the *Gita*: 'Come again, Prafulla . . . and face this world. . . . Stand before this society and say: I am not new, I am everlasting. I am that Word. I have come often, still you forgot me, so I am here again: "To save the virtuous, to destroy the evil/ To restore true religion/ I shall appear in every age . . . "'. This innovation, typically for Bankim, is slipped in at the end of a long description of the overriding value of a domesticated morality for women.[60] In *Sitaram*, too, a woman causes 'virtuous' action, a woman tries to save Hindu power and glory, a woman is wrongfully tried and humiliated. The Hindu man fails to sustain the divine energy that has driven him to create a great Hindu power. Despite Bankim's theme of the historical crime of the Muslim against the Hindu, the Hindu kingdom here breaks up from within because of the culpability of the Hindu man.[61] Bankim would not, or could not, imagine a permanent recovery of Hindu power, nor would he actualize a male agent for such redemption.

This chapter explores problems in the making of nineteenth-century political and social agendas in Bengal by focusing on the early 'liberal' half of Bankim's work. There is no space here for an exhaustive discussion of Bankim's life's work, nor of the ways in which he negotiated, in the later part of his life, the contradictory compulsions and aspirations that ruled political thinking. Bankim's critical convictions, culminating in 'Samya', are indeed dispersed from the 1880s. Yet there is no simple and final movement from one form of knowledge to another, nor can we trace the definitive making of a new agenda. For Bankim, neither Hindu faith nor Hindu nationalism offered a resolution. His predicament therefore continued, whether in his liberal inclinations or during his revivalist-nationalist turn.

The recovery, however abridged, of the history of these moves within his writings is required in order to expand the range of questions and problems with which we have become accustomed when exploring nineteenth-century political prose. Current historical enquiries often congeal at a fixed point: how various thinkers conceived the nation along lines that inexorably flowed from Western rationalism. This severely constricted enquiry evades significant anxieties which structured and

---

[60] *Debi Choudhurani, Bankim Rachanabali*, I, p. 872.
[61] *Sitaram, Bankim Rachanabali*, I, pp. 873–958.

problematized the nineteenth-century intelligentsia's negotiations between what they considered socially just and human, and all that they
saw as authentic and indigenous. Bankim's writings show, with considerable poignance, how he refuses to overcome this ambiguity. In his
relatively indigenist, later phase, when he seemed closer to a militantly
Hindu revivalist-nationalist agenda, he constantly problematizes this
same agenda with subtle, guerilla attacks. He could in fact conceive of
such an agenda only by suppressing and obliterating that part of himself which was anguished and angered by the operations of power within
Brahmanical patriarchy, and by the problems of class, caste and gender.
Later in life he keenly regretted the fact that he had ever written 'Samya'—
the questions that he had himself formulated earlier with uncompromising passion and force now needed to be evaded and silenced before he
could pose an alternative problematic. As I have been arguing, however,
the very passion of his earlier convictions refused to let them die, and
they came back to haunt and mock his new agenda.

CHAPTER FIVE

Imagining Hindu Rashtra
The Hindu and the Muslim in Bankimchandra's Writings

As we have just seen, Bankimchandra Chattopadhyay was the real founder of the Bengali novel as well as of serious Bengali discursive literature on political theory. He was also a brilliant humorist and satirist who laughed at most traditions, agendas and social types. Generally regarded as the most powerful formative influence on nineteenth-century political thinking in Bengal, he is a difficult author to read with certainty because he seems to straddle with felicity very different positions at different times[1] and seems to mock convictions and resolutions that he himself had constructed.[2]

Scholars generally regard Bankim as a crucial force in the making of both a nationalist imagination and a Hindu revivalist polemic.[3] A particularly striking instance of this dual impact is his celebrated hymn to the motherland—*Vande Mataram* (salutation to the mother), which became the most potent patriotic slogan at peak points in twentieth-century mass nationalist struggles,[4] as well as the Hindu rallying cry at moments of Hindu–Muslim violence after 1926.[5] For the Sangh Parivar,

---

[1] Tapan Raychaudhuri, *Europe Reconsidered: Perceptions of the West in Nineteenth-Century Bengal* (Delhi, 1988).

[2] Tanika Sarkar, 'Bankimchandra and the Impossibility of a Political Agenda', *Oxford Literary Review*, 16, 1994, reproduced herein as chapter four.

[3] A. Tripathi, *The Extremist Challenge: India Between 1890–1910* (Calcutta, 1967).

[4] Sumit Sarkar, *Swadeshi Movement in Bengal 1903–8* (Delhi, 1973).

[5] P.K. Datta, personal communication.

Vande Mataram, not Rabindranath Tagore's 'Jana gana mana', is the authentic Indian national anthem. The hymn is sung in its entirety, including its Bengali passages, at RSS training meetings (*shakhas*). Any change or abbreviation is strictly forbidden because the song symbolizes the undivided, inviolate body of the pre-Partition motherland; hence, an abridgment amounts to a symbolic mutilation of the sacred body, a repetition of the partition of India in 1947.[6] When the BJP came to power in Delhi during the 1993 state elections, it made singing *Vande Mataram* compulsory in Delhi's state schools.

The use of *Vande Mataram* by both Indian nationalism and Hindu communalism can lead scholars who see nationalism as an unhistorical, undifferentiated phenomenon to read the meanings of one usage into the other in their understanding of Bankim's work.[7] Bankim's work has also been split up into different, isolated components, and his concept of Hindu nationhood is read on its own as an exercise in nationalist imagination, without any reference to the Muslim in his discourse.[8] Bankim's polemical references to the Muslim are also sometimes detached from his novels. They can then be seen as a seamless whole, without internal shifts. The communal impulse is then related to his nationalism as its displaced and disfigured form.[9]

I will here explore Bankim's location of the Muslim and the Hindu nation as an interlinked formation, as one that has to be situated simultaneously within his novels and his discursive prose. The two set up an

[6]Asha Sharma, interview with the author in Delhi, December 1990.

[7]Gyanendra Pandey, *The Construction of Communalism in Colonial North India* (Delhi, 1990).

[8]Sudipta Kaviraj, 'The Myth of Praxis: The Construction of the Figure of Krishna in *Krishnacharitra*', Occasional Paper, Nehru Memorial Museum & Library, no date.

[9]Partha Chatterjee's *Nationalist Thought and the Colonial World* (Delhi, 1986) has completely ignored Bankim's novels as important ways of negotiating with political themes. Chatterjee's reading of the discursive prose too is severely limited by a literal reading of texts, without regard to Bankim's literary strategies and devices. Sudipta Kaviraj has also chosen to read each text as a fairly isolated, autonomous unit, although Kaviraj is extremely sensitive in his readings: *The Unhappy Consciousness: Bankimchandra Chattopadhyaya and the Formation of Nationalist Discourse in India* (Delhi: Oxford University Press, 1995).

internal dialogue as well as a self-interrogation that move across his earlier, relatively open-ended and often radical phase,[10] as also over his later, more dogmatic and recognizably revivalist work. I am centrally concerned with the profound breaks in thinking and expression across these two phases, as well as with the continuities preserved with narrative tropes and devices: by these Bankim continued to destabilize his seemingly unambiguous agenda of a triumphalist Hindu people. My focus will be on his last five years, when he composed three historical novels on Hindu–Muslim antagonism—*Anandamath* (first published 1882; fifth and final version, 1892), *Debi Choudhurani* (1884), and *Sitaram* (1887)—and on two polemical essays about an authentic and reinvigorated Hinduism attainable through a disciplinary regimen that Bankim spelled out in some detail—*Dharmatattva* (1888) and *Krishnacharitra* (1892).[11]

In sharp contrast to his prolific earlier phase, Bankim wrote far less in this later period. There is much less satire, caricature, and humour. For the first time, his prose remains uncompromisingly solemn, weighty, and ponderous, all of which, at least overtly, suggest a single and authoritarian polemical thrust rather than an argument that continuously poses new questions and issues to itself. *Dharmatattva*, in fact, is written in the form of a guru preaching to his disciple. The authorial voice is intrusive and cast as that of a self-proclaimed proselytizer-cum-pedagogue. One is reminded of RSS training classes—although, in *Dharmatattva*, master and disciple proceed through arguments and counter-arguments, while in RSS training sessions boys are told stories with 'correct' messages and these listeners practice silent acceptance.

This phase of Bankim's work is considered a decisive component of Hindu revivalism, and indeed it provided vital resources for late-twentieth-century Hindutva and its RSS leadership. I prefer to treat this

---

[10]Tanika Sarkar, 'Bankimchandra and the Impossibility', op. cit.

[11]Two incomplete manuscripts were posthumously published: his commentary on 'Shrimad Bhagwat Gita' (1902) and 'Devatattva O Hindudharma' (1938). Since both were incomplete and since Bankim extensively revised his writings before final publication, I have not made use of them here. All references to Bankim's writings are, as earlier, to J.C. Bagal, ed., *Bankim Rachanabali*, 2 vols. (Calcutta, 1965, 1969). All translations are mine. Page numbers are cited when required.

phase more as constituting a link between nineteenth-century Hindu revivalism in Bengal—whose Hindu supremacist agenda was not primarily turned against Muslims or Islam—and the hard, aggressive Hindutva politics that started organizing itself in the 1920s on an exclusively and explicitly anti-Muslim platform.[12] I am also concerned, however, with what has not been appropriated from Bankim's thinking on the Muslim and the Hindu nation, and with how Bankim negotiated these themes differently from those who later used his work for their own purposes.

II

Until the end of the 1870s Bankim boldly and thoroughly probed the specific forms of caste, class, and gender oppression in precolonial Indian traditions. Given the internal and structured power relations within Hinduism, which might even be loosened up somewhat under foreign rule,[13] he had even occasionally questioned the need for self-rule and nationhood for Hindus. In 'Samya' (Equality), published in 1879, he moved well beyond the notion of companionate marriage that liberal reformers had advocated for the new, educated woman: Bankim made startling suggestions about her future economic independence and about men sharing housework. He questioned the supreme emphasis that reformers, revivalists, and the colonial state placed equally on the absolute chastity of the Hindu wife—who was situated within a framework of male polygamy. He saw caste, class, and gender hierarchies as interlinked facets of a system that embodied the most absolute form of inequality anywhere in the world: 'Our country is the land par excellence of inequalities, any kind of discrimination springs into life and flourishes as soon as the seed is sown'.[14]

Even in 'Samya', however, certain kinds of freedom and oppression are dealt with in a rather cursory manner. He questioned British rule

[12]Tapan Basu, et al., *Khaki Shorts and Saffron Flags* (New Delhi, 1993).

[13]'Bharatbarshe swadhinata ebong paradhinata,' in *Vividha Prabandha, Bankim Rachanabli,* vol. 2, p. 244.

[14]Bankimchandra Chattopadhyaya, *Bankim Rachanabali,* ed. J.C. Bagal (Calcutta, 1969), II, p. 399.

and its ideas about progress in relation to persistent peasant poverty,[15] but he saw foreign rule and political freedom as a lower priority than the reform of internal stratification and oppression within Indian society. The peasant, moreover, is the object of enlightened social engineering, but political initiative is obviously beyond him. In Bankim's historical novels, too, political change is invariably initiated by kings and ascetics; when the ordinary folk initiate direct action, it degenerates into mob rioting (*Anandamath* and *Sitaram*). Demands for freedom and welfare for victims of social oppression are powerfully articulated but the agenda is left without an agent. It is the colonial state that is asked to assume a corrective role (*Bangadesher Krishak*).

In the 1870s, when Bankim was writing his socially aware and courageous prose, the absolute vulnerability of all categories of agricultural tenants in relation to rent increases, illegal cesses, and arbitrary powers of eviction by landlords had hardly been breached.[16] In the 1880s, however, plans for substantive amendments in tenancy laws had been set forth,[17] and the state was systematically compiling and classifying information about low castes with a view to improving their conditions. In 1881 Bankim was, in fact, selected by H.H. Risley to assist in preparing an ethnographic glossary with detailed research on castes and tribes for Howrah district, where he was then posted.[18] It also became increasingly difficult to regard peasants as passive victims. Powerful forms of peasant self-organization and movements against arbitrary landlord exactions had become a central feature of the agrarian scene. The spread of commercial jute cultivation, moreover, had benefited Muslim and low-caste peasants more than *rentier* groups, who constituted the base of the new middle class.[19] In addition, the failure of Bengali entrepreneurship to find space for itself in the higher rungs of trade, business and industry

---

[15]*Bangadesher Krishak* (1875), ibid.

[16]B.B. Chaudhuri, 'Agrarian Economy and Agrarian Relations in Bengal 1859–1885', *History of Bengal 1775–1905*, ed. N.K. Sinha (Calcutta, 1967).

[17]Sugata Bose, *Peasant Labour and Colonial Capital: Rural Bengal Since 1770* (Cambridge, 1993).

[18]Sekhara Bandopadhyaya, *Caste, Politics and the Raj: Bengal 1872–1937* (Calcutta, 1990), p. 33.

[19]Ibid., chapter 2.

was definitively established by the 1870s.[20] There was a keen sense of exclusion from the commanding heights of civil society for people in Bankim's own middle class. His earlier critique of the oppressive privileges of a parasitic upper-caste middle class now seemed to require a further deepening of these processes of exclusion. A partial reversal of power relations, rather than the benevolent and responsible paternalism of upper-caste landowners that he had prescribed in the 1870s, now seemed more desirable. There was now a real problem of choice.

After the late 1870s Bankim would never return to the themes of peasant poverty and caste oppression. He would repudiate 'Samya' and refuse to bring out a new edition.[21] Even without necessarily imputing narrow motives to this choice, we have to reckon with this absence and its implications for a possible radical social agenda at a time of limited but real social change. We have to recognize that the choice was made and exercised through silence, through certain excisions of his earlier concerns. It is also a fact of considerable significance that the definitive transition from a predominantly liberal to a markedly Hindu revivalist discourse was made within Bengal around the same time, and against this context Sumit Sarkar has pointed out a somewhat similar predicament in the 1920s that partly enabled a turn towards organized communalism.[22] The posing of the problem of power and exploitation was, therefore, unambiguously radical, but Bankim's radical imagining failed or refused to construct a resolution that was adequate.

If the peasant or the dispossessed low caste was not to be the subject of his own history, then the immediately realizable and convincing agency for self-improvement within Indian society—an agency that, moreover, already seemed activated—could be the middle class, with its Western education, liberal values, and reformist agenda. If the reform of Hindu patriarchy was the major concern for this group, Bankim too had his own critique of Hindu domestic norms. This critique was, if anything, far sharper than that of the reformists. Bankim was however

[20]Sabyasachi Bhattacharya, 'Traders and Trade in Old Calcutta', *Calcutta: The Living City*, ed. Sukanta Chaudhuri (Calcutta, 1991).

[21]*Bankim Rachanabali*, ed. J.C. Bagal, op. cit.

[22]Sumit Sarkar, 'Indian Nationalism and the Politics of Hindutva', *Making Indian Hindu*, ed. David Ludden (Delhi, 1996).

relentlessly critical of reformist aspirations and methods of work. He saw the reformist dependence on colonial legislation for improved family laws as morally flawed. In his view such dependence neither generated the will for change within wider society—without which reform was doomed—nor did it make 'men' of modern Hindus by vesting them with independence of effort and hegemonic capabilities. Dependence on foreign rulers perpetuated and exemplified, in fact, the very lack of a will to freedom and nationhood that had kept Hindus subject for centuries. Bankim spared no effort in mocking this dependence on alien legislation as well as the emasculation it produced. He also mocked the surrender of the new middle class to orientalist forms of knowledge on India, although he retained great respect for strands within mainstream Western social and political philosophies.[23]

Since he saw it as a class that was born retarded, Bankim refused the middle class its demands for political freedom and rights. He made himself extremely unpopular by supporting British moves to muzzle the vernacular press by suggesting it was behaving irresponsibly and needed controls.[24] He used the entire and formidable resources of his satire and caricature to make fun of the political models involved in such exercises, and to the ridiculous misadventures in handling them ('Byaghracharya Brihallangul', in *Lokrahasya*). He thereby undercut precisely the struggle for democratic and public spaces where Indians could grow through debates and the experience of organization and protest. Neither a radical nor a liberal form of democracy was compatible with the heroic agenda that held his imagination. In fact, if Bankim prefigures the trajectory of some features of Hindutva, he also powerfully embodies some aspects of a far softer and pluralistic form of liberal indigenism. The latter, out of its commitment to non-'alienated' and 'authentic' politics,

[23]See his argument against the strategy of Vidyasagar in 'Bahuvivaha,' in *Vividha Prabandha*. Satirical pieces in *Lokrahasya* (1874) make fun of the English-educated babu quite mercilessly. He criticised Indologists like Max Müller in 'Bangalir Bahubol Prabhanda Pustak' (1879). He was extremely sarcastic about dependence on Western reflections upon Indian history and religion in *Dharmatattva*. At the same time, his affiliation with Western political theories—especially radical Utilitarian and French revolutionary and socialist thinkers—was openly asserted not just in 'Samya' but even in *Dharmatattva*.

[24]*Bankim Rachanabali,* ed. J.C. Bagal, op. cit.

and with its suspicion of liberal rights and radical social protest—which derive some of their terms from post-Enlightenment political radicalism and democratic traditions—finds itself in the same space as aggressive, intolerant Hindutva in its critique of secular democratic politics. This, in the final analysis, emerges as a far more consistent and powerful strain than the critique of Hindutva, which is sporadic and milder.[25]

The thrust towards a pure and authentically Hindu site for generating the social will for change complicated Bankim's social concern. It problematized his sharp criticism of the traditional, precolonial form of Hindu domesticity and his daring imagining of the undomesticated, strong, passionate woman that had earlier marked a distance between him and his contemporary Hindu revivalist-nationalists.[26] He grew intellectually through a simultaneous and interanimated imbibing of Enlightenment universalism and Hindu philosophical resources, and he used the resources of both to interrogate both. And yet, belying the notion of hybridity which disregards the mutually transformative nature of intellectual encounters, for Bankim the compulsion to opt for a pure site of exclusively Hindu knowledge triumphed after his exchanges with the Reverend Hastie.[27]

In 1882 Hastie wrote a tract that was brutally critical of Hinduism. Bankim, who had always ridiculed orientalist pretensions about scientific knowledge on India, prepared a long, careful, and angry reply. It was after this that he repudiated 'Samya' and, in his discursive prose, became exclusively preoccupied with the theme of a reconstructed Hindu form of knowledge and leadership.

The anger was probably fuelled by the changing political environment after the mid 1870s. The post-1857 Mutiny racist repression created serious self-doubt in the Bengali middle class, which had been entirely loyal in 1857. The escalation of discriminatory colonial policies during

[25]This interpretive thrust has been well developed by Ashis Nandy in *The Intimate Enemy* (Delhi, 1983) and extended by Gyanendra Pandey in *The Construction of Communalism in Colonial North India* (Delhi, 1990) as well as Partha Chatterjee in *The Nation and Its Fragments* (Princeton, 1993).

[26]Tanika Sarkar, 'Rhetoric Against the Age of Consent', *Economic and Political Weekly*, 4 September 1993, reproduced as chapter six herein.

[27]Tapan Raychaudhuri, *Europe Reconsidered,* op. cit.

Lytton's era[28] was followed by the violent racist backlash of the Ilbert Bill agitation. Apart from this concentrated exposure to the most extreme and naked form of white racism, Bengal's middle class was also troubled by a reversal of the trends that had promised a milder climate under the viceregal policies of Lord Northbrook, and later the liberal Ripon.[29] These had seemed to point towards opening up a few minor but real opportunities for local incorporation within colonial decision-making processes.[30] The reversal of such processes led to an intensification of both liberal and Hindu revivalist forms of anti-colonial critique and organization. Liberal nationalists formed secular, open organizations for self-strengthening and formulated economic critiques of the drain of wealth, poverty, and deindustrialization; these remained foundational concepts for nationalist economic thinking down to Gandhi.[31] Hindu revivalists, on the other hand, used their anti-Western rhetoric to close off all interrogation and attempts at the transformation of power relations within the Hindu community: these now became false knowledge contaminated by alien forms of power knowledge.[32] Revivalism thus assumed a markedly fundamentalist defensiveness. Faced with this crisis of conscience, Bankim reacted by repudiating 'Samya' and by excising his earlier frontal contestations of Hindu caste, class and gender hierarchies. The excision, despite his best efforts, remained somewhat incomplete, and Bankim subsequently reinserted some of his earlier critiques insidiously into his late novels.[33]

[28]S. Gopal, *British Policy in India 1858–1905* (Cambridge, 1966); Anil Seal, *The Emergence of Indian Nationalism: Competition and Collaboration in the Later Nineteenth Century* (Cambridge, 1968).

[29]S. Gopal, *The Viceroyalty of Lord Ripon 1880–1884* (London, 1953).

[30]S. Gopal, *British Policy in India 1858–1905,* op. cit.; Anil Seal, *The Emergence of Indian Nationalism,* op. cit.

[31]Bipan Chandra, *The Rise and Growth of Economic Nationalism in India: Economic Policies of Indian National Leadership* (New Delhi, 1966).

[32]See Tanika Sarkar, 'Conjugality' (chapter six herein), and Dipesh Chakrabarty, who has recently reiterated the logic and politics of this revivalism in the same terms in his critique of contemporary 'secular feminists,' in 'The Difference/Deferral of a Colonial Modernity: Public Debate on Domesticity in Colonial Bengal', *History Workshop Journal* 35, Sept. 1993.

[33]Tanika Sarkar, 'Bankimchandra and the Impossibility', op. cit.

Historical developments as well as certain earlier political choices, then, blocked off Bankim's early inclination to consider liberal reformers as vehicles of Hindu self-improvement. As class, caste, and gender issues abruptly disappear from his work, their relative absence is filled up in the eighties by a new and coherent problematic: What constitutes authentic Hinduism? What possibilities exist within the Hinduism of the past, and in the reauthenticated Hinduism of the future, for nation building? What precisely is the culpability of the Muslim in Indian history, and how and why had Hindu power capitulated to it? It is not that these problems were not reflected on in his earlier prose, but there they had locked horns with an equally powerful set of social concerns.[34] Their centrality now becomes absolute and uncontested. Bankim looks for an ethico-religious site for a Hindu people whose dominant priority is not social justice but rather what is truly indigenous—that is, Hindu. This is explicit in *Krishnacharitra* and *Dharmatattva*. The latter, in fact, begins with the theme of poverty and hunger—a deliberate invocation of Bankim's earlier concerns. Then the guru persuades the disciple that both these ills can be overcome by the cultivation of the right Hindu disposition and knowledge. Bankim thus relocates the roots of these problems within the individual disposition and mind-set—away from social structures.[35]

Within this reoriented problematic, agency could now be restored to Brahmanic forms of knowledge and upper-caste social leadership. But this presented equally powerful problems. Bankim continued to believe that past traditions of Hinduism had not generated the impulse for freedom and nationhood: these new changes needed to be improvised and old forms of knowledge or rule would not automatically yield them. Even in his later discursive phase, he continued to polemicize against certain forms of Hindu knowledge and devotion—as, earlier, he had

[34]The themes of Hindu history and nationhood were taken up in 'Prabandha Pustak.' Many of the concerns of *Dharmatattva* and the form of its presentation had been anticipated in 'Gaurdas babajir bhikshar jhuli,' in *Vividha Prabandha* (1874). *Krishnacharitra* was originally written to form a part of *Vividha Prabandha*, but was later much altered and extended. See J.C. Bagal, II, op. cit., p. 21.

[35]*Bankim Rachanabali*, II, pp. 585–6.

critically reviewed the Sankhya traditions ('Sankhyadarshan,' in *Vividha Prabandha*). At no phase had he shown much sympathy for Vedic or Vedantist philosophies, perhaps because their quietist, reflective modes were inappropriate for a politically militant, even violent, heroic agenda, and also because these were resources that Brahmo reformers had celebrated. In *Dharmatattva*, Bankim says, 'Vaidic religion lacks the concept of devotion . . . there are only propitiatory sacrifices to attain one's earthly desires',[36] and he polemicizes against all major Hindu religious philosophies in order to assert the correctness of a reoriented bhakti.

Bankim conducted a relentless polemic against dominant Bengali forms of devotion, specially its Vaishnava form, which worshipped Krishna as a figure of erotic excess (*Krishnacharitra*); he was also critical of the quietism of Kali-devotion preached by his contemporary, Ramakrishna.[37] He chose the Puranic tradition and pulled together from it the figure of a heroic, vindictive, wily, and violent saviour figure. He used as his model the mythical-epic dimensions of the later life of Krishna, when he was no longer the shepherd boy and the great lover and had grown up into the king, the politician, the warrior (*Krishnacharitra*). Throughout his life he held lively arguments with the orthodox repositories of Brahmanic knowledge—the pandits of Bhatpara.[38] He cast doubt on the learning of the doyen of Hindu orthodoxy of his times—Pandit Sasadhar Tarkachuramani.[39] The criticality and the intellectual and polemical energies that continued to shape his writings even of the later period are of the sort that Hindutva today entirely eschews. Even in *Dharmatattva*, the guru preaches to a well-read, argumentative disciple. Contemporary RSS pedagogic principles, on the other hand, are entirely hortatory and rhetorical, and internal debates and productive differences find no space there. It is not for nothing that the RSS selects its recruits from among young children who lack the capacity to argue.[40]

---

[36]Ibid., p. 623.

[37]Sumit Sarkar, 'Kaliyuga, Chakri and Bhakti: Ramakrishna and His Times', *Economic and Political Weekly*, 18 July 1992, pp. 1543–66.

[38]Shyamali, *Bankimchandra O bhatparar panditsamaj* (Baromash, 1988).

[39]Tanika Sarkar, 'Bankimchandra and the Impossibility', op. cit.

[40]Tapan Basu, *et al.*, *Saffron Flags*, op. cit.

Existing representatives of old Hindu ruling groups—upper-caste landowners and *rentiers* who opposed the new Western learning, and leaders of Hindu religious establishments, the pandits—failed to convince Bankim that they were in any way deserving of their privilege or that they could offer a potential for active leadership. In his later novels he returned to his sharp satirical bite in portraying the classic figure of the traditional Hindu patriarch—the upper-caste parasitic landlord paterfamilias—as embodied in Haraballabh's inhuman, patriarchal orthodoxy and lack of honour and dignity (*Debi Choudhurani*). The virtuous founder of a Hindu power that he imagined in *Sitaram* could sustain neither his virtue nor his power. Contemporary sexual and financial scandals about the mohunt of the celebrated Shiva pilgrimage centre at Tarakeswar rocked Bengal in 1873 and were reported in the *Bengalee* and the *Statesman*, and there was the earlier scandal about the maharaja of the Vallabhachari sect in Gujarat: these probably made it impossible for Bankim to imagine the representatives of organized religion as saviours. Even the ascetics of *Anandamath*—his quintessentially militant patriotic novel—astonish the ordinary devout Hindu who keeps on asking them what kinds of Vaishnavas or sannyasis they are.[41]

It is notable that in this phase, as earlier, virtue, activism, and heroism are more effortlessly embodied as almost a character trait by the woman. This is true of all three novels: in the characters of Shanti and Kalyani (*Anandamath*); Prafulla, Diba, and Nishi (*Debi Choudhurani*); and Shree, the *sannyasini* (female sannyasi), and Nanda in *Sitaram*. Bankim had stopped polemicizing against the subordination of women; the bold feminist of *Samya* had buried himself. In *Krishnacharitra*, in fact, he devoted much space to justify an act of force by Arjuna—the abduction of the sister of Krishna on his advice. Krishna convinces Arjuna—and Bankim tries to convince us—that male guardians can and should override the question of the woman's consent in the interests of her own larger welfare, which they necessarily comprehend better.[42] The disproportionately large space that he devotes to justify this rather minor incident in the life of Krishna tells us how difficult he found it to persuade himself.

[41]*Bankim Rachanabali*, I, ed. J.C. Bagal, pp. 724–37.
[42]Ibid., II, pp. 498–504.

In *Dharmatattva* he overturns his earlier images of conjugality as the equal and mature mutual passion of two adults. His earlier ideas had deconstructed the revivalist-nationalist celebration of non-consensual infant marriage between a polygamous male and an utterly monogamous child wife.[43] At the same time, even in the later phase, the woman remains the locus of the nation in a far more activist way than she does within the passive, iconic role ascribed to her by revivalist-nationalists. In her submission to Shastric prescriptions and in her total insulation from new alien norms, such nationalists had seen the Hindu woman's symbolic capacity to embody and sustain the nation.[44] In Bankim, however, the only approximation of the figure of Saviour Krishna is the figure of the dacoit queen, Prafulla, who earns this capacity not by being faithful to Hindu domestic prescriptions but by surviving outside her household and by fighting against British forces. Even though the pedagogic training for the new Hindu that Bankim filled out in *Dharmatattva* is imparted to a male disciple, in *Debi Choudhurani* Prafulla actually undergoes the training. In *Sitaram*, too, the woman causes virtuous action, she tries to save Hindu power, and then suffers a wrongful trial and humiliation which together constitute a striking parallel with and an implicit critique of Rama's trial of Sita.[45]

The woman's activism, however, is occasional and exceptional even when it sustains some of the critical energies of the earlier Bankim: it is certainly not a sign of Bankim's investiture of Woman with leadership of the patriotic agenda, and it is noticeable only within his fiction. In the polemical prose, the critical energy is well contained, and even the feminine figuration of the motherland that Bankim achieved in *Anandamath* is absent. The new Hindu is emphatically a Hindu man with a difference. He is the embodiment of a rigorous, disciplinary schedule that will eventually transpose discipline from an external ethico-religious authority to a self-monitoring ethical agent who has internalized certain reinterpreted concepts of Hindu knowledge and devotional practices; these are Bankim's explanations of *anushilandharma* and bhakti. The process of training that incorporates such knowledge,

---

[43]Ibid., I, p. 620.
[44]Tanika Sarkar, chapter six herein.
[45]*Bankim Rachanabali,* I, pp. 944–8.

dispositions, physical capabilities, and devotion, replacing the privileges of birth and ritual expertise, distinguishes the new Brahman—the ideal patriot and nation-builder—from the Hindu of the old, unreformed Hindu authorities. Inherited and normative control are replaced with hard-earned leadership; Brahmanic authority is revived as intensively cultivated hegemonic aspiration. This represents Bankim's return to a higher plane, perhaps, but a return nonetheless. The imagined Hindu nation cannot, even in the imagination, be made and ruled by agents who are not male and upper caste.[46]

III

Let us now turn to certain specific dimensions within the construction of the new Hindu. Looking first at the Vande Mataram hymn, it seems quite apparent that this is a good example of the imaginative and rhetorical devices with which a militant Hindu form of patriotism is constructed. Bankim had originally composed it as a song in 1875. Later, when he finished *Anandamath*, he inserted it within the story and vested it with significant narrative functions.[47] The song, even on its own, would have been an original contribution to the deification and fetishization of the mother country. Within the novel, this sense is further heightened by other resonances, which construct a sequentiallized imagery of the deified motherland.[48] Subsequently, the hymn was detached from the novel and achieved a life of its own as a slogan in mass nationalist rallies and, later, in communal violence. The novel then came to be contained within the slogan and provided a reference point for larger messages.

The song begins in Sanskrit, then turns into Bengali, and ends with a reversion to Sanskrit passages. It begins with an evocation of the bounteous and beauteous land that nurtures its children. Bounty and physical richness turn into the image of a motherland possessing a latent strength which derives from the image of Durga, the demon-

---

[46]The RSS has very real Maharashtra Brahman origins. See Tapan Basu, *et al.*, *Saffron Flags*, op. cit.

[47]J.C. Bagal, Introduction to *Bankim Rachanabali*, I, p. 23.

[48]*Bankim Rachanabali*, I, p. 728–9.

slaying goddess; from the numerical strength of her population, compiled
in census statistics; and from the supreme sacred significance that Bankim
ascribes to the motherland within the Hindu pantheon: 'It is your image
that we worship in all temples'.[49] The land, for a while, is one with the
icon of Durga. The image of Durga then quickly and insidiously
transforms itself into that of Kali, another manifestation of the mother
goddess, but now a destructive, angry force. The hymn ends with a
reiteration of the original sense of bounty and nurture, and the goddess
exhorts her children to enrich her strength with their own. In between,
there is just a suggestion of her present weakness—'with such strength,
why are you helpless?'—but the overwhelming sense is one of power.
The power is undifferentiated and flows back and forth from the mother
to her sons, though originating always in her. In an unbroken musical
flow, the song encapsulates three distinct images of the nurturing mother:
the mother of the past, the dispossessed mother of the present, and the
triumphant mother of the future. These are developed at much greater
length within the novel.[50] Later nationalists saw the demon slayer as
pitted against the colonial power and used the song as an abbreviated
history of colonial exploitation and the patriotic struggle for liberation.
The RSS, on the other hand, certainly took it to imply a 'historical'
struggle against the Muslim. From its very inception, the RSS had stayed
away from anticolonial movements and was devoted to an exclusively
communal agenda. As a matter of fact, in the song itself, the demon is
unspecific and is eclipsed by the image of the armed mother. What is of
importance is the song's reiteration that the patriotic son is quintessentially
a soldier at war.

The novel too is ambiguous about whom the mother is fighting. It
is set at the transitional historical moment of the late eighteenth century.
Against the backdrop of the famine of 1770, armed combat rages
between marauding ascetics of the Naga Dasnami orders and a puppet
Muslim nawab indirectly controlled by the British in Bengal.[51] Bankim
makes no mention of the role of Muslim faqirs who also led plundering

[49]Ibid., p. 726.
[50]Ibid., p. 728.
[51]Ibid., p. 726.

bands of starving people. Even though historically the sannyasis were from the Shaiva orders, here they are worshipers of Vishnu, with a militant, warlike bhakti of their own. The leaders here are recruited from Bengali, upper-caste, landed folk and shown to have transformed themselves with devotional and rigorous martial training. Ascetic celibacy has been enjoined upon them for the duration of the struggle, which is meant to restore Hindu rule. Even though they do accomplish the ouster of the puppet nawab, they are also instrumental in ushering in direct and complete British dominion. A divine voice tells the supreme leader that this is providential: Hindus need apprenticeship in modern forms of power. The leader, however, remains disconsolate and unreconciled and considers the historical mission of *santans*—the ascetic leaders—as aborted, since one foreign ruler is now exchanged for another. Nationalists took this bitterness as a call for struggle against the colonial power, whereas to the RSS brigade the divine command indicates a sanction for staying away from the anticolonial struggle; the divine purpose is understood as the elimination of Muslim power.

Within the novel, the song initiates a number of political breaks and innovations. It is meant to be a sacred chant or mantra. Yet, these Hindu chants are all composed in *debbhasha* (Sanskrit)—'the language of the gods'—to which women and low castes do not have access. Mantras are also enunciated within a prescribed ritual sequence, always in front of the deity, and always by the Brahmin priest or initiated Brahmin male householder. The novel ascribes chanting mantras to an act of worship, yet the mantra here is first heard in the aftermath of a battle between British-led troops of the nawab and the santans, who lead a mob of villagers.[52] The hymn is then incorporated into the emergent cult centred on a new form of mother worship. Now it is a chant unconventionally detached from the sacred ritual sequence, and now it also functions as a song on its own, as congregational devotional music accessible to all who partake in Vaishnava gatherings. Yet, its actual public use is not devotional or contemplative but martial. The chant is unshackled from its original moorings in piety and deployed to sacralize war. As a battle cry, it transforms the congregation of devotees

[52]Ibid., p. 728.

into a monolithic and disciplined army: 'Then, in a single, resounding voice, the thousands of santan soldiers . . . sang out to the rhythms of the canon—*Vande Mataram*.'[53] If a Hindu community-for-itself is being visualized, then, from the moment of its inception, this is a community at war, unified by feelings of violence against a shared enemy. The ascetic figure of the santan, who first pronounces the words and who initiates the act of worship, merges into the figure of the military commander and strategist who leads the holy war.

There is a crucial difference between the older figure of the priest and the new priest-cum-commander. Unlike the former, the commander begins the song but he has no exclusive custody of the sacred ritual. Others—including the motley army of villagers of all castes—partake in the singing, and so the hymn moves into the vernacular. Along with this there is yet a further transformation of purpose. First a chant, then successively a song and a command, the hymn now becomes a battle cry and forms the very first political slogan in the Bengali language. The commander emerges as the political leader, the organizer par excellence.

The importance of this enterprise to aggressive Hindutva lies in its explicit enunciation of a political violence that can express itself con-vincingly as a religious cause. This is underlined in the novel when, inspired by santans, the mob begins to articulate an agenda that goes beyond simple looting: 'Unless we throw these dirty bastards [i.e. the Muslims] out, Hindus will be ruined. . . . When shall we raze mosques down to the ground and erect Radhamadhav's temple in their place?'[54]

The imaginative resources of this violent political agenda are immensely enriched precisely by its ability simultaneously to lay claim to gentle and peaceful images.[55] The song is held in place by a tension

[53]Ibid., pp. 728–9.

[54]Ibid., p. 728.

[55]This was especially evident in the way VHP ideologues simultaneously evoked the figures of the serene and the angry Ram. See the last chapter; also see P.K. Datta, 'VHP's Ram: The Hindutva Movement in Ayodhya', *Hindus and Others*, ed. Gyanendra Pandey (Delhi: 1993). The other important point of this chapter is that in bhakti philosophies, the deity's life is an object of contemplation for the devotee; it is not to be emulated. In departing from this view Bankim makes a crucial transition. He insists that Krishna's life provides a desired pattern for all Hindus. Ram too is invoked as a role model by Bankim and by Hindutva.

between contradictory impulses that constitute a delicately poised unity at the level of both sound and meaning. The land is beautiful and the mother is smiling, tender, and youthful, at the same time she is the ruthless warrior, triumphant in battle. Her loveliness, her smiles, her grace are evoked euphoniously:

> shubhrajyotsnapulokita yamineem phullakusumitadrumadalashob-hineem, suhasineem, sumadhurabhashineem, sukhadaam baradaam mataram [to the mother whose nights are gorgeous with silvery moon-light, who is decked out with trees that bloom happily with flowers, whose smile is beautiful, whose words are bathed in sweetness, who is the giver of pleasure, of bliss].

The sensuousness, the sibilance, is then abruptly replaced with quicker, jagged rhythms, by an arrangement of harsh, strident words:

> saptakotikantha kalakala ninadakarale, dwisaptakotirbhujairdhritakhar-akarabale . . . babhubaladharineem, namaami tarineem . . . [seventy mil-lion voices boom out words of doom, twice seventy million arms wield the sharp swords . . . we salute the savior mother, possessor of many kinds of strength].[56]

Classical rhetorical conventions match sound with mood. Bankim also goes further in the dramatic art of juxtaposition, via shocking and astonishing transitions within a brief and continuous space. The rhe-torical charge and power of the Hindutva project are often trivialized by assuming its simple transition from gentle quietism to violence. The song, which remains a powerful imaginative resource for the Hindutva project, complicates and widens the notion of a binary opposition be-tween peaceful, traditional Hinduism and violent Hindutva. Bankim's militant bhakti lets go of nothing, its language is supple and inventive enough to effect many movements between opposites—which is today considered by VHP thinkers to be the essence of Rama bhakti.[57]

The seemingly democratic extension of esoteric holy words into

---

[56]*Anandamath,* in *Bankim Rachanabali,* I, p. 726. The translations are mine.
[57]P.K. Datta, 'VHP's Ram: The Hindutva Movement in Ayodhya', p. 69.

slogans and songs for all has, however, certain structural limits. The leader–mob distinction is carefully underlined by the way in which each military encounter turns into chaos unless carefully calibrated by ascetic leaders. The leaders—here and in the later two novels—are carefully trained in leadership through a pedagogical scheme not available to or meant for the masses, who join the movement on account of sheer starvation and mob instinct. It is true that the ascetic leaders give up caste codes in times of war and recruit soldiers from all social strata, but, along with celibacy and asceticism, this is the last sacrifice that they must impose on themselves until the final victory is achieved. This is also described as the most difficult of sacrifices.[58] Presumably, with victory will come the restoration of the normal order of caste distinction, thereby absolving them from the pledge. The point, then, is not to overturn the social hierarchy but to qualify it in times of war. Established leaders of Hindu society may thus renew and extend their control by coming closer to ordinary folk, and by leading them to victory in the war against their common enemy. The temporary yet intimate relation that the liminal space of war offers provides legitimacy to the comprehensive training with which leaders approach the work of organization, ensuring thus that their power has a more secure base.[59]

IV

I have used the hymn and its functions within the novel as example: they reveal the rhetorical operations and structures of feeling with which Bankim delineates the politics of the reconstructed Hindu. The old Hindu suffered from the absence of physical prowess and the desire for self-rule; the new Hindu will only have arrived when he proves himself in a final battle and overwhelmingly establishes his superiority over the very Muslim who has in the past always defeated the Hindu. (This agenda of war with the Muslim occurs only in the novels.) Since the British have something to impart to the Hindu, Hindu empowerment, it seems, must unfold within an overarching colonial framework.

[58] *Anandamath*, op. cit., p. 751.
[59] On these themes, see Sumit Sarkar, 'Indian Nationalism ...', op. cit.

It is the Muslim, the vanquisher of generations of past Hindus, who will be the great adversary of the new Hindu. This is the concluding note and message of *Anandamath*.[60]

The Muslim is the adversary for yet another reason. I would like to suggest that Bankim made a distinction between the historical experience of Muslim rule on the one hand, and Islam as an organized religion and the Muslim as a personality type on the other. Muslim rule, in his view, brought neither material nor spiritual improvement to India, it merely emasculated and defeated Hindus. Yet Islam and the Muslim— with his supposedly violent commitment to religion and his desire for power—had much to teach the Hindu. 'By imbibing these principles . . . the Hindu will be . . . as powerful as the Arabs in the days of Mohammad.'[61] In his polemic on world religions, Bankim seems to grant perfection to Hinduism only as an ideal, whereas, through a series of oblique half-statements, Islam is endowed with perfection in historical times. If universal love is taken to be the highest human ideal, then, says Bankim, Hinduism has it in the largest degree. Yet throughout history this has led to a dangerous quietism, to an inadequate comprehension of national dangers, to subjection, and to degeneration of the community. Islam and Christianity have both avoided this particular problem. Between the two, Islam forged far ahead of Christianity in attaining greater unity within its own boundaries and emerged as the more successful political model. By combining different sets of values we can, he suggests, construct a single uniform scale wherein Islam transcends the particular problems of both Christianity and Hinduism (even though Hinduism and Islam are not directly compared with each other).[62]

In a crucial and conclusive part of *Dharmatattva*, Islam is dropped from the explicit comparative scheme and there is a new triangular contest for virtues among Hinduism, Buddhism, and Christianity: 'If Jesus or Sakya Singha had been householders and yet leaders of world religions, then their systems would have been more complete. Krishna as ideal man is a householder. Jesus or Sakya Singha are not

---

[60] *Bankim Rachanabali*, I, p. 787.
[61] *Dharmatattva*, in ibid., II, p. 647.
[62] Ibid., p. 648.

ideal men.'[63] If Hinduism scores over the two other religions on these grounds, there is also a third, unmentioned presence, another leader of a world religion who was a householder and who yet transcended his mundane ties—Muhammad. Islam, or rather the figure of the Prophet, is the sunken middle term in the diagram. If the prophet implicitly shares the honour of having founded a perfect religion (alongside Krishna), he has the further advantage of having done this within the accepted hagiography of Islam, and within the single, universally acknowledged version of that religion. This is the image of Muhammad to be found in a well-known Western text much used in Bankim's time: Thomas Patrick Hughes's *Dictionary of Islam* (1885).

Bankim was painfully aware that his ideal Krishna was an appropriation and construction solely of his own heroic and intellectual efforts, and that in this construction he was going against the grain of dominant Hindu interpretive schemes: *Krishnacharitra, Dharmatattva,* and *Anandamath* argue hard against the other models of bhakti. Bankim's Krishna is a householder-king, a warrior, a politician. He is overwhelmingly a man of action, strong enough to be wily in a higher cause and resorting to seemingly amoral strategies for the higher good of his people. He is entirely unlike the morally pure or philosophically questioning Christ and Buddha. He is equally unlike the figure of love and play celebrated in Vaishnava hagiography. Bankim's Krishna stands closest to Muhammad. In fact, Islam's silent influence on Bankim's construction is exact in particular features as well as in the total conception, so that one may even be tempted to speculate that Bankim's Krishna could have been constructed out of a biography of the prophet Muhammad. By asserting that with a correct application of bhakti Hindus will be transformed into the Muslims of Muhammad's time, Bankim hoped that a reinterpreted life of Krishna would bring into play for Hindus the same historic role played originally by Islam.

V

His discursive prose of later years obliquely draws upon what Bankim regarded as the enviable resources and energies of Islam. If he did not

[63]Ibid., p. 647.

engage in sustained polemic against Islam in his essays on religion, in his fiction he did evolve a denunciatory mode around Muslim rule in India. While his notions of ideal Hinduism informed nineteenth-century Hindu revivalism, the particular language that he, more than any other writer of that time, developed to describe the Muslim inflected the rhetoric and aspirations of violent Hindu communalism over the next century.

Bankim bestowed the Muslim unprecedented centrality in his historical and political scheme, thereby starting a tradition. The revivalist climate of the times was shaped decisively by anti-reformist and anti-missionary propaganda, and there were even clashes with missionaries in the early 1890s: there are references to an attack on missionaries at Tarakeswar in 1891,[64] and other minor attacks were reported from Calcutta and Bankura over the same year. During the Age of Consent Bill agitation of the 1880s and early 1890s, Muslims were written about as fellow sufferers and victims of colonialism.[65] The nationalist vernacular press usually took care to distinguish between the integrated, indigenized nature of 'Muslim rule' and the alien nature of the colonial government. This is not to say that Bengal was immune from the communal violence that was sweeping across parts of northern India in the 1890s. Muslims had recently gained a few educational concessions. W.W. Hunter's thesis on Muslim backwardness promised more,[66] and, with Muslim self-modernization moves (of the Aligarh variety), the possibility of sharpened competition in the sphere of the new education and jobs—where Bengali Hindus had so far enjoyed a decisive edge—seemed imminent. So far, however, Muslims had remained a rather marginal worry and Hindu revivalism had not targeted the Muslim as its main enemy.

Bankim bequeathed a set of historical judgments on the nature and consequences of Muslim rule in Bengal: 'How does our Muslim ruler protect us? We have lost our religion, our caste, our honour and family name, and now we are about to lose our very lives. . . . How can Hinduism survive unless we drive out these dissolute swine?'[67] These ideological

[64] *Dainik O Samachar Chandrika,* 19 April 1891.

[65] *RNP* (1890).

[66] Mushirul Hasan, 'The Myth of Unity: Colonial and National Narratives', *Making India Hindu,* op. cit.

[67] *Anandamath,* op. cit., p. 727.

moves do not need proper historical authentication since they are posed fictionally. The pseudo-historical comments, however, carry the immense weight of conviction, particularly as Bankim was known for the historicist thrust of his discursive prose. Such comments in his fiction therefore seem insidiously authenticated, and they then justify political rallying cries of extreme virulence: 'Kill the low Muslims' is a refrain raised repeatedly in *Anandamath*.[68] Even though Bankim never made use of theories on the drain of wealth, he used the same motif to describe the flight of money from Bengal to Delhi in the form of the heavy revenue burden of Mughal times.[69]

Perhaps the most significant way in which Bankim served as a bridge between nineteenth-century Hindu revivalism and later, anti-Muslim, violent politics was by providing a powerful visual image of communal violence and giving this the status of an apocalyptic holy war. He stamped this image indelibly on the imagination of communal politics by fusing the impulse for community violence and revenge into the spectacle of a female body: In his last novel, *Sitaram*, Gangaram, the brother of the heroine Shree, is unjustly charged and sentenced to execution by a tyrannical Muslim faqir and a *qazi* (judge). Unable to stop this mockery of justice, Shree goes to the place of execution where a big crowd, including many Hindus, has gathered to watch the event. In despair, Shree tries to rally them to save their fellow Hindu, to instil a sense of brotherhood and mutual responsibility. She points out the fact that a man of their community is being killed by another community. Shree does not invoke justice, nor does she try to rally the crowd against tyranny and misrule. Quite spontaneously, the words that rise to her mouth are words of community solidarity and violence:

Then Gangaram saw a goddess-like figure among the green leaves of the huge tree. Her feet resting on two branches, her right hand clutching a tender branch, the left swirling her sari, she was calling out: 'Kill, kill . . .' Her long, unbound tresses were dancing in the wind, her proud feet were swinging the branches up and down, up and down, as if

[68]Ibid., p. 784.

[69]'Bangalar Itihasa', *Vividha Prabandha, Bankimchandra Rachanabali*, II, p. 332.

Durga herself was dancing upon a lion on the battlefield. Shree had no more shame left, no consciousness, no fear, no rest. She kept calling out—'Kill, kill the enemy . . . The enemy of the country, the enemy of Hindus, my enemy . . . kill, kill the enemy . . .' That straining arm was such a lovely arm . . . such beauty in her swollen lips, her flaring nostrils, sweat-drenched stray locks falling across a perspiring forehead. The Hindus kept looking at her and then streaming towards the battlefield with 'glory to Mother Chandika' on their lips.[70]

In an instant, Shree transforms a scattering of Hindus with no previous sense of mutual connectedness into an army with a single violent purpose, a community-for-itself created through the invocation of vengeance against another. The spectacle of violence derives from the image of a passionate feminine body that metaphonically gives birth to violence. If political passion is produced through feminine agency, there is little doubt about the kind of image in which this passion is cast. The woman's body moving 'up and down, up and down', 'that straining arm', 'her swollen lips, her flaring nostrils', 'sweat-drenched locks,' and 'perspiring forehead'—these are well-remembered classical conventions to describe a woman at the moment of sexual climax. The superimposition of the icons of Durga and of Chandika, the goddess of war, on this body provides a sacred frame to the whole. It tightly controls yet obliquely heightens the flow of sexual energy from which the image derives its power. The beginnings of a violently communalized imagination may then have something to do with a variety of male fantasizing which fuses sexual passion and political violence within a single and encompassing idea of pleasure.

VI

The consequences of such imagination do not entirely exhaust the logic of Bankim's discourse on the Muslim. We have seen that his serious discursive prose refers to Islam with respect, Bankim's novels deal equally with Hindus and Muslims, and their relations with one another. The fiction seems ranged side by side, next to one another, providing

[70]*Sitaram*, in ibid., I, p. 881. For similar images in our own times, see the last chapter herein.

dramatic and tense encounters between man and man, man and woman, woman and woman, as communities, nations, armies, as loving, fighting, making peace, arguing, negotiating. If all the novels on this inter-community theme are taken to compose a single novel, and the arrangements between people of the two religions as relations between two composite individuals, then the obvious simile is that of a conjugal, wildly emotional, dangerously fluctuating sexual relationship that may simultaneously include great intimacy along with great violence. This is a far cry from the way white people encounter Indians in Bankim's novels—those encounters provide moments of sheer comedy.[71]

In his first novel, *Durgeshnandini* (1865), there is a striving for an almost mechanical symmetry of virtue and vice on both sides of the Hindu–Muslim encounter. The aim is to establish a shared code of conduct, be it for the heroes, the heroines, the villains or the cowards. Hindus and Muslims are not two monolithically integrated peoples: political alliances and expediency cut across religious boundaries.[72] Interestingly, Bankim—who experimented boldly with rather transgressive possibilities in sexual relationships beyond Hindu domestic and conjugal prescriptions—found the Muslim woman, who seemed unbounded by the norms of monogamic faithfulness, a productive ground for playing on utterly new registers of sexual morality and commitment. The characters of Ayesha in *Durgeshnandini*, Zebunnisa in *Rajasingha* (1882), and Dalani in *Chandrasekhar* (1875) provide striking and diverse examples.

From his third novel, *Mrinalini*, the possibility of a shared enterprise vanishes and the Muslim becomes the great historical adversary of the Hindu. Battles between individuals are now loaded with destiny for nations. In *Rajasingha* the Muslim adversary is a hated and dreaded enemy—he is no less a man than the fanatical Aurangzeb: 'He was born to hate the Hindus, he found Hindu offences unpardonable'.[73] There are references to all of Aurangzeb's well-thumbed sins in the opening chapter—*jeziya*, temple-wrecking, cow-slaughter, forced conversions.

[71] *Chandrasekhar*, in ibid., p. 405; *Muchiram Gurer Jibancharit*, in ibid., II, pp. 126–7. Here is material for high drama or tragedy.

[72] *Bankim Rachanabali*, I, pp. 53–138.

[73] Ibid., p. 664.

This seems a typical case of stereotyping. Yet let us remember the first appearance of this presumed enemy of Hindus: we meet an elderly man in white, quiet, dignified, assured, respecting strength in his enemy. All the characteristic historical associations are revived and made familiar in the first chapter. Gradually, however, the stereotype is defamiliarized, redeemed, and humanized, especially by Aurangzeb's gentle, melancholy love for a Hindu serving-maid. This is no monster but a great adversary. He has been defeated in a historic battle, and herein lies the true glory of Mewar.[74] Unlike the anonymous, faceless English troops, Muslim adversaries, even the worst, have human faces in which complex emotions are often delicately sketched.

In *Sitaram*, the last novel, the Muslim combatant has, in contrast, become largely an abstraction, an absence; yet battles with such a Muslim now fill up the entire novelistic space. Has Bankim, then, at the end of his life, managed to formulate and congeal an agenda to the point of blind hatred, to a position where the enemy sheds his human features and is reduced to a simple figure of malevolence?

I think Bankim found it impossible to form or celebrate an agenda with sustained conviction even in his last, dogmatic, markedly authoritarian phase. If the agenda seems to be coherent and complete, he proceeds to fracture it from within, to dissolve his own statement of conviction. Sitaram is defeated by his own inner flaws. The Hindu leader, whether a commander, a king, a Brahmin, or a patriarch, remains weak, treacherous, greedy, and cowardly across historical and social differences. The most significant and problematic thing about the last novel, I think, is Sitaram's brutality against Hindu women, which is conventionally ascribed to the stereotypical Muslim. When Sitaram's Hindu kingdom breaks up, Hindu women celebrate the event with vindictive glee. An erstwhile tolerant Muslim faqir leaves his kingdom, vowing never to live under Hindu rule. The stereotyped notion of Muslim intolerance is turned upside down, for it is Sitaram who, by his own villainy, had forced this conclusion on the faqir.

The novel, which is charged with shrill intensity, ends with uncharacteristic bathos. Bankim had never before used the device of a chorus

[74] *Rajsingha*, ibid., pp. 672–4.

composed of ordinary people. Here we find two common men, Ram and Shyam, uttering the last words.

Ram: How goes it, brother? Have you heard any news about Mohammad-pur? [Sitaram's kingdom].

Shyam: Different people say different things. Some say the king [Sitaram] and the queen could not be captured. . . . The wretched Muslims executed a false king and a false queen.

Ram: . . . That sounds like a Hindu fiction, a mere novel.

Shyam: Well, who knows whose story is a fiction. Your story may well be a Muslim tale. Anyway, we are ordinary people, all this doesn't concern us. Let us enjoy a smoke in peace.

Let Ramchand and Shyamchand enjoy their pipe of tobacco. We shall end our narrative at this point.[75]

This is an uncharacteristic narrative closure for Bankim: he had always been intensely concerned with historicity, with political bias and partisanship vitiating historical truth. All his familiar concerns are blown away with a few puffs of smoke, with rumours recounted by two ignorant and rather uninterested men who dismiss all history as ultimately unknowable, as equally uncertain versions of certain events, and, finally, as supremely irrelevant to the likes of them.

What exactly is involved in this major departure? One can only speculate at several levels: it can denote a final failure of hope in the heroic, redemptive exercise, in the possibility of nation-building. It can, on the other hand, indicate a recognition of the autonomy of the imaginative domain. The Brechtian alienation device, the underlining of the fictional nature of the work by talking about 'novels and fictions', may point to the constructedness of all writings, historical and fictional. Or is it, after a long gap and after many changes, a return to the theme of 'Samya', which in the meantime had been overtaken by dreams of Hindu glory? Does it question the materiality of notions like political freedom and nationhood in the context of the everlasting peasant problem, grounding the failure of the nation in the disjunction between the two?

[75] *Sitaram*, op. cit., pp. 957–8.

Bankim formulates and fills out a violent Hindu agenda and immediately proceeds to deconstruct it. He powerfully projects religious militancy as a resolution to the problem of colonization; yet he has an equally powerful certainty about the untenable future of this resolution. It is inevitable, then, that while outlining this agenda in intensely heightened colours and proclaiming it with a brutal stridency that nearly reaches breaking point in his last novel, he must also immediately counterpose to these convictions an alienating scene that drags the shining vision of Hindu triumph down into the realms of idle rumour and gossip.

CHAPTER SIX

Conjugality and Hindu Nationalism
Resisting Colonial Reason and the Death of a Child-Wife

At the risk of provoking startled disbelief, I propose to place ideas about Hindu conjugality at the very heart of militant nationalism in Bengal.[1] Historians have seen the centrality of debates around colonial laws relating to women and marriage in the discourse of liberal reformers. Thus far, however, they have not located these themes within early Hindu nationalism.

I will examine three interlocking themes in this chapter. First, I believe that in the last four decades of the nineteenth century a fairly distinct political formation had emerged, which could loosely be called revivalist-nationalist. This was a mixed group of newspaper proprietors, orthodox urban estate-holders of considerable civic importance within Calcutta, and pandits as well as modern intellectuals whom they patronised. Such people used an explicitly nationalist rhetoric against any form

---

[1] I use the term 'militant nationalism' in a somewhat unconventional sense here: not as a part of a definite and continuous historical trend but as a moment of absolute and violent criticism of foreign rule that was developed by a group of Hindus in the late 1880s and early 1890s, largely over Hindu marriage controversies. Certain newspapers, especially the *Bangabashi*, took the lead in mobilising protest, organising mass rallies, and provoking official prosecution. That particular group, however, soon withdrew from the scene of confrontation. In the Swadeshi Movement of 1905–8, the *Bangabashi* would remain quiescent, even loyal to the authorities. I owe this piece of information to Sumit Sarkar. For an excellent study of the newspaper, see Amiya Sen, 'Hindu Revivalism in Bengal' (Ph.D. thesis, Delhi University, 1980).

of colonial intervention within the Hindu domestic sphere. Their rhetoric marked them off from the broader category of revivalist thinkers who did not necessarily oppose reformism in the name of resisting colonial knowledge. At the same time, the revivalist-nationalist group's commitment to an unreformed Hindu way of life separated them from liberal nationalists of the Indian Association and Indian National Congress variety. Needless to say, the groups spoken of here were not *irrevocably* distinct or mutually exclusive. Yet, despite the overlaps, there was clearly a distinctive political formation of nationalists who contributed to the emerging nationalism a highly militant agitational rhetoric and mobilising techniques that were built around a defence of Hindu patriarchy.

The second theme involves exploring why the revivalist-nationalists chose to tie their nationalism to issues of conjugality, which they defined as a system of non-consensual, indissoluble, infant marriage.

And, finally, in relation to the third theme, we need to dwell upon the arguments they fabricated. We find that the age of consent issue forced a decisive break in their discourse. It made it imperative for revivalist-nationalists to shift to an entirely different terrain of arguments and images, moving from the realm of reason and pleasure to that of discipline and pain. My elaboration of these themes is intended to widen the context of early nationalist agitations and provide them with an unfamiliar genealogy.

A few words are necessary to explain why, in the present juncture of cultural studies on colonial India, it is important to retrieve this specific history of revivalist-nationalism, and to work with a concept of nationalism that incorporates this history. Edward Said's *Orientalism* has fathered a received wisdom on colonial studies that has proved to be as narrow and frozen in its scope as it has been powerful in its impact. Said's work proceeds from a conviction about the totalising nature of a Western power-knowledge which gives to the entire Orient a single image with absolute certainty. Writings of the Subaltern Studies pundits and of a group of feminists, largely located in first-world academia, have come to identify this singular structure of colonial knowledge as the originary moment for all possible kinds of power and disciplinary formations. Going hand in hand with 'Orientalism', this concept is seen by such academics to reserve for itself the whole range of hegemonic capabilities. This unproblematic and unhistoricised 'transfer of power' to structures of colonial knowledge has three major consequences: first, it constructs a monolithic, unstratified colonised subject who is powerless and without an effective or operative history of his/her own. The only history that she is capable of generating is 'derivative'. As a result, the colonised subject is absolved of all complicity and culpability in the makings of structures of exploitation over the last two hundred years of Indian colonial history: the subject's only culpability lies in the surrender to colonial knowledge. As a result, the lone political agenda for a historiography of this period shrinks into native contestations of colonial knowledge—since all power supposedly flows from this single source. Every species of contestation, by the same token, is taken to be equally valid. Today, with the triumphalist growth of aggressively communal and/or fundamentalist identity politics in our country, such a position comes close to indigenism. In fact it comes close to being intellectually Fascist in its authoritarian insistence on the purity of indigenous epistemological and autarkic conditions.

The Saidian magic formula has weird implications for the feminist agenda as well. The assumption that colonialism had wiped out all past histories of patriarchal domination, replacing them neatly and exclusively with Western forms of gender relations, has naturally led on to an exclusive identification of patriarchy in modern India with the project of liberal reform. While liberalism is made to stand in as the only vehicle of patriarchal ideology (since it is complicit with Western knowledge), its opponents—the revivalists and the orthodoxy—are vested with a rebellious, even emancipatory agenda, since they prevented colonisation of the domestic ideology. And since, for such academics, colonised knowledge is regarded as the exclusive source of all power, all that contests it is supposed to possess an emancipatory possibility for women. By easy degrees, then, we reach the position that while opposition to widow immolation was complicit with the colonial silencing of non-colonised voices and, consequently, was an exercise of power, the practice of widow immolation itself was a contestatory act outside the realm of power relations since it was not sanctioned by colonialism. In a country where people will still gather in their lakhs to watch and celebrate the burning of a teen-aged girl as sati, such cultural studies are grim with political implications.

It is apparent that colonial structures of power compromised with—and indeed learnt much from—indigenous patriarchy and upper-caste norms and practices which, in certain areas of life, retained considerable hegemony. This indubitable fact opens out a new context against which to revaluate liberal reform. Above all, we need to remember that other sources of hegemony, far from becoming extinct, were reactivated under colonialism and opposed the liberal-rationalist agenda with considerable vigour and success. The historian cannot view the colonial past as an unproblematic arena within which all power was on one side and all protest on the other. It is necessary to take into account a multi-faceted nationalism (and not simply its liberal variant), all aspects of which were complicit with power and domination even when they critiqued Western knowledge and challenged colonial power.

II

A summary of controversial legislative activity pertaining to Hindu marriage in the late nineteenth century will help map our discursive field. The Native Marriage Act III of 1872 was, for its times, an extremely radical package which prohibited polygamy, legalised divorce and laid down a fairly high minimum age of marriage. It also ruled out caste or religious barriers to marriage. Predictably, the proposed bill raised a storm of controversy. Its jurisdiction was eventually narrowed down to such people as would declare themselves to be not Hindus, not Christians, not Jains, not Buddhists and not Sikhs. In short, its scope came to cover the Brahmos alone, whose initiative had led to its inception in the first place.[2]

Furious debates around the bill opened up and problematised crucial areas of Hindu conjugality—in particular the system of non-consensual, indissoluble infant marriage whose ties were considered to remain binding upon women even after the death of their husbands. This polemic hardened in 1887 when Rukma Bai, an educated girl from

[2]Charles H. Heimsath, *Indian Nationalism and Hindu Social Reform* (Princeton: Princeton University Press, 1977), pp. 91–4; Ajit Kumar Chakraborti, *Maharshi Debendranath Tagore* (Allahabad, 1916; Calcutta, 1971), pp. 406–35.

the lowly carpenter caste, refused to live with her uneducated, consumptive husband, claiming that since the marriage was contracted in her infancy it could be repudiated by her decision as an adult. She was threatened with imprisonment under Act XV of 1877 for non-restitution of conjugal rights. The threat was removed only after considerable reformist agitation and the personal intervention of Victoria.[3] The issue foregrounded very forcefully the problems of consent and indissolubility within Hindu marriage.[4]

In 1891 the Parsi reformer Malabari's campaign bore fruit in The Criminal Law Amendment Act 10 which revised Section 375 of the Penal Code of 1860, and raised the minimum age of consent for married and unmarried girls from ten to twelve.[5] Under the earlier penal code regulation a husband could legally cohabit with a wife who was ten years old. The revivalist Hindu intelligentsia of Bengal now claimed that the new act violated a fundamental ritual observance in the lifecycle of the Hindu householder—that is, the 'garbhadhan' ceremony, or the obligatory cohabitation between husband and wife which was meant to take place immediately after the wife reached puberty. Since puberty, in the hot climate of Bengal, was quite likely to occur before she was twelve, the new legislation meant that the ritual would no longer remain compulsory. If the wife reached puberty before attaining the age of consent, then obviously garbhadhan could not be performed. This in turn implied that the 'pinda', or ancestral offerings, served up by the sons of such marriages would become impure and that generations of ancestors would be starved of it. The argument provided the central ground for a highly organised mass campaign in Bengal. The first open mass-level anti-government protest in Calcutta and the official prosecution of a leading newspaper were its direct consequences.[6]

[3]The act of 1877 was a colonial intervention to tighten up the marriage bond which the Hindu orthodoxy strongly defended on the grounds that it coincided with and reinforced the true essence of Hindu conjugality.

[4]See Dagmar Engels, 'The Limits of Gender Ideology: Bengali Women, the Colonial State, and the Private Sphere, 1890–1930', *Women Studies, International Forum*, vol. 12, 1989.

[5]Heimsath, pp. 147–75.

[6]See extracts from *Bangabashi* and *Dainik O Samachar Chandrika* between 1889 and 1891 in *RNP*.

This summary might be taken to suggest, Cambridge School fashion,[7] that nationalist initiative was actually a mere reflex action, following mechanically upon the legal initiatives of the colonial state. This was far from being the case. Not only was colonial initiative itself generally a belated and forced surrender to Indian reformist pressure, Hindu revivalist reaction against both was ultimately constituted by a new political compulsion: it was coterminus with a recently acquired notion of the colonised self which arose out of the 1857 uprising, the post-Mutiny reprisals, Lyttonian discriminatory policies in the 1870s, and the Ilbert Bill racist agitations in the 1880s. These experiences collectively modified and cast into agonising doubt the earlier choice of loyalism that the Bengali intelligentsia had made, fairly unambiguously, in 1857. Our understanding of responses to colonial legislation can make only very limited and distorted sense unless they are located within this larger context.

Whereas early-nineteenth-century male liberal reformers had been deeply self-critical about the bondage of women within the household,[8] the satirised literary self-representation of the Bengali 'baboo' of later decades recounted a very different order of lapses for himself: his was a self that had lost its autonomy and now willingly hugged its chains. Rethinking about the burden of complicity with colonialism hammered out a reoriented self-critique as well as a heightened perception about the meaning of subjection. It is no accident that even the economic critiques of drain, deindustrialisation and poverty would come to be developed by the post-1860s generations.

With a gradual dissolution of faith in the progressive potential of colonialism, a dissolution that accompanied political self-doubt and the failure of indigenous economic enterprises,[9] there was also a disenchantment with the magical possibilities of Western education. Earlier reformers had been led to look hopefully at the public sphere

[7]For this version of Cambridge historiography on Indian nationalism, see Gallagher, Seal and Johnson, *Locality, Province and Nation* (Cambridge, 1973).

[8]I have discussed this in 'Hindu Household and Conjugality in Nineteenth-Century Bengal', paper read at the Women's Studies' Centre, Jadavpur University, Calcutta, 1989.

[9]N.K. Sinha, *Economic History of Bengal* (Calcutta, n.d.), vol. I.

as an arena for the test of manhood, of genuine self-improvement. But now, with activities shrinking into parasitic petty landlordism and tenure-holdings, or to mechanical chores within an oppressive and marginalised clerical existence, the bhadralok household increasingly resembled a solitary sphere of autonomy, a site of formal knowledge where—and only where—education would yield practical, manipulable, controllable results. The Permanent Settlement had generated a class of parasitic landlords with fixed revenue obligation whose passivity was reinforced by uninhibited control over their peasants' rent. The gap between a fixed sum of revenue and flexible rent procurement in a period of rising agricultural prices cushioned an existence of fairly comfortable tenure holding. The Rent Acts of 1859 and 1885, however, breached that security. Organised tenant resistance of the late nineteenth century led to heightened anxieties and uncertainties among the landed gentry. The household, consequently, became doubly precious and important as the only zone where autonomy and self-rule could be preserved.[10]

In the massive corpus of household management manuals that came to occupy a dominant place in the total volume of printed vernacular prose literature of these years, the household was likened to an enterprise to be administered, an army to be led, a state to be governed[11]—all metaphors rather poignantly derived from activities that excluded colonised Bengalis. Unlike Victorian middle-class situations, then, the family was not a refuge after work for the man. It was their real place of work. Whether in the Kalighat bazaar paintings[12] or in the Bengali

[10]See my Introduction within the present volume.

[11]See for instance Prasad Das Goswami, *Amader Samaj* (Serampore, 1896); Ishanchandra Basu, *Stri Diger Prati Upadesh* (Calcutta, n.d.); Kamakhya Charan Bannerji, *Stri Shiksha* (Dacca, 1901); Monomohan Basu, *Hindur Achar Vyavadhar* (Calcutta, 1872); Chandranath Basu, *Garhasthya Path* (Calcutta, 1887); Bhubaneswar Misra, *Hindu Vivaha Samalochan* (Calcutta, 1875); Tarakhnath Biswas, *Bangiya Mahila* (Calcutta, 1886); Anubicacharan Gupta, *Grihastha Jivan* (Calcutta, 1887); Narayan Roy, *Bangamahila* (Calcutta, n.d.); Chandrakumar Bhattacharya, *Bangavivaha* (Calcutta, 1881); Pratapchandra Majumdar, *Stri Charitra* (Calcutta, n.d.); Purnachandra Gupta, *Bangali Bau* (Calcutta, 1885); and many others.

[12]See the preponderance of this theme in the collection of W.C. Archer, *Bazaar Paintings of Calcutta* (London, 1953).

fiction of the nineteenth century, workplace situations remain shadowy, unsubstantial, mostly absent. Domestic relations alone constitute the axis around which plots are generated, in sharp contrast with, for example, Dickensian novels.[13]

The new nationalist worldview, then, reimaged the family as a contrast to and a critique of alien rule. This was done primarily by contrasting two different versions of subjection—that of the colonised Hindu male in the world outside, and that of the apparently subordinated Hindu wife at home. The forced surrender and real dispossession of the former was counterposed to the allegedly loving, willed surrender and ultimate self-fulfilment of the latter.[14] It was in the interests of this intended contrast that conjugality was constituted as the centre of gravity around which the discursive field on the family organised itself. All other relations, even the mother–child one (which would come to take its place as a pivotal point in later nationalist discourse) remained subordinated to it up to the end of the nineteenth century. It was the relationship between the husband and wife that mediated and rephrased, within revivalist-nationalism, the political theme of domination and subordination, of subjection and resistance as the lyrical or existential problem of love, of equal but different ways of loving.

The household generally, and conjugality specifically, came to mean the last independent space left to the colonised Hindu. This was a conviction that was both shaped and reinforced by some of the premises of colonial law. English legislators and judges postulated a basic division within the legal domain: British and Anglo-Indian law had a 'territorial' scope and ruled over the 'public' world of land relations, criminal law, laws of contract, and evidence. On the other hand, there were Hindu and Muslim laws which were defined as 'personal', covering persons rather than areas, and ruling over the more intimate areas of human existence—family relationships, family property and religious life.[15]

[13]See, for instance, plots in the novels of Bankimchandra, *Bankim Rachanabali*, vol. I.

[14]Prasad Das Goswami, op.cit.

[15]See, for instance, Sir William Markby, Fellow, Balliol College and erstwhile judge in Calcutta High Court, *Hindu and Mohammadan Law* (1906; reprinted Delhi, 1977), pp. 2–3.

Early nationalists chose to read this as a gap between on the one hand the *territory* or the *land* colonised by an alien law, and on the other the *person*, still ruled by one's own faith. This was a distinction that the Queen's Proclamation of 1859, promising absolute non-interference in religious matters, did much to bolster.[16] Even in subjected India, therefore, there could exist an interior space that was as yet putatively inviolate.

Far from trying to hegemonise this sphere and absolutise its control, colonial rule, especially in the post-1857 decades, tried to keep its distance from it, thus indirectly adding to the nationalist conviction. The earlier zeal for textualisation and codification of traditional laws was gradually replaced by a recognition of the importance of unwritten and varied custom, of the inadvisability of legislation on such matters, and of urging judicial deference, even obedience, to local Hindu opinion.[17] Towards the end of the century, a strong body of Hindu lawyers and judges came to be formed whose conformity to Hindu practices (Hindutva) was often taken to be of decisive importance in judicial decision-making, even though their professional training was in Western jurisprudence, not in Hindu law.[18] There was, moreover, an implicit grey zone of unwritten law whose force was nevertheless quite substantial within law courts.[19] Take a Serampore court case of 1873, for instance, where a Hindu widow was suing her brothers-in-law for defrauding her of her share in her husband's property by falsely charging her with 'unchastity'. Her lawyer referred frequently to notions of kinship obligations, ritual expectations from a Hindu widow and moral norms and practices of high-caste women.[20] Clearly, these arguments

[16]See frequent reference to the Queen's Proclamation in the agitational writings in the nationalist press, *RNP*, 1887–91.

[17]Markby, op.cit., for a convergence of the views of this Orientalist scholar-cum-colonial judge with Hindu legal opinion; and c.f. Sripati Roy, *Customs and Customary Law in British India*, Tagore Law Lectures, 1908–9 (reprinted Delhi, 1986), pp. 2–6.

[18]See J.D.N. Derrett, *Religion, Law and the State in India* (London, 1968).

[19]For a clarification of the notion of unwritten law, see Robert M. Ireland, 'The Libertine Must Die: Sexual Dishonour and the Unwritten Law in the 19th Century United States', *Journal of Social History*, Fall 1989.

[20]*The Bengalee*, 7 March 1873.

were thought to possess value in convincing the judge and the jury, even though overtly they had little legal significance. Far from laughing peculiarly Hindu susceptibilities out of court, English judges, even the Privy Council, seriously rationalised them. Referring to the existence of a Hindu idol as a legal person in a different law suit, an English judge commented: 'Nothing impossible or absurd in it . . . after all an idol is as much of a person as a corporation.'[21] Legal as well as ritual niceties about the proper disposition of idols were seriously debated, and sacred objects were brought into courts of law after due ritual purification of the space.[22] The introduction of a limited jury system between the 1860s and the 1880s in Bengal further strengthened the voice of local Hindu notables, and, consequently, of local usages and norms. An official recommendation of 1890 curtailed the powers of the jury in many directions but left the powers of settling marriage disputes intact in their hands.[23]

Nor did colonial legislators and judges form a unified, internally coherent body of opinion on proper Hindu norms and practices which they would then try to freeze. A substantial debate developed over a proposal in 1873 to transfer the cognisance of cases connected with marriage offences, especially adultery, from criminal to civil courts. While Simson, the Dacca commissioner, recommended the repeal of penal provisions against adultery, Reynolds, the magistrate of Mymensingh strongly demurred: 'I have always observed with great aversion the practice of the English law in giving damages in cases of adultery and seduction, and wanted it to remain a criminal offence.'[24] About cases of forfeiture of property rights by 'unchaste widows', there was a clear division between the high courts of Allahabad on the one hand and

---

[21]Markby, op.cit., p. 100.

[22]This relates to a case involving the disposition of a Shalgram-shila in case of Surendranath Bannerjee *vs* the chief justice and judges of the High Court at Fort William, July 1883. See an account in Subrata Choudhary, 'Ten Celebrated Cases Tried by the Calcutta High Court' in the *High Court at Calcutta, Centenary Souvenir 1862–1962* (Calcutta, 1962).

[23]Sharmila Bannerjee, *Studies in the Administrative History of Bengal, 1880–1989* (New Delhi, 1978), pp. 151–5.

[24]Cited in *The Bengalee*, 26 April 1873.

those of Bombay, Madras and Calcutta on the other.[25] The divisions reflected the absence of any monolithic or absolute consensus about the excellence of English legal practice as a model for Indian life.

These decades had in England seen profound changes in women's rights *vis-à-vis* property holding, marriage, divorce, and the rights of prostitutes to physical privacy.[26] Englishmen in India were divided about the direction of these changes and a significant section felt disturbed by the limited, though real, gains made by contemporary English feminists. They turned with relief to the so-called relative stability and strictness of Hindu rules. The Hindu joint-family system, whose collective aspects supposedly fully submerged and subordinated individual rights and interests, was generally described with warm appreciation.[27] Found here was a system of relatively unquestioned patriarchal absolutism which promised a more comfortable state of affairs than what emerged after bitter struggles with Victorian feminism at home.

The colonial experience, in its own way, mediated and reoriented debates on conjugal legislation in England. There were important controversies: the best known being between John Stuart Mill and James Fitzjames Stephen on the issue of consensus *vs* force and authority as the valid basis for social and human relations. Stephen, drawing on his military-bureaucratic apprenticeship in India, questioned Mill's premise of complementarity and the notion of the companionate marriage.[28]

There was no stable legal or judicial model that could, therefore, be imported into India. Prior to the Judicature Act of 1873 there were four separate systems of courts in England, each applying its own form of law, and these were often in conflict with each other.[29] In any case,

[25]See extracts from *Murshidabad Patrika, Dacca Prakash* and the *Education Gazette* in April 1875, *RNP.*

[26]See Phillipa Levine, *Victorian Feminism, 1850–1900* (London, 1987), pp. 128–43. Also see Holcombe, *Wives and Property—Reform of the Married Women's Property Law in 19th Century England* (Oxford, 1983).

[27]Markby, op.cit., p. 100.

[28]Mendus and Rendall (eds), *Sexuality and Subordination, Interdisciplinary Studies of Genders in the 19th Century* (London: RKP, 1989), p. 133.

[29]See also Holcombe, 'Victorian Wives and Property: Reform of the Married Women's Property Law, 1857–82' in Martha Vicinus, *A Widening Sphere: Changing Roles of Victorian Women* (London: Methuen, 1977).

the prolonged primacy of case-law and common-law procedures within England itself made English judges in India agree with Indian legal and nationalist opinion that customs, usages and precedents were far more valid sources of law than legislation.[30]

A general consensus about the differentiated nature of colonial law, then, postulated a fissure within the system wherein Hindus could insert their claims for a sectoral yet complete autonomy, for a pure space. The specific and concrete embodiment of this purity seemed to lie more within the body of the Hindu woman rather than the man—a conviction shaped, no doubt, by the growing self-doubt of the post-1857 Hindu male. Increasingly, irony and satire, a kind of black humour, became the dominant form of educated middle-class literary self-representation. There was an obsessive insistence on the physical manifestation of this weakness. The feeble Bengali male physique became a metaphor for a larger condition. Simultaneously, it was a site of the critique of the ravaging effects of colonial rule. 'The term Bengali is a synonym for a creature afflicted with inflammation of the liver, enlargement of the spleen, acidity or headache.'[31] Or, 'Their bones are weak, their muscles are flabby, their nerves toneless.'[32] Or, 'Bengal is ruined. There is not a single really healthy man in it. The digestive powers have been affected and we can eat but a little. Wherever one goes one sees a diseased people.'[33] Through the grind of Western education, office routine[34] and enforced urbanisation, with the loss of traditional sports and martial activities, the male Bengali body was supposedly marked, maimed and completely worn down by colonialism. It was the visible site of surrender and loss, of defeat and alien discipline.

The woman's body, on the other hand, was still held to be pure and unmarked, loyal, and subservient to the discipline of shastras alone. It was not a free body by any means, but one ruled by 'our' scriptures, 'our'

---

[30]Markby and Sripati Roy, op.cit.

[31] *The Amrita Bazar Patrika*, 4 February 1873.

[32] *The Hindoo Patriot*, 16 August, 1887.

[33] *The Amrita Bazar Patrika*, 28 January, 1875, RNP Bengal, 1875.

[34]See Sumit Sarkar, 'The Kalki-Avatar of Bikrampur: A Village Scandal in Early Twentieth-Century Bengal', in Ranajit Guha (ed.), *Subaltern Studies VI* (Delhi, 1989).

custom. The difference with the male body bestowed on it a redemptive, healing strength for the community as a whole. An interesting change now takes place in the representation of Hindu women in the new nationalist discourse. Whereas for liberal reformers she had been the archetypal victim figure, for nationalists she had become a repository of power, the Kali rampant, a figure of range and strength.[35]

What were the precise sources of grace for Hindu women? A unique capacity for bearing pain was one. So was the discipline exercised upon her body by the iron laws of absolute chastity, extending beyond the death of the husband, through an indissoluble, non-consensual infant form of marriage, through austere widowhood, and through her proven capacity for self-immolation. All these together imprinted an inexorable disciplinary regimen upon her person that contained and defined her from infancy to death.

Such discipline was not entirely confined to the normative or conceptual sphere. Bengal, with the exception of the Central Provinces and Berar, and Bihar and Orissa, had the highest rate of infant marriages—a custom that cut across caste and community lines and did not markedly decrease even after the Act of 1891.[36] Before it was banned, Bengal had also been, as we know, the heartland of the practice of sati. The Hindu woman's demonstrated capacity for accepting pain thus became the last hope of greatness for a doomed people. As we saw, Bankimchandra linked sati with national regeneration:

> I can see the funeral pyre burning, the chaste wife sitting at the heart of the blazing flames, clasping the feet of her husband lovingly to her breasts. Slowly the fire spreads, destroying one part of her body and entering another. Her face is joyful . . . The flames burn higher, life departs and the body is burnt to ashes . . . . When I think that only some time back our women could die like this, then new hope rises up in me, then I have faith that we, too, have the seeds of greatness within us. Women of Bengal: You are the true jewels of this country.[37]

[35]See 'Nationalist Iconography' in this volume.

[36]*Report of the Age of Consent Committee, 1928–29*, Government of Bengal (Calcutta, 1929). For some statistical observations on this matter, see pp. 65–6.

[37]*Kamalkanter Daptar*, op.cit.

Bankim had plenty of reservations on other aspects of Hindu conjugality,[38] but he seemed to identify with it at its most violent point of termination, through a highly sensualised spectacle of pain and death, a barely disguised parallel, as we have seen in the previous chapter, between the actual flames destroying a female body and the consuming fires of desire.

III

There were two equally strong compulsions and possibilities in the construction of Hindu womanhood—love and pain—which produced deep anxieties within early nationalism.

The accent on love had, from the beginning, underlined acute discomfort about mutuality and equality. Pandit Sasadhar Tarkachuramani, the doyen of Hindu orthodoxy, argued that a higher form of love distinguished Western from Hindu marriages. While the former seeks social stability and order through control over sexual morality, the latter apparently aspires only towards 'the unification of two souls.' 'Mere temporal happiness, and the begetting of children are very minor and subordinate considerations in Hindu marriage.'[39] The revivalist-nationalist segment of the vernacular press, polemical tracts and manuals translated the notion of marriage of souls as mutual love lasting practically from cradle to funeral pyre. This uniquely Hindu way of loving supposedly anchored the woman's absolute and lifelong chastity.[40] Yet the very emphasis on love, so necessary as a critique of alien oppression and misunderstandings of the Hindu order, was a double-edged weapon: once it was raised, sooner or later the question of the

[38]Tanika Sarkar, 'Bankimchandra and the Impossibility of a Political Agenda' in this volume.

[39]*Bangabashi*, 9 July 1887, *RNP*, 1887. For a critical discussion of such views see Rabindranath Tagore, *Hindu Vivaha* (*c.* 1887). Rabindranath himself, in this extremely convoluted logical exercise, grants a practical purpose to infant marriage purely for better breeding purposes but, in the process, Hindu conjugality is denied all effective or spiritual pretensions. *Rabindranath Rachanabali*, vol. 12 (Calcutta, *c.* 1942).

[40]Chandrakanta Basu, *Hindu Patni and Hindu Vivaha Bayas O Uddeshya*, cited in *Hindu Vivaha*, op.cit., also by the same author, *Hinduttva*, op.cit.

mutuality of such love was bound to arise. Was it equally binding on both partners? If not, and since Hindu males were allowed to be polygamous, could its jurisdiction on women be anything more than prescriptive? Particularly if marriage was imposed on her at birth, without the question of her consent or choice?

Nothing in the Hindu shastras would confirm the possibility of mutually monogamous ties. To redeem this absence there appeared, for the first time in the history of Hindu marriage, a wave of polemical literature that valorised, indeed insisted on, male monogamy: 'We find tracts that advise widowers never to remarry.'[41] Manuals advocating self-immolation for the adult widow now simultaneously advise that child widows should be remarried; they have no obligation towards a husband whom they have not, as yet, come to love.[42] Not just sacred texts but custom too now allows a wide spectrum of castes to make a second marriage possible for men if the first wife is barren or bore no sons.[43] Yet in the absence of a shastric or custom-based injunction against polygamy, and given the reluctance among Hindu revivalist-nationalists to invite reformist legislation, male chastity was fated to remain normative rather than obligatory, while the woman's chastity was not a function of choice or willed consent. This was a compromise that became fundamentally difficult to sustain.

Through much of the 1880s we find a studied silence on this uncomfortable equation within the Hindu marriage and a self-mesmerising repetition of its innately aesthetic qualities. The infant-marriage ritual is drenched in a warm, suffusing glow. 'People in this country take a great *pleasure* in infant-marriage. The *little bit* of a woman, the infant bride, clad in red silk, her back turned towards her boy husband . . . The drums are beating, and men, women and children are running in order to glimpse that face . . . from time to time she breaks forth into *little* ravishing smiles. She looks like a *little lovely* doll.'[44] (italics mine) The key words are little, lovely, ravishing, pleasure, infant,

---

[41]See for instance Prasad Das Goswami, op.cit., Bhubaneshwar Misra, op.cit., Kalimoy Ghatok, *Ami* (Calcutta, 1885).

[42]Monomohan Basu, op.cit.

[43]Ibid.

[44]*Sulabh Samachar O Kushadahe*, 22 July 1887, *RNP*, 1887.

and doll.[45] They are inserted at regular intervals to make the general account of festivities draw its warmth from this single major source— the delight-giving and delighted infant bride. The community of 'men, women and children' that forms for the occasion is bonded together by a deeply sensuous experience, by great visual pleasure, by happiness. The radiant picture of innocent celebration is rounded off through the cleverly casual insertion of the phrase 'boy husband'. Yet infant marriage was prescriptive only for the girl. The groom of the 'lovely doll' could be, and frequently was, a mature, even elderly man, possibly much-married already. A strategic and organising silence lies at the heart of this image of desire and pleasure.

Even if the quality of Hindu love was assumed to be 'higher', Hindu marriage was still placed firmly within mainstream developments in the universal history of marriages which had supposedly trodden a uniform path from the 'captive' stage to fairly permanent, often sacramental, systems. Consent-based alternatives, whether in ancient Indian or in class-based modern Western traditions, were dismissed as aberrations or minor variations.[46] A long editorial, significantly entitled 'The Bogus Science', questioned the sources and authenticity of reformist knowledge: the nature of their evidence, of deduction, of arrangement of proof.[47] A powerful eugenics-based argument against infant marriage (infant marriages produce weak progeny) was countered by a climatic view of history:[48] irrespective of the age of the parents, a tropical climate was in any case bound to produce weak children: reformers were thereby accused of casuistry or weak logic. And since the penal code had earlier laid down ten as the minimum age of consent, how would raising it to twelve ensure genuine consent? 'A girl of fourteen or sixteen is not

---

[45]Far from invariably evoking a sense of superiority and disgust among Englishmen, the spectacle would very often arouse similar sentiments. Compare a description of a marriage procession by an English tourist with our earlier account: 'It was the prettiest sight in the world to see those gorgeously dressed babies . . . passerbys smiled and blessed the little husband and the tiny wife'; John Law, *Glimpses of Hidden India* (Calcutta, *circa* 1905).

[46]*The Hindoo Patriot*, 25 July 1887.

[47]Ibid., 16 August 1887.

[48]Ibid., 12 September 1887.

capable of legally signing a note of hand for 5 rupees and she is, *ipso facto,* a great deal more incompetent to give her consent to defile her person at twelve.'[49] It was also considered more than a little dishonest to place such importance on the woman's consent in this one matter since, within post-marital offences, 'in the case of the wife the point does not turn on consent, for, if that had been the case, there would have been no such offence as adultery in the Penal Code.'[50] A high premium was thus placed on the rule of rationality in the defence of Hindu marriage.

Hindu rationality was represented as more supportive than reformist or colonial projects. Given the physical and economic weakness of women, an indissoluble marriage tie had to be her only security. This contention conveniently overlooked the fact that, in a polygamous world, indissolubility was binding, in effect, on women alone. A clear-eyed kulin brahmin widow had remarked: 'People say that the seven ties that bind the Hindu wife to the husband do not snap as they do with Christians or Muslims. This is not true. According to Hindu law, the wife cannot leave the husband but the husband may leave her whenever he wants to.'[51] It was also maintained that consent was immaterial since parents were better equipped to handle the vital question of security than an immature girl.[52] Security also largely depended upon perfect integration with the husband's family, so the sooner the process began, the better it was for the girl.[53]

Hindu marriage, in the rather defensive discourse of the 1880s, then, was more pleasurable and more beautiful, kinder and safer, more rational, and guaranteed by a sounder system of knowledge. In any case, it was essentially a part of universal developments in the history of civilisations: differences in marriage systems between the Hindu and the non-Hindu were played down, if not obliterated.

The Rukma Bai episode of 1887 made it imperative at last to rewrite

[49]Ibid., 1 August 1887.

[50]*Surabhi O Patrika,* 16 January 1887, *RNP,* 1887.

[51]Nistarini Devi, *Sekaler Katha,* first published serially in *Bharatbarsha* between 1913 and 1914. Jana and Sanyal (eds), *Atmakatha* (Calcutta, 1982), p. 11.

[52]Chandrakanta Basu, op.cit.

[53]*The Hindoo Patriot,* 19 September 1887.

this narrative of love and pleasure in the language of force. The earlier lyricism in relation to such 'love' had already been ruptured from time to time to underline and recuperate the basic fact of non-consensuality. At a meeting convened at the palace of the Shova Bazar Raj, Rajendralal Mitra had insisted: 'in it [Hindu marriage] there is no selection, no self-choice, no consent on the part of the bride. She is an article of gift, she is given away even as a cow or any other chattel.' Approving laughter greeted his exposition and he went on: 'There is in Hinduism not the remotest idea of choice and whoever changed any small part of it was no Hindu.'[54] Rukma Bai's action violently foregrounded the sexual double standards and made a mockery of the notion of the loving heart of Hindu conjugality. A lot of the debate centred around the vexed question of whether a woman could sue for separation from an adulterous husband. 'Among the Hindus, unchastity on the part of the husband is certainly a culpable offence but they set much higher value upon female chastity': its erosion would lead to the loss of family honour, growth of half-castes and the destruction of ancestral rites.[55] Bare, stark bones that formed the basic foundation of Hindu marriage now began to surface, threatening to blow the edifice of love away. 'A good Hindu wife should always serve her husband as God even if that husband is illiterate, devoid of good qualities and attached to other women. And it is the duty of the government to make Hindu women conform to the injunctions of the Shastras.'[56] The basis of conjugality now openly shifts to prescription.

Rukma Bai had forced a choice upon her community—between the woman's right to free will and the future of the pristine essence of Hindu marriage: the two could no longer be wedded together as a perfect whole. Revivalist-nationalists had to treat the two as separate, conflicting units, and indicate their own partisanship.

That came forth in no time at all. 'It is very strange that the whole of Hindu society will suffer for the sake of a very ordinary woman.'[57] Or, 'kindness to the female sex cannot be a good plea in favour of the

[54]Cited in The Hindoo Patriot, ibid.
[55]Dainik O Samachar Chandrika, 22 June 1857.
[56]Bardhawan Sanjivani, 5 July 1887, RNP, 1887.
[57]Dhumketu, 4 July 1887, RNP, 1887.

proposed alteration.'[58] Interestingly, the episode had shown up another fault in the image of the Hindu community. Rukma Bai belonged to the carpenter caste, where divorce had been customary. Whose custom must colonial law recognise now? Was Hinduism a heterogeneous, indeed, self-divided, self-contradictory formation, or was it a unified monolithic one? The revivalist-nationalist answer, once again, was unambiguous. 'The Brahmin caste occupies the highest position and all laws and ordinances have been formed with special reference to that. All the other castes conduct themselves after the fashion of the Brahminical castes.'[59] Or, 'it is true that divorce obtains among some low-caste people and the government should be really doing an important duty as a ruler if it should make laws fixing and negotiating the uncertain and unsettled marriage customs of the people.'[60]

The debate prised open the imagined community along lines of caste and gender and delineated the specific contours of the revivalist-nationalist agenda. This could no longer base its hegemonic claims on its supposed leadership of the struggle of a whole subjected people for autonomy and self-rule in their 'private' lives. Its nationalism became more precisely defined now as the rule of brahmanical patriarchy. Its rationality was based on the forced and absolute domination of upper-caste, male standards, not universal reason leading towards freedom and self-determination for the dispossessed. If it aspired to detach Hindus from colonised reason and lead them to self-rule, it would only do so by substituting for it a brahmanical, patriarchal reason based on scripture-cum-custom, both of which were disciplinary and oppressive for the ruled subjects—as was the colonial regime in the sphere of political economy. The contestation of colonisation was no simple escape from or refusal of power: nor had colonialism equally and entirely disempowered all Indians. Resistance was an agenda itself irrevocably tied to schemes for domination, an exercise of power that was nearly as absolute as that which it resisted.

[58] *Sambad Prabhakar*, 30 June 1887, *RNP*, 1887.
[59] *Bangabashi*, 25 June 1887, *RNP*, 1887.
[60] *Nababibhakar Sadharani*, 18 July 1887, *RNP*, 1887.

IV

Curiously, one possibility within Hindu marriage had not occurred to reformists or to Bengali Hindu militants—the possibility of the sexual abuse of infant wives. There had been, from time to time, the occasional stray report. The *Dacca Prakash* of June 1875 reported that an 'elderly' man had beaten his child wife to death when she refused to go to bed with him. Neighbours had tried to cover it up as suicide but the murder charge was eventually proved. The jury, however, let off the husband with a light sentence.[61] The *Education Gazette* of May 1873 had reported a similar incident when the 'mature' husband of a girl of eleven 'dragged her out by the hair and beat her till he killed her' for similar reasons. He was let off with a light sentence as well.[62] Reporting remained sporadic and the accounts were not picked up and woven into any general discussion about Hindu marriage as yet. The controversy over the right age of consent continued to hinge on eugenics, morality, child rearing and family interests.

In 1890 Phulmonee, a girl of about ten or eleven, was raped to death by her husband Hari Maiti, a man of thirty-five. Under existing penal code provisions, however, he was not guilty of rape since Phulmonee had been well within the statutory age limit of ten. The event, however, added enormous weight and urgency to Malabari's campaign for raising the age of consent from ten to twelve. The reformist press began to systematically collect and publish accounts of similar incidents from all over the country. Forty-four women doctors brought out long lists of cases where child-wives had been maimed or killed because of rape.[63] From the possible effects of child marriage on the health of future generations, the debate shifted to the life and safety of Hindu wives.

Phulmonee was the daughter of the late Kunj Behari Maitee, a man from the 'Oriya Kyast' caste, who had been a 'Bazar Sircar' at Bow Bazar Market. It was a well-paid job and it seems that, by claiming 'Oriya Kyast' status, the family was aspiring to a superior caste position in consonance with their economic viability: Maitees were otherwise

[61] *Dacca Prakash*, 8 June 1875, *RNP*, 1875.
[62] *Education Gazette*, 11 May 1873, *RNP*, 1873.
[63] Heimsath, op.cit.

categorised as a low Sudra group. The family frequently referred to its specific caste practices in court with some pride. They said that while they adhered to child marriage, they forbade cohabitation before the girl's menstruation and that, in this respect, Phulmonee had not come of age. Their version was that the newly-married couple had been kept apart according to caste rules, and that Hari, on a visit to his in-laws, had stolen into Phulmonee's room and had forced himself upon her, thereby causing her death. Hari Maiti, however, insisted that since their marriage she had spent at least a fortnight at his house and they had slept together all the time. He made no mention of caste rules against pre-menstrual cohabitation. It seems, then, that caste customs remained loose and flexible, and that each family would allow considerable manipulation within them.

Even though Hari Maiti had insisted that on the last night they had not had intercourse, medical opinion was unanimous that the girl had died of violent sexual penetration. If the court accepted that Hari was right and that Phulmonee had slept with him earlier, then it could go a long way to show that since nothing untoward had happened earlier, on the fatal night in question Hari would not have had any reason to suspect that more vigorous penetration might lead to violent consequences. He would, in fact, have been able to seem convinced that intercourse was perfectly safe. The English judge, Wilson, clearly indicated that he chose to accept Hari's version, thus exonerating him from the charge of culpable homicide. The charge of rape, in any case, was not permissible since the penal code provisions ruled out the existence of rape by the husband if the wife was above the age of ten. The judge was equally opposed to any extension of the strict letter of the law, in this case to devise exemplary punishment for a particularly horrible death: 'Neither judges nor juries have any right to do for themselves what the law has not done.'

The judge built up his case on the hypothetical argument that the couple had slept together earlier. He chose to ignore the version given by the women in the girl's family—of Radhamonee, Bhondamonee and Sonamonee, the mother, aunt and grandmother of the girl.

I think it is my duty to say that I think there exists hardly such solid and satisfactory ground as would make it safe to say that this man must have had knowledge that he was likely to cause the death of the girl . . . You will, of course, in these, as in all matters, give the benefit of any doubt in favour of the prisoner.

The weight of concern is, very blatantly, on the exoneration of the man rather than on the fate of the woman. The law itself was shaped so as to preserve custom as well as the male right to the enjoyment of an infantile female body.

What needs to be particularly noted here is that, throughout the trial, the judge was saying nothing about a husband who insisted on sleeping with a child, or about the custom which allowed him to do so with impunity. Above all, he was not making any judgmental comparison between the ways of husbands, Eastern or Western. In fact, he bent over backwards to exonerate the system of marriage that had made this death possible: 'Under no system of law with which Courts have had to do in this country, whether Hindu or Mohammedan, or that formed under British rule, has it ever been the law that a husband has the absolute right to enjoy the person of his wife without regard to the question of safety to her.'[64]

Both the Hindu husband and the Hindu marriage system are generously exempted from blame and criticism. There is, in fact, an assertion about a continuity in the spirit of the law from the time of the Hindu kingdoms to that of British rule.

A significant body of English medical opinion confirmed the clean bill of health that the colonial judiciary had advanced to the Hindu marriage system. Even in a strictly private communication, meant for colonial officialdom alone, the secretary to the Public Health Society wrote to the Government of Bengal:

The council direct me to lay special stress upon the point . . . that they base no charge against the native community.

They reverently cited the work on Hindu law by Sir Thomas Strange to evoke, in near-mystical terms, the supreme importance of his marriage

[64]Bengal Government Judicial J C/17/, Proceedings 96–102, 1892, Nos 101–02. File J C/17–5. Honourable Justice Wilson's charge to jury in the case Empress *vs* Main Mohan Maitee, Calcutta High Court. Report sent by Arcar, Clerk of the Crown, High Court, Calcutta, to Officiating Chief Secretary 90B, No. 6292-Calcutta, 8 September 1890.

rules to the Hindu, and the inadvisability of external interference with them.

The council admit that our native fellow subjects must be allowed the fullest possible freedom in deciding when their children should be ceremonially married. That, in the constitution of Hindu society, is a matter with which no Government could meddle and no Government ought to meddle.

They proceeded to review the considerable medico-legal data on sexual injuries inflicted on child wives and concluded that, whatever the weight of evidence on the matter, the system of infant marriage must continue unabated. The age of commencing cohabitation could be raised *only if Hindus themselves expressed a great desire for change* (emphasis mine).

Contrary to received wisdom, then, there is hardly here a vision of remaking the Hindu as a pale image of his master, nor of designs of total change and reform. Macaulay's notorious plan of recasting the native as a brown sahib was not necessarily uniformly dominant for the entire spectrum of colonial rule. Even when dominant, it had to make crucial negotiations with other imperatives and value preferences and, above all, with the everlasting calculations of political expediency. If, at the time of Macaulay, the Anglicist vision of a Westernised middle class had appeared as the strongest reservoir of loyalism, soon enough other alternatives emerged and were partially accommodated, modifying the earlier formula and crucially mitigating its reformist thrust. Our moment of the 1890s comes after a long spell of middle-class agitation over demands on constitutional rights, of Indianisation of the services, of security against racial discrimination and abuse. It comes after the outburst of white racism over the Ilbert Bill issue, when the educated middle class was temporarily vested with the possibility of standing in a position of judicial authority over Europeans. Empowering the Indian through Westernisation, consequently, came to be envisaged as the most threatening menace to colonial racial structures.[65] It was a moment when the slightest concession to Indian liberal reformism would be

[65]See Mrinalini Sinha, *Colonial Masculinity: The 'Manly Englishman' and the 'Effeminate Bengali' in the Late Nineteenth Century* (Manchester: Manchester University Press, 1995), pp. 33–69.

made most unwillingly and only in the belief that it represented a majority opinion.

The new legislation was conceived after the reformist agitation had convinced the authorities that the 'great majority' was ready for change.[66] After the Phulmonee episode, revivalist-nationalists were maintaining a somewhat embarrassed silence; this was broken only after the proposed bill came along. During the interval the reformist voice alone was audible. Since this, for the moment, looked like the majority demand, political expediency coincided temporarily with reformist impulse and the government committed itself to raising the age of consent. At the same time, official opinion in Bengal did not extend the terms of the specific reform to larger plans for invasive change. On the contrary, it displayed a keenness to learn from the codes of Hindu patriarchy. Did a recognition that they were confronted with the most absolute form of patriarchal domination evoke a measure of unconscious respect and fellow feeling among the usually conservative, male English authorities, rather than the instinct for reform? As the secretary to the Public Health Society put it: 'The history of British rule and the workings of British courts in India manifest a distinct tenderness towards . . . the customs and religious observances of the Indian people.'[67]

There was still the mangled body of 'that unhappy child, Phulmonee Dassee,' a girl of ten or eleven, sexually used by a man whom she had known only a few weeks, twenty-nine years her senior, a man who had already been married (aunt Bhondamonee's evidence in court). There was the deposition of her mother Radhamonee: 'I saw my daughter lying on the cot, weltering in blood. Her cloth and the bed cloth and Hari's cloth were wet with blood.'[68] There was unanimous medical opinion that Hari had caused the death of a girl whose body was still immature and could not sustain penetration. She died after thirteen hours of acute pain and continuous bleeding. The dry medi-

---

[66]Bengal Government Judicial NF J C/17/, Proceedings 104–17, June 1893. From Simmons, honorary secretary, Public Health Society of India to chief secretary, Government of Bengal, Calcutta, 1 September 1890.

[67]Ibid., C.C. Stevens, officiating chief secretary 90B, to secretary, home department, Government of India, Darjeeling, 8 November 1890.

[68]Letter from Simmons, op.cit.

cal terminology somehow accentuates the horror more than words of
censure:

> A clot, measuring 3 inches by one-and-a-half inches in the vagina . . . a
> longitudinal tear one and three quarters long by one inch broad at the
> upper end of the vagina . . . a haematoma three inches in diameter in the
> cellular tissue of the pelvis. Vagina, uterus and ovaries small and unde-
> veloped. No sign of ovulation.[69]

Phulmonee's was by no means an isolated case. Dr Chever's investigations of 1856 mentioned at least fourteen cases of premenstrual
cohabitation that had come to his notice, and the subsequent finding
incorporated in Dr McLeod's report on child marriage amply corrob-
orated his data.[70] We may presume that only such cases as would have
needed police intervention or urgent medical attention entered the
records. These were, then, cases of serious damage that resulted from
premature sexual activity. An Indian doctor reported in court that 13
per cent of the maternity cases that he had handled involved mothers
below the age of thirteen. The defence lawyer threw a challenge at the
court: cohabiting with a pre-pubertal wife might not have shastric
sanction, yet so deep-rooted was the custom that he wondered how
many men present in court were not in some way complicit with the
practice?[71]

The divisional commissioners of Dacca, Noakhali, Chittagong and
Burdwan deposed that child marriage was widely prevalent among all
castes, barring the tribals, in their divisions. The commissioner of
Rajshahi division found that only in Jalpaiguri district 'Mechhes and
other aboriginal tribes do not favour child marriage . . . amongst the
Muhammadans and Rajbungshis, females being useful in field work,
are not generally married until they are more advanced in age'. On the
whole, the practice was more common among lower castes. The average
age of marriage for upper-caste girls was slowly moving up to twelve
or thirteen due to the relatively large spread of the new liberal education

[69]Bengal Government Judicial, J C/17/, op.cit.
[70]Ibid.
[71]*McLeod's Medical Report on Child Wives*, Bengal Government Judicial, ibid.

among them, and, ironically, to the growing pressures of dowry which forced parents to keep daughters unmarried till they could put together an adequate amount of dowry.[72] In fact, the compulsion to delay marriage till the dowry could be collected would have found a convenient ally in the new liberalism. Among the lower castes, on the other hand, emulation of brahmanical orthodoxy rather than of liberal values would be a more assured way of claiming pure ritual status. Wherever infant marriage prevailed, there was no way of ensuring that cohabitation would be delayed till the onset of puberty.

While both scriptural and customary injunctions were too strongly weighted in favour of early marriage to allow a raising of the age of marriage for girls, certain parts of the shastras did prescribe against pre-pubertal cohabitation among married couples. Nobinchandra Sen, poet and district magistrate of Chittagong, suggested that this injunction could be reinforced with legislation. Official opinion tried to distinguish between two distinct levels in marriage; the wedding ceremony itself was interpreted as a sort of a betrothal, after which girls remained in their parents' homes. It was only after the onset of puberty that they went through a 'second marriage' and went off to live with their husbands. A group of 'medical reformers' (Indian as well as European doctors who advocated changes in marriage rules on strictly medical grounds) as well as administrators advised legislation to ban marital cohabitation before the performance of the second marriage. They hoped that there was sufficient shastric as well as customary sanction behind the practice.[73]

It was soon clear, however, that too much was being made of the 'second marriage'. It was not generally taken to constitute a distinct separate stage within marriage as a whole. While there was widespread recognition that girls should begin regular cohabitation only after they attained puberty, the custom was customarily violated. Once the marriage had been performed, domestic (especially female), pressure pulled the wife into the husband's family. In any case, it was difficult to decide exactly at what age girls attained puberty or make sure that

[72]Ibid.
[73]Ibid.

no girl was sent off to her husband any earlier. Viable legislation would have to spell out a definite age at which puberty started rather than indicate a general physical condition.

The definition of puberty proved to be the stumbling block. According to custom, it was equated with the onset of regular menstruation. And here, revivalist-nationalists were treading delicate ground. While they wanted to oppose the proposed age of twelve, they could not push the age too far back, since they had not opposed the earlier penal code ban on marital cohabitation before the girl was ten. If they now chose to construe the earlier ban as an oppressive intrusion which had already interfered with Hindu marriage practices, then they could no longer sustain their present agitational rhetoric to the effect that the current intervention was the first fundamental violation of Hindu conjugality, and therefore spelt the beginning of the end of the only free space left to the Hindu. Without this sense of a new, momentous beginning of doom, the pitch of the highly apocalyptic rhetoric would fall flat. If the new legislation were to be seen as merely a part of a long-drawn-out process, then opposition to it could hardly invest itself with a life-or-death mission. They therefore insisted that 'true puberty' only occurred between the of ages of ten and twelve. Even if menstruation occurred earlier, it was a fluke and not a regular flow. The earlier penal code regulation had not therefore interfered with the garbhadhan ceremony. Since, in the hot climate of Bengal, menarche was sure to start between ten and twelve, further raising the age of consent would constitute the first real breach in ritual practice.

Reformers argued that puberty sets in properly only after twelve. In this, they used a different notion of puberty. While revivalist-nationalists unequivocally equated puberty with menarche, medical reformers argued that puberty was a prolonged process and menarche was the sign of its commencement, not of its culmination. The beginning of menstruation did not indicate the girl's 'sexual maturity'—which meant that her physical organs were developed enough to sustain sexual penetration without serious pain or damage. Until that capability had been attained, they argued, the notion of her consent was meaningless.

It is remarkable how all strands of opinion—colonial, revivalist-nationalist, medical-reformer—agreed on a definition of consent that pegged consent to a purely physical capability, divorced entirely from free choice of partner, from sexual, emotional or mental compatibility. Consent was put into a biological category, a stage when the female body was ready to accept sexual penetration without serious harm. The only problem lay in establishing when this stage was reached.

It would be simplistic, however, to conclude that there was complete identity of patriarchal values between reformers and revivalists. Whatever their broader views, reformers always had to struggle along with a minimalist programme since nothing else would have the remotest chance of acceptability either with the legislative authorities or in Hindu society. We only have to remind ourselves about the explosive protests that this legislation provoked. Reformist campaigning for legislation was more a consciousness-raising device, a foregrounding of issues of domestic ideology than pinning effective hopes of real social change to acts. Nor was the minimalist programme of insisting on the woman's physical safety an insignificant matter, under the circumstances. Revivalist-nationalists on the other hand, grounded their agenda on the most violently authoritarian regime of patriarchal absolutism. Their insistence upon self-rule in the domestic sphere coincided with their insistence that the Hindu girl should sacrifice her physical safety, and even her life if necessary, to defend the community's claim to autonomy.

As the reformist campaign gathered momentum and as the government, by the end of 1890, seemed committed to Malabari's proposals, Hindu militants were faced with two options. They could accept a radical reorientation of their earlier emphasis: that is, they could admit of a basic problem within present marriage practices and then separate them from past, supposedly authentic, norms. This way, they could still maintain their distance from reformers by insisting on reform from within in place of alien legislation from outside. While this would have amounted to an honourable face-saving device, it would still have implied an assault on the totality and inviolability of what had so far been exalted as the essential core of the system. Worse still, it would have amounted to a surrender to missionary, reformist and rationalist critiques of Hindu conjugality. On the other hand, it could come to terms with the phenomenon of violence and build its own counter-campaign around its presence. If difference was found to lie not in superior rationality, greater humanism, pleasure or love, but rather in pain and coercion, then these constituents of difference should be admitted and celebrated.

V

The Age of Consent Bill could have reasonably been faulted on many counts. It was an unbelievably messy and impractical measure. The reporting and verification of violations were generally impossible in familial situations. Even if the girl—provided she survived—and her parents were willing to depose against the husband, neighbours, whose evidence was crucial in such cases, usually protected the man. Proving the girl's age was fairly impossible in a country where births, even today, are not often registered. Medical examination was often inconclusive. Where matters did eventually reach the court, the jury, and British judges, fearful of offending custom, rarely took a firm stand. In 1891 the mother of a young girl had pressed for legal action in such a case and the girl herself gave very definite evidence in court. On the basis of a dental examination the English magistrate, however, could not be absolutely certain that she was not over twelve. The husband was consequently dischargd.[74] Unnerved by the massive anti-bill agitations, the government hastened to undermine the scope of the act. Five days after its enactment, Lord Lansdowne sent circulars instructing that enquiries should be held by 'native Magistrates' alone, and in any case of doubt prosecution should be postponed.[75]

The nationalist press referred to these problems from time to time but used them as auxiliary arguments rather than as central ones. Certain other kinds of political criticism found a stronger resonance. There was a powerfully articulated fear about the extension of police intrusion right into the heart of the Hindu household.[76] There was also strong opposition on the grounds that an unreformed and unrepresentative legislature should not legislate on such controversial

---

[74] *The Bengalee*, 21 March 1891.

[75] Dagmar Engels, op.cit.

[76] *Surabhi O Patrika*, 16 January 1891, *RNP*, 1891.

matters[77]—a criticism that sought to link the anti-Bill agitation with (Moderate) Congress-type constitutional demands. These protests too remained rather marginal to the true core of the Hindu revivalist-nationalist debate, which was carried on by hardliners like the newspapers *Bangabashi, Dainik O Samachar Chandrika* and *The Amrita Bazar Patrika.*

Hindu nationalists started on a very familiar note that had been struck on all sorts of issues since the 1870s: a foreign government was irrevocably alien and immune to the meaning of Hindu practices. And where knowledge does not exist, there power must not be exercised. A somewhat long illustration from the *Dainik O Samachar Chandrika* sums up a number of typical statements on the matter.

That a woman should, from her childhood, remain near her husband, and think of her husband and should not even think of or see the face of another man . . . are injunctions of the Hindu Shastras, the significance whereof is understood only by 'sasttvik' [pure] people like the Hindus. The English look to the purity of the body. But in Hindu opinion she alone is chaste and pure who has never even thought of one who is not her husband. No one who does not see with a Hindu's eye will be able to understand the secret meaning of Hindu practices and observances . . . . According to the Hindu the childhood of a girl is to be determined by reference to her first menses and not to her age . . .[78]

The first point made here is a methodological one that disputes the attempt to comprehend any foreign system of meaning through one's own cognitive categories (and immediately proceeds to do so itself by generalising on English attitudes about the body and the soul). The meaning of Hindu female childhood is then made different through a different arrangement of medical, sexual, moral and behavioural conditions. While revivalist-nationalists do not, as yet, insist on complete autonomy in the actual formulation and application of personal laws, they do claim the sole and ultimate right to determine their general field of operations. The claim is justified by breaking up and dispersing the sources of Hindu conjugality among numerous and ever-shifting

[77] *The Bengalee,* 21 March 1891.
[78] *Dainik O Samachar Chandrika,* 14 January 1891, *RNP,* 1891.

points of location. Some could be based on written texts, some located in oral traditions, yet others in ritual practice, and—most problematic of all—a whole lot could be simply embedded in an undefinable, amorphous, diffused Hindu way of life, accessible to Hindu instincts alone. The intention is to disperse the sources of Hindu law and custom beyond codified texts, however authoritative or authentic those might be. Even an ancient authority like Manu, who advocated sixteen as the upper limit of marriage age for girls, was dismissed as someone who wrote for the colder northern regions—where puberty came later. Charak and Susruta were dismissed even more summarily as near-Buddhists who had scant regard for true Hindu values. The process of wide dispersal renders Hindu customs opaque and infinitely flexible, to the point of being eternally elusive to colonial authorities.

The crucial emphasis lay in the reiteration that the proposed law was the first of its kind to breach and violate the fundamentals of Hinduism. The argument could only be clinched by derecognising the importance of earlier colonial interventions in Hindu domestic practices. Sati, it was argued, was never a compulsory ritual obligation and its abolition therefore merely scratched the surface of Hindu existence. The Widow Remarriage Act had a highly restricted scope, simply declaring children born of a second marriage to be legal heirs to their fathers' properties.[79] Reformers replied that the new bill was no unprecedented revision of custom either, since the penal code had already banned cohabitation for girls before the age of ten. Since girls could attain puberty before that age, the sanctity of the garbhadhan ceremony had already been threatened. Hindu revivalist-nationalists retaliated with a reference to the elusive sources of Hindu custom and a notion of the Hindu 'normalising' order which could be grasped by pure-born Hindus alone: 'It seems they [the reformers] do not know the meaning of *Adya Ritu* [real menses]. Mere flow of blood is no sign of *Adya Ritu*. A, girl never menstruates before she is ten and even if she does the event must be considered unnatural.'[80] This took care of the 1860 Penal Code provision against cohabiting with a girl under ten. An 'authentic' Hindu girl,

[79]*Nabayug*, January 15, 1891, *RNP*, 1891.
[80]*Dainik O Samachar Chandrika*, 15 April 1896, *RNP*.

according to revivalists, does not reach puberty before she is ten. The earlier ban had therefore not really tampered with Hindu practices. Were the ceiling to be extended to twelve, a serious interference would occur. The meaning of physicality itself is constituted differently and uniform biological symptoms do not point to a universal bodily developmental scheme, since Hindus alone know what stands for the normal and the abnormal in the body's growth.

The insistence that the English were about to commit a primal sin against Hinduism, that an unprecedented attack was going to be mounted on the last pure space left to a conquered people, was necessary to relocate the beginnings of true colonisation here and now—so that a new chronology of resistance could also begin from this moment, redeeming the earlier choice of loyalism. 'The Indians have felt for the last two centuries that India is no longer theirs, that it has passed into the hands of the Yavanas. But the Indians have, up to this time, found solace in the thought that though their country is not theirs, their religion is theirs'.[81]

Or, even more forcefully and explicitly, 'No, no, a hundred battles like that of Plassey, Assay, Multan could not in terribleness of effect compare with the step Lord Lansdowne has taken'.[82] With the possibility of protest in the near future, apocalyptic descriptions of subjection became common: 'The day has at length arrived when dogs and jackals, hares and goats will have it all their way. India is going to be converted into a most unholy hell, swarming with hell worms and hell insects . . . . The Hindu family is ruined.'[83]

It was this language of resistance and repudiation that gave the Age of Consent controversy such wide resonance among the Bengali middle class. The *Bangabashi*, in particular, formulated a rhetoric in these years with phenomenal success,[84] becoming in the process the leading Bengali daily, changing over from its weekly status, and pulling a whole lot of erstwhile reformist papers into its orbit for some time. Even Vidyasagar, the ideal-typical reformer figure, criticised the bill.[85]

[81] *Nabayug*, op.cit.

[82] *Bangabashi*, 21 March 1891, *RNP*, 1891.

[83] Ibid.

[84] See Amiya Sen, op.cit.

[85] Mentioned in *The Bengalee*, 7 March 1891.

The response of a fairly pro-reform journal, the *Bengalee*, epitomises the way in which the new agitational mood reacted on a potentially reform-minded, yet largely nationalist, intelligentsia. It had supported the bill quite staunchly up to the end of January 1891, after which there seemed to occur an abrupt change of line. In February, after reporting on 'an enormous mass protest meeting, the largest that had ever been held', it started to find problems with the legislation—albeit more of a constitutional kind, with reflections upon the unrepresentative nature of the legislature.[86] In March it covered yet another mammoth protest meeting and then redefined the grounds of its own opposition. 'It is no longer the language of appeal which opponents of the Bill address to the rulers of the land . . . . However much we may differ from the opponents of the measure, we cannot but respect such sentiments.'[87]

We therefore turn to the 'language' of the opponents, to the *Bangabashi*. Here was a radical leap from mendicant appeals, from oblique and qualified criticism and from guilt and shame-ridden self-satirisation. Here was the birth of a powerful, self-confident nationalist rhetoric. 'Who would have thought that a dead body would rise up again? Whoever thought that millions of corpses would again become instinct with life?'[88] There was an exhilarating sense of release in the naming of the enemy.

The Englishman now stands before us in all his grim and naked hideousness. What a grim appearance. How dreadful the attitude . . . The demons of the cremation ground are laughing a wild, weird laugh. Is this the form of our Ruling power? Brahmaraksharh, Terror of the Universe; Englishmen . . . do you gnash your teeth, frown with your red eyes, laugh and yell, flinging aside your matted locks . . . and keeping time to the clang of the sword and bayonet . . . do you engage yourselves in a wild dance . . . and we . . . the twenty crores of Indians shall lose our fear and open our forty crores of eyes.[89]

Very confidently, almost gleefully, every former trapping of rationalisation was peeled away from the core message. Admittedly, sanction for

---

[86] *The Bengalee*, 28 February 1891.
[87] Ibid., 21 March 1891.
[88] *Bangabashi*, 28 March 1891.
[89] Ibid.

infant marriage came from Raghunandan alone, who was a late and local authority. It might well lead to other deaths.[90] It did, in all likelihood, weaken future progeny and lead to racial degeneration; but 'the Hindu prizes his religion above his life and short-lived children'.[91] Hindu shastras undoubtedly imposed harsh suffering on women: 'This discipline is the pride and glory of chaste women and it prevails only in Hindu society'.[92] There were yet other practices that might bring on her death.

Fasting on *Ekadashi* [fortnightly fasting—without even a drink of water—to which widows are meant to ritually adhere] is a cruel custom and many weak-bodied widows very nearly die of observing it . . . it is prescribed only in a small 'tatwa' of Raghunandan. Is it to be banned, too, for this reason, and the guardian of the widow arraigned in front of the High Court and pronounced guilty by the Baboo jurors?[93]

There would be other Phulmonees who would die similar violent deaths through infant marriage. Yet:

the performance of the garbhadhan ceremony is obligatory upon all. Garbhadhan must be after first menstruation. It means the first cohabitation enjoined by the shastras. It is the injunction of the Hindu shastras that married girls must cohabit with their husbands on the first appearance of their menses and all Hindus must implicitly obey the injunction. And he is not a true Hindu who does not obey it . . . If one girl in a lakh or even a crore menstruates before the age of twelve it must be admitted that by raising the age of consent the ruler will be interfering with the religion of the Hindus. But everyone knows that hundreds of girls menstruate before the age of twelve. And garbhas [wombs] of hundreds of girls will be tainted and impure. And the thousands of children who will be born of those impure garbhas will become impure and lose their rights to offer 'pindas' [ancestral offerings].[94]

Even in translation the power of the voice comes through. The repetitive short sentences joined by 'ands', the frequency of the word 'must',

[90]*Dainik O Samachar Chandrika*, 15 January 1891.
[91]*Bangabashi*, 25 December 1890.
[92]*Dainik O Samachar Chandrika*, 14 January 1891.
[93]Ibid., 11 January 1891.
[94]Ibid.

the use of vast and yet vaster numbers to build up inexorably towards a sense of infinite doom—all add up to an incantatory, mandatory, apocalyptic mode of speech that is the typical vehicle for a fundamentalist millennarianism. All external reasoning has been chipped away, just the bare mandate is repeated and emphasised through threats and warnings. This is an immensely powerful, dignified voice, aeons away from timid mendicancy or morbid self-doubt. This is the proud voice of the community legislating on itself in total defiance of foreign rule and alien rationalism. It speaks the authoritative word in the appropriately authoritarian voice. The Hindu woman's body is the site of a struggle that for the first time declares war on the very fundamentals of an alien power-knowledge system. Yet it is not merely a displaced site for other arguments but remains, at this moment, the heart of the struggle. Bengali Hindu revivalist-nationalism, at this formative moment, begins its career by defining itself as the realm of unfreedom.

This contestation of alien reformism and rationalism, this defence of community custom, represses the pain of women whose protest was drowned to make way for a putative consensus. It is no longer possible to resurrect the protest of Phulmonee and of many, many other battered child-wives who died or nearly died as a result of marital rape. We have, however, several instances when cases were lodged at the initiative of the girl's mother, sometimes forcing the hands of the male guardians—for those times a rare demonstration of the woman's protest action. We also have a court deposition left by a young girl who was severely wounded and violated by her elderly husband.

'I cannot say how old I am. I have not reached puberty. I was sleeping when my husband seized my hand . . . . I cried out. He stopped my mouth. I was insensible owing to his outrage on me. My husband violated me against my will . . . . When I cried out he kicked me in the abdomen. My husband does not support me. He rebukes and beats me. I cannot live with him.'

The husband was discharged by the British magistrate. The girl was restored to him.[95]

[95] *The Bengalee*, 25 July 1891.

CHAPTER SEVEN

A Pre-History of Rights?
The Age of Consent Debates
in Colonial Bengal

'I saw my daughter lying on the cot, weltering in blood . . .'[1]

—Evidence given in court by Radhamonee, mother of eleven-year-old Phulmonee, who died of marital rape by her husband in 1890. Her death was widely reported and discussed, and in 1891 Indian reformers persuaded the colonial government to raise the minimum age of consent for married girls to twelve.

'It is the injunction of the Hindu *shastras* that married girls must cohabit with their husbands on the first appearance of their menses . . . and all Hindus must implicitly obey the injunction . . . And he is not a true Hindu who does not obey it . . . If one girl in a lakh or even a crore menstruates before the age of twelve, it must be admitted that by raising the age of consent the ruler will be interfering with the religion of the Hindus . . .'[2]

—Extract from a Bengali newspaper which furiously opposed the Age of Consent Bill.

We saw in the previous chapter that the nineteenth century in colonial Bengal was not a time when individual rights existed,

[1]Letter from Simmons, Honorary Secretary, Public Health Society of India, to Chief Secretary, Government of Bengal, Calcutta, 1 September 1890, Bengal Government, Judicial, NF JC/17/Proceedings 104–17, June 1893.

[2]*Dainik O Samachar Chandrika*, 14 January 1891.

even within her home, for the woman. The idea of an inalienable, public and explicit claim that a woman could articulate for herself did not exist. The woman was not seen, as yet, to be in possession of an individuated identity or self—separable from the family-kin-community nexus—to which rights could adhere. Yet, an immunity of sorts for her life was slowly emerging as a perceived necessity in the free-ranging, self-reflexive debates within the emergent public sphere. Over the next few decades that immunity gradually came to declare itself as her right to life. This was an important and contentious beginning, and the long nineteenth century was, in a way, a long debate over the claims of her community/family/caste to the right to inflict death upon her. In controversies about widow-immolation and the age of consent, her physical survival was the issue, and in the widow remarriage debate her sexual death was at stake.

In the 1890s the fledgling notion to a title over one's life was expressed in the word 'consent': a polyvalent, mid-term word, containing the seeds of concepts about personhood and right. The Age of Consent debates in Bengal in 1891, and the many meanings that were attached to the woman's consent, convey the intricacies of the transition.

To understand the full range of the possibilities of modern laws, however, we need to go beyond the state and its legal-judicial apparatus and locate their reception in the public sphere.[3] More than that, we need to go beyond the debates on law, and the related debate on community, and start with a little girl's death, and with the multiple representations of this event. Nineteenth-century Indian liberal reformers had focussed on particular aspects of the Hindu woman's condition, hoping to change especially coercive aspects of it through state legislation.[4] Their action led to the outlawing of widow immolation and to the legalising of widow remarriage. Even when framed within obligatory

[3]For legal reforms, see J.D.M. Derrett, *Religion, Law and the State in India* (London, 1968); Also, Sir William Markby, *Hindu and Mohammadan Law* (Calcutta, 1906, Delhi, 1977); Sripati Roy, *Customs and Customary Law in British India*, Tagore Law Lectures, Calcutta University (Calcutta, 1908–9, Delhi, 1986). For an excellent study of early colonial lawmaking, see Radhika Singha, *A Despotism of Law* (Delhi, 1998).

[4]For a study of reforms and reformers, see Charles H. Heimsath, *Indian Nationalism and Hindu Social Reform* (Princeton: Princeton University Press, 1964).

references to shastras, and *achar* (custom),[5] a commitment to certain universal and absolute moral categories, nonetheless, seeped in irrepressibly through the dense scriptural exegesis, the sanctity of the woman's life being an early and abiding concern within this. Hindu orthodoxy, as we saw, opposed the new reformed laws on account of ritual imperatives based on life-cycle rites, arguing that these constituted the Hindu group ethic. The orthodox refused to accept any wider self-evaluative criteria that would be universal rather than particularistic.

In the last years of the century, however, a more complex vocabulary of opposition was put together by modern cultural nationalists—or Hindu revivalists, as they are generally known. The ritual sphere remained for them the source of authentic meaning and value, the site of difference and uniqueness. Its preservation was now seen as all the more significant because political autonomy was already lost. It was particularly the Hindu woman's submission to community discipline, they said, that would ensure that last remnants of authenticity wherein also lay the promise of future nationhood.

The autonomy of the Hindu man having been irrevocably colonised by alien culture and education, the Hindu woman's body became a deeply politicised matter—it alone could signify past freedom and future autonomy. As we saw, this body became tied to a shastric and custom-based regimen of non-consenting and indissoluble infant marriage. The woman needed to be strictly faithful even if her husband abandoned her, remarried many times, and even if the marriage was not consummated, and even if he died.[6] Such arguments bore much fruit. They certainly curbed the effectiveness of the new reformist laws. For widow remarriage, though legalised since mid century, continued to lack moral sanction within the community. The custom of sati, on the other hand, which had been legally outlawed, remained enshrined

---

[5]From the late eighteenth century, the colonial state held on to its stand that there would be no change made in matters of religious belief, practice and matters of marriage, inheritance and succession, unless the different religious communities themselves suggested alterations in present practice. Moreover, even then changes would need to base themselves on better interpretations of, or new evidence from, the sacred texts or custom. See Radhika Singha, op. cit.

[6]For a discussion of these arguments, see chapters 1 and 6 of this book.

within community memory as a signifier of the Hindu woman's moral strength, the ultimate proof of Hindu greatness.

Derived from brahmanical prescriptions, these customs had become widespread and entrenched among most low castes as well. By the late nineteenth century, upwardly-mobile segments from most low and even untouchable groups frowned upon widow remarriage and practised the marriage of infant girls, even though their own caste custom had been far more flexible in the past.[7] Upper-caste patriarchal practices constituted a horizon of 'clean' norms that aspiring low castes could draw upon in order to claim better ritual standing. In practice, a variety of local and caste-related usages prevailed, but the pull was always towards upper-caste norms. An orthodox newspaper made this clear: 'The Brahmin caste occupies the highest position . . . All other castes conduct themselves after the fashion of the Brahmanical castes.'[8] What the revivalists argued was, therefore, perfectly true. The highly diversified, caste-divided Hindu community did derive much of its commonality from brahmanical patriarchal norms and practices: it was what upper-caste women did that held the community together as one, despite enormous internal stratification.

Given this, the politics of cultural nationalism was bound to oppose any further abridgement of Hindu domestic discipline by alien or reformist legislation. The domestic realm was all that they could rule within colonialism. The community leadership—inevitably, male, upper-caste, landowning middle class—was divorced from agricultural as well as industrial, commercial and financial entrepreneurship and from administrative decisions and legislative and military power by colonial racial discrimination. By the latter half of the century, with the crisis of investment having become acute, the shrinking scope for self-expression through 'male' enterprise, alongside the militant nationalist self-organisation of the late nineteenth century, gave the Age of Consent debates their extraordinary charge.[9] Around this issue we find the beginnings of mobilisation, mass meetings, and demonstrations of

[7]See H.H. Risley, *Tribes and Castes of Bengal: Ethnographic Glossary*, vol. 1 (Calcutta, 1891; 1981), XCIII.

[8]*Bangabashi*, 25 June, 1887; *RNP,* 1887.

[9]See chapter 1.

unprecedented scale and strength. We find the first stirrings of a modern anti-colonial agitational nationalism.

What was the role of the colonial state? It is usually seen as an agency of modernisation, trying to acquire cultural hegemony by outlawing the culture of the colonised, by refusing the particularities of lived practices in the name of a counterfeit universal reason that was actually white, male and Enlightenment-generated.[10] I take a different view. The colonial state had always promised that the entire sphere of belief, religious observance, and domestic practices like marriage and inheritance—in short the region of personal laws—would be codified according to the religious norms, scripture and custom of the different communities. This, then, was an arena that the state itself assigned to the local community. All changes relating to sati and widow remarriage, indeed, followed only upon strenuous—and often dubious—reinterpretations of local scripture by liberal reformers. A senior and influential colonial bureaucrat, H.H. Risley, wrote about infant marriage in 1891: 'Many things have been said of infant marriage . . . Much of the criticism . . . seems to be based on considerable ignorance of . . . Oriental life . . . it is the only way that accords with the lines of oriental life . . . and it were folly to dream of making all things new.'[11] The politics of recognition that Charles Taylor recommends for the survival and self-reproduction of subordinated communities[12] was indeed guaranteed by the colonial state in the field of domestic practice.

Elaborated and spelt out, such a politics of recognition would imply that community norms would not depend on extraneous issues such as moral implications derived from universal criteria. The community would live by its own laws without being required to explain its particular self-understanding according to external norms.[13] The compact between

[10]For a serious qualification of this modernising image, even in the realm of production and property relations, see D.A. Washbrook, 'Law, State and Society in Colonial India', in Baker, Johnson and Seal, eds, *Power, Profit and Politics* (Cambridge: Cambridge University Press, 1981).

[11]Risley, *Tribes and Castes of Bengal/Ethnographic Glossary*, vol. 1, XCIII.

[12]See Charles Taylor, 'The Politics of Recognition' in Amy Gutman (ed.), *Multiculturalism* (Princeton: Princeton University Press, 1994).

[13]Such safeguards to the privileged control of the community over intra-communal relations and decisions are recommended as a viable political alternative

the state and the community, therefore, allowed very little room for social change. Reformers could address only a few areas where alternative scriptural rulings or readings were just about possible, but the scope was inelastic. In any case, the procedure of the compact doubly reaffirmed the rule of scripture and custom, for laws could not be made, remade, or unmade on grounds other than scripture or custom.

Somewhat outside the spaces of the state and the community—though overlapping and intersecting with both—certain countervailing institutional developments were taking place. Modern conditions of communication, especially the press, print media and vernacular prose, allowed the expression of alternative values, and their articulation and elaboration through constant debates and arguments. Even when the arguments were instruments of a purposive, manipulative rationaliy, they needed to sustain themselves before a public tribunal, they needed to convince.

I suggest that two momentous political changes came out of a public sphere where opinions were exchanged, debated, revised, publicised. One was that even though the state exempted the community from explaining and justifying its discipline, the procedures of the public sphere insisted that this be publicly defended. Given the presence of the informal tribunal, the community—if it had any hegemonic aspirations—was forced to constantly explain itself. The other change was that, in the process, the exchange of arguments broke down the given-ness of community rule and rendered all norms post-conventional—that is, they became norms that now required discursive justification. Neither religious injunctions nor state legislation could any more belong to the realm of non-negotiable articles of faith or unquestioned, sedimented deposits of common sense. The structuring principles of individual life and of nation were taken apart, debated, argued over,

---

to uniform citizenship notions by Partha Chatterjee for present times as well. He also suggests complete freedom to communities for settling inter-community relations and conflicts according to norms generated entirely within group ethics and without any recourse to universalisable reason. See 'Secularism and Toleration' in *Economic and Political Weekly,* 9 July 1994. For a critical reflection, see Sumit Sarkar, 'The Decline of the Subaltern in *Subaltern Studies*' in *Writing Social History* (Delhi: Oxford University Press, 1997).

problematised. What emerged was not so much fresh democratic laws or a higher reason as a weakened basis of all injunctions that could no longer command via majestic authority, but that would now have to argue every inch of their way. Even if all voices were more or less patriarchal, authoritarian, power-laden and manipulative, their incessant mutual interrogation loosened the grounds of their authority, their mutual criticism made transparent the ideological foundations of the system.

Meaning now seemed uncertain rather than fixed or explicit. The public sphere, through its pluralised nature, offered opportunities for moral choices to a politically interested public. Colonised Indians lacked formal citizenship rights but, within the public sphere, they arrogated to themselves some of the *capabilities associated with citizenship*. Habermas has postulated that ideal laws are those whose addressees know themselves as possible or potential authors of the laws. Colonised Indians were not citizens in any real sense. In 1890–1 they had not come to acquire even the most nominal representation in legislating bodies. At the same time, the state allowed self-governance in the realm of personal laws. Even though that perpetuated the discipline of high-caste patriarchal norms, these were under considerable strain from public debates.[14] Given the immunity enjoyed by personal laws, and given the argumentative quality of the public sphere, something like an access to specific law-making capacities occurred in this realm of personal laws in late-nineteenth-century Bengal—within the overarching, anti-democratic colonial context.

There were other voices and arguments that forced themselves upon the compact over personal laws reached between community and state. Liberal reformers like Malabari had agitated for the abolition of child marriage for a long time on humanitarian grounds, or on the grounds of universal moral laws. This was something that the colonial state would not admit in the domestic sphere. Reasons of political expediency, as well as the fear of Victorian feminism at home (from which Indian patriarchies seemed to offer a more secure refuge) have been seen already.

---

[14]Jurgen Habermas, 'Struggles for Recognition in the Democratic Constitutional State' in *Multiculturalism,* op. cit., p. 122.

In 1890, however, the colonial state was forced to depart from its accustomed endorsement of community rule with Phulmonee's death. Hindu law admitted cohabitation with child-wives, and the colonial penal code had laid down that intercourse with wives under ten alone would be counted as rape. Phulmonee's husband Hari Maiti was thus exempted from the murder charge as well as from the charge of rape and was found guilty of causing death inadvertently, by a rash and negligent act.

The death was, as we saw within the earlier context of revivalist-nationalism, a crucial event in the public sphere. It brought together and re-energised continuing debates on Hindu domestic norms and the need for legislative reform. A huge controversy was sparked off in the press over the issue of child marriage and over the custom that enabled cohabitation with a child-wife. Child-marriage was not only customary, it was far too strongly recommended by authoritative religious codes. The state, therefore, was not ready to intervene. The only intervention that could expediently occur was over the age of consent within marriage. The Phulmonee episode made it difficult to skirt the possibility of a new age of consent entirely. It added fuel to the reformist camp and temporarily embarrassed and silenced revivalists. The government misread the silence to assume that there was a favourable climate of opinion for reformist legislation.

Cultural nationalists, however, gathered strength soon and retaliated with massive protest campaigns. They argued that a higher age of consent would violate the garbhadhan ritual, the first of the ten fundamental life-cycle rites for high-born Hindus.[15] If the rule is violated, her womb is polluted, her future sons will not be able to offer pure ritual offerings to ancestral spirits, and the sin of foeticide will be visited upon her father and her husband. In short, it would be death for the community, for it would nullify the first principle of Hindu domesticity. An excerpt from *Bangabashi*, the newspaper that played a leading role in the anti-state campaign, provides a fairly typical example of the rhetoric which

---

[15]For a more old-fashioned orthodox statement, see its presentation and refutation in Ramnath Tarkaratna, *Opinion on the Garbhadhan Ceremony according to Hindu Shastras—Delievered to Government* (Calcutta, 1891).

was fundamentalist as well as a powerful challenge to the state. 'The day has at length arrived when dogs and jackals . . . will have it all their way. India is going to be converted to a most unholy hell, swarming with hell worms and hell insects . . . The Hindu family is ruined.'[16] Or: 'The Englishman now stands before us in his grim and hideous nakedness. How dreadful the attitude . . . Terror of the Universe, Englishmen: do you gnash your teeth, frown with your red eyes, laugh and yell . . . keeping time to the clang of bayonets . . . and we . . . the twenty crores of Indians shall lose our fear and open our forty crores of eyes.'[17]

The rhetoric is death-defying, yet what powers the defiance is the male right to enjoy immature female bodies. A few years later, when a mass movement was initiated in Bengal over an arbitrary state decision to partition the province, the same *Bangabashi* stood loyally behind the Raj.[18] This, I suggest, is a characteristic of cultural nationalism—then, as now. The politics of cultural recognition turns out to be a fundamentalist defence of internal power structures—patriarchy, caste, class—rather than a systemic critique of these.

Other characteristic conditions for cultural nationalism become evident here. The subject is an upper-caste, affluent, powerful male voice from the dominant religious community. However, its design for power is based on its evocation of a fear of imminent death, and its hegemony derives from a claim to its own imminent powerlessness, to the prospect of extinction. It compels surrender and submission of the individual to the community by flaunting its fragility in face of a far more triumphalist hegemonic authority: Western Reason, which claims the entire human universe for itself.[19] I suggest that, in colonial and post-colonial situations, leaders of communities ensure their power over the lives of individuals through suggestions of the imminent death of their community. They then authorise the abdication of all individual claims and rights that are separate and distinct from the community's

[16] *Bangabashi*, 21 March 1891, *RNP*, 1891.
[17] Ibid., 28 March 1881.
[18] See chapter 6.
[19] This suggests a modest and timid variant of Social Darwinism: instead of a race for survival through assertion of power over other nations, what is recommended here is survival of the nation through a preservation of identity.

commands and injunctions. Community leaders demand a human sacrifice in the name of the threatened community.[20]

There was in the discourse of cultural-nationalists an implicit weighing of the relative importance of the two deaths. It was not that they condoned or sympathised with Hari Maiti. Their repugnance against his act merely paled into insignificance when they contemplated that countervailing measures might lead to an abridgement of the community's totalitarian rule. Could the death of a girl be equivalent in import to the death of an entire cultural system? As a revivalist newspaper had put it on an earlier occasion (over the matter of a Hindu woman's claim to repudiate a non-consensual infant marriage): 'It is very strange that the whole Hindu society will suffer for the sake of a very ordinary woman.'[21]

The great reform campaigns of the nineteenth century revolved, one way or the other, around the question of the woman's death; sati and the age of consent both related to the violent destruction of her physical body, while the widow remarriage issue was centred on her sexual death. The question was not really whether the community or the state should have the power to inflict death on the woman, though quite often this is how it was posed. The real issue was whether she as a person enjoyed an immunity from violent death when community laws allowed such a death to occur. The question was also whether she was, in fact, legally and politically, a person at all, a person whose claim to life would be self-authenticating because of her personhood. Finally, the issue was about the relative importance of two units: the *person* as a right-bearing individual, *vs* the *community* as a culture-bearing entity. Since the Hindu community had placed supreme emphasis on the woman as the vehicle of its cultural authenticity, would she be acknowledged as a bearer of culture or as a bearer of individual immunity, if not of right? There were, in other words, looped discourses on the politics of *recognition* and *the meaning* of survival: who should be

[20]Imminent death as a dominant motif in cultural-nationalist discourses has been discussed in the context of early-twentieth-century Hindu militant politics by P.K. Datta, *Carving Blocs: Communal Ideology in Early Twentieth-century Bengal* (Delhi: Oxford University Press, 1999).

[21]*Dhumketu*, 4 July 1887; *RNP*, 1887.

granted survival if both claims came from threatened species and if the two claims contradicted each other?

II

In colonial deliberations we find deep embarrassment and discomfort on this matter. The Age of Consent Act was a halfway house compromise which tried to reaffirm community discipline and also ensure the physical safety of the woman. It criminalised cohabitation with a wife under the age of twelve, arguing that this would ensure that consummation occurred after puberty: girls rarely started their menarche before that age. The garbhadhan ceremony would then be enacted at the right time and pre-pubertal girls would also be made safe from premature intercourse. The compromise pleased none, and the law was, indeed, exceptionally clumsy and inept. Orthodox pandits and cultural nationalists grumbled that this made nonsense of garbhadhan, for most girls menstruated before twelve. The Hindu domestic order had, therefore, been dealt its death blow. Liberal reformers, on the other hand, argued that a lot of girls menstruated after twelve, and in any case menarche did not mark the full puberty and physical and mental maturity necessary for safe intercourse. The law therefore still exposed girls to brutal damage and death.

The colonial government would go so far and no further. Moreover, it took good care to surround the act with safeguards so that neither domestic privacy nor the husband's privilege would be abused by the state.

III

I have identified five levels in the discourse around the age of consent. The first and the most immediate was the trial proceedings of the Hari Maiti case, especially the charge of Justice Wilson to the jury. Second, we come to the opinion of the medical establishment, largely European. Third, the opinion of administrators, reporting to Government of Bengal the conditions and problem of child marriage and premature cohabitation in their respective districts. Fourth, statements from Indian men

men of importance, whose opinion was solicited by the government before the new law was drafted. As yet, provincial legislative bodies had no Indian representation. The government therefore invited a large and mixed group to advise it on the law, drawing upon leaders of political associations, social reformers, well-known journalists, lawyers, and a very broad group of pandits. Finally, there were discussions in the public sphere, in journals, newspapers, tracts and theatrical representations.

What is striking is that the government neither asked for womens' opinions nor requested Indian correspondents to consult the opinion of women of the family on the matter. None of the Indian correspondents—not even the reformists—suggested that they had done this on their own. One of the reasons for this lack is that womens' organisations had not yet come into being. In their absence, it was far too delicate a matter for individual women to express their opinion. Nor do we find specific references to the matter in the discursive writing by women that had started to appear in print from the 1860s. Is it true, then, that the reformist campaign for raising the age of consent was more a male concern about the nature of future nationhood than a concern for the problems of women as perceived by themselves?

I would suggest a more finely tuned reading of what appear to be large silences. Womens' writings, especially autobiographical ones, portray the initiation into married life as a time of great fear. At the same time, they describe middle age—the onset of the infertile period when the sexual connection was usually terminated—as a time of relative power, freedom, status and happiness.[22] The contrast between the felt terror over the beginning of the sexual connection, and the sense of release associated with its conclusion, could be one way of referring to the unmentionable traumatic episode. At least one early woman writer, Basantakumari Dasi, was quite explicit. Non-consensual child marriage makes chastity both mechanical and difficult, she said, for physical intimacy is a form of horrible coercion for the child wife, especially in

[22]This comes out very clearly in the first full-length autobiography in the Bengali language, Rashsundari Debi's *Amar Jiban* (Calcutta, 1875). I have translated it and incorporated the translation in *Words to Win: Amar Jiban, A Nineteenth-Century Autobiography* (Delhi: Kali for Women, 1999).

the total absence of familiarity and compatibility. 'They are not animals, they too are human beings'.[23]

Young wives were sometimes killed by enraged husbands when they refused to go to bed with them. Newspaper reports of these events record something of the strength of revulsion. In May 1873 the 'mature' husband of a girl of eleven 'dragged her out by the hair and beat her till he killed her' because she would not come to his bed. He was let off with a light sentence.[24] In June 1875 an elderly man beat his young wife to death for similar reasons. Neighbours tried to cover it up as a case of suicide, but a charge of murder was eventually brought against him. The jury let him off with a light sentence.[25] In several court cases of forced intercourse that resulted in physical damage, the girl herself, as well as her mother, would very forcefully and elaborately depose in the courtroom, even though it was considered grossly improper for women to appear in court at all, or to refer to things like menstruation and intercourse in public. Phulmonee's mother, aunt and grandmother gave graphic and angry descriptions of her suffering, her husband's culpability. In another case, reported by the *Bengalee* in July 1891, the girl herself gave a detailed account of the rape. So judicial records did preserve the actual words of women, even when legal discourse failed to specifically reserve a space for them. Newspapers made these words reverberate in the public sphere. The reformist *Bengalee* repeated the evidence given by a girl at court: 'I have not reached puberty . . . My husband violated me against my will . . . When I cried out, he kicked me in the abdomen . . . He rebukes me and beats me. I cannot live with him.' The elderly husband, as we noted, was discharged by the British magistrate and the girl restored to him.[26]

Official documents did not seek out the woman's opinion, and the absence of a notion of female personhood ensured a broad silence. Nonetheless, interesting representational possibilities were encoded within legal-judicial and administrative discourses and procedures through which the girl-child and her experience could force an entry.

[23]Basantakumari Dasi, *Jositvigyan* (Barisal, 1875), p.2.
[24]*Education Gazette,* 11 May 1873, *RNP,* 1873.
[25]*Dacca Prakash,* 8 June 1875, *RNP,* 1875.
[26]*The Bengalee,* 25 July 1891.

The entry was least evident in the words of the judge when he summed up the evidence on the Hari Maiti trial. In his charge to the jury, Justice Wilson dwelt only on the man's action: whether he had previous intercourse with Phulmonee, whether he knew that vigorous penetration could be fatal, whether he knew she had not yet started menstruating. He also made it a point of criticising neither Hari Maiti's nature (which inclined him to enjoy a child), nor the domestic-conjugal custom that allowed him to do so. 'Under no system of law . . . whether Hindu or Mohammedan . . . has it ever been the law that a husband had the absolute right to enjoy the person of his wife without regard to the question of safety to her.'[27] The judge's focus was on a man's actions on a specific night, and he bent over backwards to give him every benefit of doubt.

European members of the medical establishment, similarly, made it a point to exempt Hindu marriage custom from all blame. The British Secretary to the Public Health Society wrote to the Government of Bengal: 'The Council direct me to lay special stress upon the point . . . that they base no charge against the native community . . . The Council admit that our native fellow subjects must be allowed the fullest possible freedom in deciding when their children should be ceremonially married. That, in the constitution of Hindu society, is a matter with which no Government could meddle and no Government ought to meddle.'[28]

At the same time, the very nature of their evidence compelled them to focus their gaze on the corpse of the 'unhappy child Phulmonee Dassee' who had died after thirteen hours of profuse bleeding.[29] They had to record the precise traces of a brutal and fatal penetration, they had to agree that even at eleven, that is over the statutory age of ten,

[27]Justice Wilson's charge to jury in the case of Empress *vs*. Hari Mohan Maitee, Calcutta High Court. Report sent by Acrar, Clerk of the Crown, High Court Calcutta, to Officiating Secretary, Government of Bengal, Calcutta, September 1890. Bengal Government, Judicial, JC/17/, Proceedings 90–102, 1892, Nos 101–102, File J C/17–5.

[28]Letter from Simmons, 1 September 1890, Calcutta, Bengal Government Judicial NF/17/, Proceedings 104–17, June 1893.

[29]Ibid.

Phulmonee's body was sexually immature. More, they had to generalise beyond the individual body. They admitted that even menarche did not prepare the body for safe intercourse, and that premature maternity was extremely dangerous. They talked of difficult and delayed labour, of the laceration of genital passages, of extreme exhaustion and the frequent death of child-mothers—when they had agreed that there should be no legislative interference with either child-marriage or the custom of early cohabitation. They thought that about 20 per cent of the births in Bengal happened to mothers between eleven and thirteen. They cited medico-legal data to show that in 1872 alone there were 205 recorded cases of infant death from sexual violation.[30]

While medical opinion focussed on damaged infantile bodies, administrators reported on the ubiquity of the custom, in all places, among all castes and communities. On the whole, it was more common among lower castes. Among upper castes, due to the growing pressure of dowry demands, the age of marriage for girls was going up slowly because parents needed more time to put together an adequate dowry.[31]

Some Bengali observers added intimate and painful detail: how the little girl was forced against her will to go to her husband's bed, how the older women of the family hoped for as early an appearance of the new generation as possible, how the girl's vagina could be mechanically dilated and bleeding artificially induced to make her ready for intercourse and conception. They interpreted the tears of the little girl when she returned to the matrimonial home from a visit to her natal one as tears induced by fear of the husband's advances. They read her wan face, her premature ageing, and her fatigue and early death as induced by premature sexual contact and childbearing. A few of them also very occasionally talked of mental and sexual incompatibility, of something as cruel as rape, even though they found it difficult to accept—or to even conceive of—a concept such as marital rape. If the female voice

[30]Ibid.

[31]See, for instance, letters from F.R.S. Collier, District Magistrate, Midnapore, 4 February 1891; D.R. Lyall, Commissioner, Chittagong Division, 5 February 1891; E.E. Lowis, Chief Commissioner Rajshahi Division, 3 February 1891; H. Savage, Magistrate of Backergunje, 1 February 1891, and many others, Files J 7A/2, Judicial, Political and Appointments Depts, Judicial, 1891.

could not be admitted yet, a hermeneutics of deciphering women's physical signs, gestures and emotions did develop and was incorporated in deliberations over the making of a new law.[32]

All we have here are male representations of women's experiences. But these mediated, refracted male representations nonetheless refer to a female lifeworld. These representations had to be debated extensively and authenticated in the public sphere, where some women had already appeared as critical observers and commentators on domestic custom. What is historically significant about this departure is that, in the process, the masculine gaze was expanded and altered. A new way emerged of looking at the woman's sexual or maternal body. We must remember that Bengal had an old, established classical literary tradition for describing both in wonderfully lush, rich detail. Now, we find deconstructive descriptions of both these iconic images: instead of a nubile, youthful body, the broken body of a mere child; instead of the sacred, lustrous maternal body, the emaciated, exhausted body of a child-mother. The materiality of pain and damage peeled away the iconic layers.

In the process, also, the home and the family were reinscribed as places of danger, of death—whether for satis, or for widows barred from remarriage, or for child-wives. This was a crucial departure, since both ancestral tradition and colonial law consigned the woman to her home. If the home now appeared not as her refuge but as her torture chamber, her grave, then was there a justification for confining her within it? Hindu cultural nationalists had contrasted the loving heart of the Hindu home with the loveless, coercive nature of colonial rule. They had seen domestic arrangements as a matter of willed love and surrender on the part of the woman, in contrast to the forced submission of the Indian man to the colonial order. Bankimchandra, as we saw, eroticised the spectacle of sati.[33] Widows supposedly spent a lifetime of sexual

[32]See especially, Ishan Chundra Mitra, Government Pleader, Hooghly, 2 February 1891, to the Chief Secretary, Government of Bengal; Duaraka Nath Ganguly, Assistant Secretary, Indian Association, 6 February, 1891, to Chief Secretary; B.C. Seal, Sessions Judge of Bankura, 6 February 1891, to Chief Secretary; Manomohan Ghose, Barrister and Advocate, Calcutta High Court, 6 February 1891, and many others, ibid.

[33]*Kamalakanta*, Calcutta, 1875; Jogeshchandra Bagal (ed.), *Bankim Rachanabali*, II (Calcutta: Sahitya Sansad, 1954), p. 73.

asceticism exalted by memories of their husbands: widowhood was a time not of deprivation but of joyous expectations of reunion with him.[34] The child bride was a delightful little doll.[35] The entire system— of widow immolation, of celibate widowhood, of non-consensual, indissoluble infant marriage—had been bathed in shared pleasure and sensuality to make a stark and telling contrast with other systems of marriage, and with the heartlessness of colonialism.

So the deliberations over the age of consent struck more than a jarring note. They brought the glowing edifice down, they relentlessly refocussed the complacent male gaze upon a broken young female body. The Hindu home could no longer provide easy contrast to the colonial order; worse, it almost seemed to provide a justification for colonialism, as many women's writings between the 1860s and the 1890s indeed claimed: 'Men, you have done a terrible wrong to the women of your country and, for that, you are condemned to live as exiles in the land of your birth.'[36] Whether revivalist or reformist, the Hindu male gaze was now less a voyeuristic and more a very anxious gaze. A new possibility also forced itself, adding to the discomfort: Were they talking of the woman, or of a mere child yoked in untimely marriage? Was there a separate stage in the woman's life called childhood? If yes, was it compatible with marriage? A newspaper opposing the bill argued that the Hindu girl's biological development should be differently assessed: 'According to the Hindu, the childhood of a girl is to be determined by reference to her first menses and not to her age . . .'[37] Reformers linked childhood to a stage anterior to the full maturation of all the sexual, procreative organs. A minimum age, they said, would be a safer index.

Significantly, lawmaking in the domestic realm gave short shrift to the divide between private and public. Conjugal connections, the woman's concrete mode of being, her body, indeed the vagina itself, were now matters of lawmaking. A whole range of newspapers was

---

[34]Chandrakanta Basu, *Garhasthya Path* (Calcutta, 1887).

[35]Description of a wedding in *Sulabh Samachar O Kushadaha,* 22 July 1887, *RNP,* 1887.

[36]For citations of many such views by the first generation of writing women, see *Words to Win,* op.cit.

[37]*Dainik O Samachar Chandrika,* 14 January 1891, *RNP,* 1891.

started to report on laws relating to sati and widow remarriage. The fortunes of the *Bangabashi* were made out of its stand on the age of consent. The *Amrita Bazar Patrika* turned itself from a weekly newspaper into a daily one during the campaign. And, as we saw, farces lampooning the new law were enacted with roaring success in the new public theatres of Calcutta.

Feminists have noted that the entire domain of interactive relationships—of love, nurture and care—are usually excluded from moral and political considerations, ensuring a split between the male sphere of public justice, ethics and morality, and the female sphere of affect, emotions, nurture.[38] In the Indian colonial public sphere, however, questions of political justice and rights were articulated, and even conceived of, very largely in and through discussions of the intimate sphere, of domestic arrangements, of the nature, virtue and ideals of different kinds of human relationships. These were often a metaphor for the larger questions of the politics of colonialism—whose effects were read and evaluated through the grid of power relations between Indian men and women.

Women were entirely socialised by and restricted to family-kin-community. The notion of a legal right to life, or the right to a sexual life, implicitly, gave her notionally an immunity that was neither promised nor conveyed to her by the community or the family. It gave the woman a new identity as a legal person over and beyond her group membership, an identity contested by her established guardians. It was an identity formed outside the latter's control, exercised in an arena which was not created by them. The woman as notionally a legal person sat somewhat at odds with her old masters. The ideological apparatus was fractured—just a little bit.

This is an implication of legal personhood absent in the other variant of revivalism—that of the Arya Samaj. The Samaj accepted most reformist proposals but the new Arya community handed them to the woman as a matter of its own consideration and will. It knitted the woman far more closely to the family-community nexus, it did not

[38]See Carol Gilligan, *In a Different Voice: Psychological Theory and Women's Development* (Cambridge: Harvard University Press, 1982).

leave an additional, potentially uncontrollable space for her. The Samaj did not stimulate her sense of herself as a right-bearing individual, the sense that, at least notionally, she derived from gaining a legal identity.

IV

The word consent was used in peculiar ways in all these discourses. Medical, legal, reformist and nationalist opinion agreed to attach to it a certain physical capacity when a girl could sustain intercourse without much damage. Differences arose over subsidiary issues: when was this capacity achieved; did menarche signify full puberty and did either menarche or puberty indicate sexual maturity? What happened if the girl began menstruating before twelve, and could not perform garbhadhan due to the new law? Above all, there were differences over whether a statutory age of consent was necessary, and whether it ought to be made mandatory that the wife be allowed to visit her husband only after she first menstruated.

At this point the question of self-choice or compatibility did not seem to inflect the notion of consent anywhere. The immunity that the woman's person would enjoy would depend on when her body signified a certain readiness. So it was her body that signified consent, and it was her body that would enjoy legal immunity till then. The protected person was nothing more than a protected body. Personhood for her did not extend to anything beyond her sheer physical existence.

The interesting question is, why was this particular word, 'consent', then used at all, with all its connotations of an informed assent? The Bengali term for the Age of Consent Act was *sammati ain,* which also meant assent based on intelligent understanding. If we say that this was a mechanical replica of the phrasing used in the British law of consent of 1885, we need to look beyond this particular moment. The words 'assent' and 'consent'—or a synonym—were used again and again in the debates on sati and widow remarriage. Both the warring camps argued that they represented the authentic *assent* of the woman: while reformers argued that widows feared burning or a sexless life, the orthodox insisted that she was impatient to rejoin her husband in heaven, or that she could not contemplate sex with another man. The Petition Against the Abolition of Suttee of 1829 declared: 'Hindu widows perform

of their own accord and pleasure . . . the sacrifice of self-immolation.'
Later, the Bill to Remove all Legal Obstacles to the Marriage of Hidu
Widows stated: 'In the case of the widow who is of full age . . . her own
consent shall be sufficient to constitute her remarriage lawful.'[39] The
notion of assent, not simply obedience, had become central to both
fundamentalism and reform.

However strategically limited to a physical state, or represented by
men, it seems that, one way or the other, the woman was supposed to
signify consent—to community discipline, or to new laws. And this
was a very new thing indeed. Her consent had been, so far, entirely
absent as a constituent element for lawmaking—whether for the ancient
codes of Manu or of Parashar or in the later edicts of Raghunandan,
or in the eighteenth-century sacred text of *Mahanirvanatantra*, much
used by Rammohan Roy. We find ourselves, therefore, on the threshold
of a new understanding about the nature of ideal laws, shared, ironically,
between reformers and revivalists. By now anti-colonial nationalism
had developed far enough to make the principle of self-governance by
Indians a normative ideal, as both general good and general right.

Even the notional admission of a principle of consent was thus an
important departure. Once incorporated as a principle, it would inevitably open the door to more radical demands, as indeed it did: that
women signify their assent in their own words and from an organised
forum which was meant to represent women's collective voice and interest; that women mobilise themselves on a public platform to do so; that
women be separately consulted by lawmakers; that women themselves
become part of the lawmaking procedure. When the question of child-
marriage was reopened in 1927, we find that all of these things had
already happened, in less than thirty years.

This enormous transformation indicated the formation of new female competences. A handful of educated women had already appeared
in the public sphere of print, writing critical, reproachful polemic against
Hindu marriage practices.[40] I suggest that the emergent possibilities
made it imperative to include the term 'consent', even as its scope was

---

[39]Cited in Radha Kumar, *The History of Doing: An Illustrated Account of
Movements for Women's Rights and Feminism in India, 1800–1990* (Delhi: Kali for
Women, 1993), pp. 12 and 18.

[40]I have discussed these writings in *Words to Win*. See also Rosalind O'Hanlon,

read restrictively. The possibilities gathered strength in the next two decades, which saw the first beginnings of organised womens' movements. They also saw a far more articulate notion of gender rights, spelt out as such. At the time of the age of consent agitations, however, we stand at the confluence of different possibilities, at the point of a slow, faltering, but real transition towards a sense of the woman as a right-bearing person.

Beyond its very limited and distorted application in the legal arena in 1891, then, the nomenclature itself showed that the discourse on the woman's personhood had started shifting. It was a shift that the community had to accommodate, at least in its rhetoric. Its leaders might claim exemption from the idea of a universal ethic on the grounds of their cultural particularity and difference. But they could no longer openly say, without severe cost to their hegemonic designs, that the assent of their women was not necessary.

The tension between their own laws and their public rhetoric put intolerable strains on the Hindu community's discourse. The age of consent debates were a single, exceptional moment when such people were forced to say that community discipline was more important than the woman's consent, more, that this discipline need not base itself on such consent. Rajendralal Mitra could say it only ironically: 'Hindu women are given away as cattle are, how can their consent make any difference to marriage transactions?'[41] A newspaper leading the campaign said even if a hundred Phulmonees died, the custom must be retained.[42] Another ideologue said that Hindu custom was painful and did extract a severe price from its women. But its glory lay in its severity: 'This discipline is the pride and glory of chaste women and it prevails only in the Hindu society', said another stalwart anti-bill newspaper.[43] If difference was seen to lie in greater discipline than in love, then this discipline had to be exalted as the sign of cultural authenticity. The older argument about woman's pleasure, however, was one that cultural

---

A Comparison between Women and Men: Tarabai Shinde and the Critique of Gender Relations in Colonial India (Madras: Oxford University Press, 1994).

[41]Cited in *Hindoo Patriot,* 25 December 1890.

[42]*Bangabashi,* 25 December 1890, *RNP,* 1890.

[43]*Dainik O Samachar Chandrika,* 14 January 1891, *RNP,* 1891.

nationalists were forced to surrender. This diminished their critique of the alien state and darkened the bright picture they had painted of the Hindu home and the Hindu woman. It weakened the moral basis of their nationalism. In the next century, at the time of mass politics and mammoth anti-colonial struggles, the organised leadership of nationalism would pass from their hands into another: into the hands of those ready to combine the liberal universalist arguments with systemic critiques of colonial rule.

The nineteenth-century's contentions can now be related to contemporary debates on individual rights and community rights. There is a growing worry that the modern state vaults over the realm of community existence by distributing rights between two poles; the individual, the culturally unmarked citizen who is the repository of rights; and the state which guarantees rights. Excluded from a properly secured legal personhood, the *community* cannot—it is felt— expect survival and continuity through future generations. Hence community laws—which in normal times ensure cultural authenticity—turn pathological in a situation of imminent death.

It was to avoid this that Charles Taylor argued the necessity of ensuring the continuity of minority cultures, not merely of their survival. That involves the conferring of certain powers over the individual and her choices within the community.[44] In the Indian context, controversies surround the classification of dominant and minority cultures. Partha Chatterjee has tried to refuse all such distinction between indigenous dominant and minority cultures in the face of the all-pervasive dominance of the West. Going by his reoriented, single-axis polarity between indigenous/subaltern and Western/dominant, we run into a problem.[45] What ground is there to separate out and defend the right to life of an individual if we do not ascribe to certain rights the status of universal and general good, even when they run counter to the claims made upon individual lives by 'threatened' cultures? The notion of rights

[44]See his 'Politics of Recognition' in Amy Gutman (ed.), *Multiculturalism* (Princeton: Princeton University Press, 1995).

[45]See Chatterjee, *Nationalist Thought and the Colonial World: A Derivative Discourse?* (Delhi, Oxford University Press, 1986), and *The Nation and Its Fragments* (Princeton: Princeton University Press, 1993).

as a universal claim becomes urgent and substantial only at this point of conflict, where, unless given absolute priority over the other, it dies.

Taylor does indeed set apart certain 'invariant conditions' where cultural claims will not apply, and a matter of life and death would, obviously, be the first of them.[46] However, where do we ground such invariant conditions when we privilege them over a culture's demands? We can only refer to the claim to life as an absolute imperative, but if we do this we have already conceded the most vital and enduring claim of universal rights. The claims of the community will henceforth be parasitic upon the residue that is left over from the domain of rights. To argue on these lines does not mean wiping individual lives clean of community and cultural influences. It means simply not allowing them mandatory powers even when the individual refuses certain aspects of them. It also allows the individual to select, move away, and deny aspects of the culture she is born into. Only within a horizon of freedom can she have a meaningful relationship with her cultural lifeworld.

In a very important qualification made by Seyla Benhabib to the notion of rights, a continuity is posited between the embedded and embodied individual self that can only derive its full identity from a collective, communitarian identity.[47] Habermas suggests a similar convergence by pointing out the organic link between the individual and her lifeworld: so that the two are not conflicted but are complementary identities. A fuller realisation of the rights of the former will lead on to a larger fullness of the rights of the latter.

Reflections on the necessary connections between the individual and collective selves are entirely valid. At the same time, they conceal a part of our problem by overlooking the possibility of rupture and choice. It is not enough, when conflict occurs, to fall back upon the categorical sanctity of invariant conditions. It is necessary also to recognise that they are universal in nature and demand a greater claim over and above particular considerations, however urgent.

Benhabib has pointed out that critiques of universalism choose to

[46]Charles Taylor, op. cit.

[47]'The Generalized and the Concrete Other: The Kohlberg-Gilligan Controversy and Moral Theory', in S. Benhabib, *Situating the Self: Gender Community and Postmodernism in Contemporary Ethics* (Oxford: Polity Press, 1992), pp. 164–70.

use 'substitutive' rather than 'interactive' conceptions of the concept.[48] The latter would, indeed, take care of many of the questions posed by the critique. For, while 'substitutive' conceptions evoke a false universalism by substituting a particular culture for the universal, interactive notions base universal norms on something like a genuine fusion of normative horizons. Interactive universalism comes about through an acknowledgement of 'concrete others' who are culturally and historically embedded in different traditions and histories. This is indeed a most necessary and pertinent corrective to a 'substitutive universalism' where a masked culture masquerades as universalisable norms, and where a total abstraction from concrete histories makes others disappear as concrete entities, embedded in different, particular histories.

At the same time, there is still a danger that an over-accented notion of difference may lead to the assumption that tradition, community and inherited conditions constitute the sole source of authentic meaning and value, outside of which there can only be a loss of identity.[49] Where do we fit the politics of transformation into this scheme? History must not become destiny.

[48]The entire question of the nature of identity which is mortgaged to a community discipline has acquired a sinister aspect in the present Indian context. A militaristic and intolerant political formation—a variant of Hindu nationalism—has emerged as the dominant partner within the ruling coalition government at the centre. A mass-front organisation of this party masterminds violent campaigns against Indian Muslims and Christians, arguing that these minority communities are the products of conversion away from Hinduism—which is claimed as the sole authentic religion of the Indian people, the repository of her cultural identity. Any stepping away from the identity threatens the imminent loss of India's cultural distinctiveness. Conversion, therefore, is something that cannot be allowed among Indian people. See Sumit Sarkar, 'Hindutva and the Question of Conversions' in K.N. Panikkar (ed.), *The Concerned Indian's Guide to Communalism* (Delhi: Viking, 1999).

[49]For an excellent discussion of certain forms of universalisability, and of the problems that arise when they are denied, see Martha C. Nussbaum, Introduction, and Martha Chen, 'A Matter of Survival: Womens' Right to Employment in India and Bangladesh' as well as Roop Rekha Verma, 'Family, Equality and Personhood' in M. Nussbaum and J. Glover (eds.), *Women, Culture and Development; A Study of Human Capabilities* (Clarendon Press, 1995), pp. 37–61; 426–33.

CHAPTER EIGHT

Nationalist Iconography
The Image of Women in Nineteenth-Century Bengali Literature

Patriotic themes came to constitute a significant domain in Bengali literature from about the 1880s,[1] and the corpus went through many developments and mutations down to Gandhian times. A constant preoccupation was with the figure of the woman. She dominates Bengali works through the conceptualisation of the country itself in her image; by investing the ideal patriot with womanly qualities; and by the reconstruction of feminine roles and duties—and, consequently, of the familial universe by the nationalist enterprise.

The literature that has been surveyed here—songs, poems, plays, novels and short stories—was usually brought out by inferior presses in Calcutta, district towns, even villages. Some of these writings belonged to a particular strand within popular literature, most notably those connected with the Battala presses of Calcutta[2]—clumsily written cheap broadsheets or books, commenting on current sensations. Some others have gained an important status within the history of Bengali literature: the plays and songs of Mukunda Das, the author of many celebrated songs and Swadeshi 'jatras' (roving theatres) from Barisal, for instance.[3] Hardly any of them developed new imaginative forms or themes. Their

[1]Bankimchandra Chattopadhyaya's *Anandamath* was first published in 1882, *Bankim Rachanabali*, I (Calcutta, 1963).

[2]On this see Bireshwar Bandopadhyay, *Heto Bai Heto Chhara* (Calcutta, 1984).

[3]Introduction, *Charan Kabi Mukunda Daser Granthabali* (Calcutta, n.d.).

weight lies in the very dullness of constant repetition, in sharing and reworking many of the literary and social conventions that informed the rest of popular or folk literature. Literary masterpieces on patriotism—by Bankim for instance—have been used here only when they provided major imaginative norms and devices for the other category of works.

Rather belatedly, historians have started to explore how, within a subaltern domain of politics (as distinct from mainstream Congress leadership)[4] women created a separate and problematic space for themselves.[5] We still need to know how these processes and departures were conceptualised on the basis of new, sacred principles that nationalists constructed to reorder the terms of human relationships.

The first such principle and cultural artefact is the concept of the Motherland—*Deshmata*. As is usual with other nationalist discourses, the country is not just a piece of land with people living on it. It is abstracted from the people and personified as the Mother Goddess, the most recent and most sacred deity in the Hindu pantheon. The people, then, are not the 'desh' itself, but are sons of the Mother—detached from an imagined entity and put in a subordinate relation to it. Through long and continuous usage this concept has acquired such a seeming naturalness that its disjunction as a cultural construct is worth emphasizing. The process of deification is essentially a process of self-estrangement, of fetishisation.

The country was sacralised and feminised. The empire, symbolised by the lion, had often represented itself in strong, male terms. The standard British sneer against Bengali 'baboos' was that, unlike the 'manly', virile, British public schoolboy-cum-administrator, and unlike the Indian martial races, the Bengali babu was a weak, effeminate creature. Bengali nationalism, as an oppositional ideology, therefore, defiantly worshipped and gloried in the female principle. Feminisation also marked a point of departure in political consciousness. Imperialism had produced its own Mother Goddess, the figure of the Great Queen Victoria, on

[4]On a definition of this domain see Ranajit Guha, Preface in Ranajit Guha (ed.) *Subaltern Studies I: Writings on South Asian History and Society* (Delhi, 1982).

[5]Kapil Kumar, 'Baba Ramchandra and the Women's Question: Rural Women in Avadh', unpublished paper.

whom a formidable load of emotional effusion was lavished by Bengali poetasters in the 1870s and 1880s:

> Where are you, Mother Victoria, I touch your feet
> Mother, what kind of a mother are you, why have you forgotten your child?

Or:

> Where are you, our mother the Great Queen
> We have no other shelter but you
> Mother, we call out to you and we all look up to you
> For what sort of pleasure have you abandoned us?[6]

The slightly reproachful tone of the hurt yet loving child is clearly drawn from the popular devotional songs of the eighteenth-century Shakta poet Ramprasad Sen—songs of pleading for Mother Kali.[7] A significant new stage occurred when this literature transposed such addresses from an unseen, remote and foreign mother to Mother India instead—a mother more authentic, more giving and very close to the Indian child.[8]

For Bengalis, accustomed to the worship of a variety of female cults, emotional resonances connected with an enslaved mother figure tended to be particularly powerful. During the Salt Movement, for example, the alienation of salt-making rights from Indians was expressed through a representation of the salt earth as the full breasts of the Mother to which none other than the child ought to have access.

> Of course we'll make salt, it has nothing to do with you,
> What claims do you have to the honey produced by my mother's breasts?[9]

[6]Gita Chattopadhyay, *Bangla Swadeshi Gan* (Delhi, 1983), p. 243.

[7]See Shibaprasad Bhattacharya, *Bharatchandra O Ramprasad* (Calcutta, 2nd edition, 1967).

[8]A more complex and problematic and much more self-conscious transfer was effected in the course of the Philippines liberation struggle when the Spanish motherland was transformed into the Philippines mother. See Raynaldo Ileto, *Payson and Revolution: Popular Movements in the Philippines 1849–1940* (Manila, 1981), p. 192.

[9]Prabhat Chandra Maity, *'Swaraj Sangeet', Proscribed Book* (Calcutta, 1931).

Or:

Our Mother is now in the hands of the foreigner.[10]

The mother, however, is not just a figure signifying enslavement. Feminine cults also represent power, an image of resurgent and fearful strength, irrevocably associated in the Bengali Hindu mind with the concept of Shakti, on whose grace depends the success of the patriotic enterprise. There is a curious blending, as we shall see, of the principles of abject victimhood and triumphant strength in the polysemic iconography deployed around the mother.

Benedict Anderson has described the quality of the political love within nationalism in terms of the language with which nationalism describes its object; nationalism deploys the vocabulary of kinship (here, a matriarchal connection) or the vocabulary of the home, where again the figure of the Mother is dominant. Both idioms point in the same direction, towards an object to which one is naturally tied and which one does not choose on grounds of self-interest.[11]

Colonial subjection forced an exposure to a radically new civilisation as also necessarily and axiomatically superior. This induced within the local intelligentsia a simultaneous attraction to that civilization and a need to escape from it to one's own past, to one's own roots. These roots, however, seem to have become tarnished by comparison, doubt, criticism and a questioning induced by that exposure to a more successful cultural order. A new, acute consciousness of the inexorable march of history (with which India had never kept in step), of teleological time with a Westernised notion of progress as its goal—these produced intolerable anxieties and a violent desire to break out of colonialism's iron frame by a return to a past. This meant a return to one's mother, a reversion to the womb, to a state of innocence and pleasure, to a zone where the infant is as yet undifferentiated from the mother, as yet unaware of his own distinct self.[12] The agonised, anxious quest that began

[10]Bejoylal Chattopadhyay, *Damaru, Proscribed Book* (Calcutta, 1930).

[11]Benedict Anderson, *Imagined Communities: Reflections on the Origin and Spread of Nationalism* (London: Verso, 1983).

[12]For a distinction between the time of linear history and time as female subjectivity, 'monumental time' of cycles, gestations, and the eternal recurrence

in the nineteenth century for the construction of this authentic past is deeply poignant precisely because such a search itself is a product of a self which is irredeemably differentiated. The past, the mother figure, to be reappropriated either as religion or as motherland, can no longer be a state of doxa,[13] a moment of effortless ease anterior to the anxious questioning or creation of an orthodox tradition, before even the question of acceptance or rejection of tradition comes up.[14]

Bankim represented the past, present and future states of the Mother through three main iconographic sets which, with variations, decisively influenced all later nationalist imaginings.[15] The Mother in the past was an uncomplicated, glorious figure of abundance, peace and benevolence—a Jagaddhatri (nurturer of the world) or an Annapurna (the giver of food).[16] The opening lines of Mukunda Das's play *Palliseva* associate her most particularly with a superlative abundance of food.[17] A hint of past richness persists in the physical features of a rich soil, a still green and fertile land whose bounty, however, is no longer available for her children. The struggle for freedom, in fact, gets expressed again

---

of a biological rhythm, see Julia Kristeva, 'Women's Time' in Rosaldo and Gelpi (ed.), *Feminist Theory: A Critique of Ideology* (Harvester Press, 1981). Such cyclical and monumental temporality is traditionally linked to feminine and maternal subjectivity.

[13]For an explication of the notion of 'doxa' see Pierre Bourdieu, *Outline of a Theory of Practice* (Cambridge: Cambridge University Press, 1972).

[14]It is interesting to note that the stern rationalism of the Brahmos gave way to a phase dominated by the emotionalism of Keshub Chandra Sen: the doctrinal expression of this change was the change from a notion of God the Father of Rammohun Roy to the conceptualisation of God as Mother by Keshub. At a deeper level the change perhaps signified an abdication of earlier optimism of the universality of historical progress and its accessibility to Indians—and a consequent search for an alternative frame of being, beyond progress, beyond history. For a discussion of this phase of emotionalism, mother-worship and kirtan music, see Bankabihari Kar, *Mahatma Vijaykrishna Goswamir Jivabrittanta* (Calcutta, 1921). For a discussion of this enterprise in Ramakrishna's life, see Sumit Sarkar, 'The *Kathamrita* as Text: Towards an Understanding of Ramakrishna Paramhansa', Occasional Paper No. 22, Nehru Memorial Museum and Library, 1985.

[15]See *Anandamath*, op. cit., p. 759.

[16]Ibid., pp. 728–9.

[17]Mukunda Das, *Palliseva, Mukunda Rachanabali*, op.cit.

and again as a struggle for food. Food and cloth, the two basic necessities, were the strongest metaphors in the nationalist imagination.

Past radiance then finds its perfect antithesis in the image of total darkness and ruin within the colonial present. Two contradictory icons are used simultaneously to depict this state: in one the mother is the archetypal helpless female victim, the 'Bharatmata' painted by Abanindranath—pale, tearful, frail. Early nationalist poetry struck a note of deep gloom and mourning around this figure.[18] In later nationalist poetry the metaphor of the disrobing of Draupadi at the Kaurava court lies concealed behind persistent depictions of Gandhi as the saviour Krishna, who covers the shame of the country with an endless supply of cloth produced by his charkha—his version of Krishna's 'Sudarshanchakra'.

A humiliated Bharat desires you
Come, Murari, with your Sudarshanchakra.[19]

Sometimes the metaphor is explicit—like Dushashan, the wicked steal her clothes. He (Hari, i.e. Gandhi) provides an endless flow of cloth, from the charkha in his hand.[20]

A more common and powerful image, however, is that of Kali. Although used earlier by Bankim, this figure becomes universalised from Swadeshi times, due perhaps to a more clearly and openly articulated sense of anger. The meaning of Kali is comprehended in two very different ways. Bankim saw in her a measure of our shame, deprivation and exploitation. Kali is a have-not figure, a woman who has abandoned her femininity and even a basic sense of shame. 'She is trampling upon her own Shiva herself, alas our Mother!'[21] The woman on top signifies a total collapse of the ordered world, a violence directed basically against

[18]'A mournful Mother India weeps day and night, tears streaming down her face, a shaft of sorrow piercing her breasts.' (Anon); Or: 'Look at our Mother, disease-ridden, skeletal, a withered body . . .' Jyotirindranath Tagore.
See Gita Chattopadhyay, op.cit., pp. 250, 309.

[19]Jayadev Goswami, *Charankavi Mukunda Das* (Calcutta, 1972), p. 229.

[20]Kamalakanta Chakravarty, *Yugavatar Shri Shri Mahatma Gandhir Ashtottar Shatanam Grantha* (Tripura, 1932).

[21]*Anandamath*, op.cit., p. 729.

the self. Other poets, like Mukunda Das, have, however, gloried in her power, in her capacity to destroy evil and transcend death.

> Our Mother is drunk with blood
> And wants to drink the blood of her children
> Unless you awake, Shyama, no one is going to wake up.[22]

The wrath of Kali also evoked a powerful image of a transformation of the rich country into a desolate, awesome cremation ground.

> Mother, come with your fierce aspect
> Come with your awful spirits
> Come and dance on this vast cremation ground
> Which is Bharat.[23]

Through her thirst for revenge, through her insistence on the martyrdom of her sons, Kali will make a nation of heroes out of slumbering Indians. The two modes of representing Kali indicate, perhaps, an inner tension within nationalism about the principle of female strength and about the violence and destructiveness latent in it.

After the final victory of Kali through blood and death, the country comes into her own once more. Bounty and nurture are grafted upon the principle of power in the triumphant image of Mahishasurmardini Durga, the most popular form in which the mother goddess is worshipped in Bengal. There is, however, a curious mismatch between how she looks and what she does. Durga is supposedly a warrior goddess who has killed a dreaded *asura*. Yet the icons depict a smiling, matronly beauty, a married woman visiting her natal home with her children at her side—the archetypal mother and daughter, fundamentally at odds with the dying demon at her feet and the weapons in her hands. In the juxtaposition of diverse images exists the hint of triumphant strength but it is overlaid, and the overwhelming final impression is that of domesticated and gentle femininity. Bengali nationalists finally appropriated this by transforming the traces of militancy and sexuality into something more 'innocent'—into the ideal mother figure, the pre-

---

[22]Jayadev Goswami, op.cit.
[23]Ibid., p. 218.

siding deity of Bengali kitchens and the sickbed. Bepin Chandra Pal, the extremist leader, found it comfortable to reinterpret the semantics of the image:

> This is nothing but a mother's beauty . . . My mother is not a *sanyasini* but is hungry for affection, tirelessly serving others . . . This is the way Bengalis have seen their mother every morning in the kitchen. The hair piled on top of the head does not denote the state of a yogini but that of the busy cook going about her business. The heavy breasts indicate a plenitude of milk awaiting the infant. The parted lips denote the ecstasy experienced at the moment of suckling the child.[24]

Once the mother, whether through her wrath, or through her calm strength, arouses her sons, the struggle for leadership passes out of her hands into those of her sons: so, ultimately, the woman has a specific and limited role and there is no final and absolute transgression. Kali reverts back to Durga, Durga becomes a household drudge. Debi Choudhurani lays down the glorious garb of the robber queen and turns to dish-washing.[25]

If relief and regeneration depend on the will and moral fibre of the sons, who, then, are the true *santans* (patriotic sons)? Bankim and revolutionary terrorists simplified the search through the device of substitution. The entire patriotic cause was vested in the hands of an elect band of saviour heroes, of world-renouncing holy leaders inspired by a single purpose and refusing to recognise other commitments, authority, deference structures.[26] Gandhian movements, however, expanded the boundaries of involvement and participation, and extended the range of activities by incorporating strategies of sustained agitation and organisational work. What, then, of the *grihi santan*, the householder who has to alternate between complete surrender of worldly ties at moments during the upsurge, but who remains anchored in a given social order and everyday relations of domination and subordination for the rest of his life? A much more subtle and delicate worldview was necessary

[24]Bepin Chandra Pal, *Sahitya O Sadhana*, vol. II (Calcutta, 1960), p. 25.

[25]Bankimchandra Chattopadhyay, *Debi Choudhurani, Bankim Rachanabali*, op.cit., p. 869.

[26]*Anandamath*, op.cit.

here to develop an appropriate self-image and an image of the moral universe.

If the mother is potentially and ideally a life-affirming principle, a source of nurture and plenty, then the true santan should, to an extent, incorporate these attributes. On the basis of such criteria, the authentic santan is identified in much post-Swadeshi nationalist literature with women and peasants: the earth, productive, endlessly giving and suffering, transcending ego completely in the interests of nurture. Both are invested with qualities of motherhood: the woman, by virtue of her biological state and functions; the peasant, because of the nature and purpose of his labour. The pull of Vaishnavite, hagiographic literature was powerful and paradigmatic: the devotee has to feminise himself through a constant flow of tears since feminine love is the highest form of love and surrender to attain the divine. The ideas find a not-too-remote resonance in certain kinds of current feminist thinking which postulates a separate feminine domain of affect and emotion, shaped by the experience of motherhood, and intrinsically superior to dry, male rationality.[27]

The mother's mantle now falls on the 'race of mothers'—*mayer jati*—without whose awakening and participation national regeneration remains an impossible goal.[28] The sequence of the process remains the same; the first initiative will be seized by flesh-and-blood mothers, there will be a raising of patriotic consciousness, and when this resurgent patriotism of mothers irradiates the son, her task is complete and the burden of regeneration passes on from the mother to the son. 'If a nation of true mothers can be built then true sons will abound in every household.'[29] In most plays and novels the figure of a sanyasi, however, performs the original ritual to trigger off a chain reaction in the awakening process: he simultaneously pleads with the mother goddess to awake and awaken, and instruct Bengali mothers in their mission.[30]

[27]See Julia Kristeva, op.cit. Also Susan Bordo, 'The Cartesian Masculinisation of Thought', *Signs*, vol. II, No. 3, Spring 1986.

[28]'Bangamata is summoning you, listen to her: Awake, all my daughters' (p. 249); and: 'Arouse a "jati" of mothers, Build up a nation of mothers' (p. 249). Mukunda Das, in Jayadev Goswami, op.cit.

[29]Mukunda Das, *Karmakshetra* (Barisal, 1930), p. 5.

[30]Mukunda Das, *Palliseva, Karmakshetra, Brahmacharini, Mukunda Daser Granthabali*, op.cit.

There is a remarkable thematic uniformity, even monotony, in the plots. Against the broad, though somewhat shadowy, backdrop of a freedom movement (often visualised as constructive Swadeshi[31]) a major subplot is that of a more intimate struggle within the household/local rural community. The focus is not so much on the irrevocably antagonistic relationship with the British, but on what is seen as a non-antagonistic contradiction between the woman and the peasant on the one hand and the temporary villain of the plot on the other—the urbanised babu, the absentee landlord, the Shylockian usurer. When his exploitative and thoughtless hedonisn plunges the family into ruin, his wife, the tenants, and the disinterested, patriotic sanyasi pool their initiative, resources and wisdom to save him. There is, eventually, a change of heart, and a final return of the hero to the village and the bosom of the family. Order is restored, cosmic and social imbalances corrected, and a healing process begins to work within the shattered family and community.[32]

There is an interesting correspondence between the broader, more public movements and the inner, private struggle. The well-worn theme of a drain of wealth is recreated within indigenous society: there is a drain within a drain, so to speak, with the wealth, talent and leadership siphoned off from the village—the real India of authentic peasant and familial virtues—to Calcutta, the citadel of foreign power, education and culture, where family morality is pulled out of joint, wives lord it over hapless mothers-in-law, prostitutes are given priority over wives, and the cash nexus rules over all.

Kaliyuga is now indeed, rampant,
Otherwise how is it that the mother has become a maid-servant
And the man carries his wife proudly on the head?[33]

The struggle to make the natural guardians of society take up their divinely ordained role corresponds to moderate attempts at persuading the British to give up un-British unpractices. During Gandhian struggles, even after the patriotic perspective changed to Purna Swaraj, the strategy

---

[31]For a discussion of this trend in the Swadeshi Movement, see Sumit Sarkar, *The Swadeshi Movement in Bengal 1903–1908* (New Delhi, 1973).

[32]Mukunda Das, *Samaj, Palliseva, Karmakshetra, Brahmacharini*, op.cit.

[33]Jayadev Goswami, op.cit., p. 212.

remained persuasion, effected by the dramatic spectacle of suffering—a traditionally feminine strategy.

The plays of this period are not just an elaborate and devious attempt to restore a given order of power relations. They are about radical breaks and fundamental departures. Even if the woman is not given a direct role in the public domain, the moral initiative given to her irrevocably alters notions about hegemony and authority within the family. The fact that the male patriarch regains his moral status through the intervention of the woman ultimately transforms earlier models of patriarchal power by making this crucially dependent on the woman's superior understanding. Mukunda Das's plays do not portray even one negative female character. *Debi Choudhurani*, Bankim's historical-cum-patriotic novel about a woman rebel-leader at the time of the Sanyasi uprisings, ends with a plea for the return of such a woman on Indian soil: it is significant that she is vested with the mission that Krishna himself is meant to perform and that the invocation repeats the language of the *Gita*. Only among several women in Bankim's patriotic novels can some crucial attributes of the saviour Krishna be seen, the Krishna whom Bankim constructed in his *Krishna Charitra*.[34]

Norms about new expectations were fleshed out in an ideal type of the patriotic woman, whose construction absorbed much of this literature. The nineteenth-century reformist stress on formal education is rejected strenuously. A report on the work of the Gandhian Abhay Ashram indicates that there were plans for primary education for Muslim village boys, peasants and untouchable scavengers, but none at all for girls or women of any social strata.[35] A model training centre in a play by Mukunda Das excluded even the works of Bankim from its curriculum since their study requires a high level of formal education: the end might be laudable but the means are far too dubious.[36] Women's education

---

[34]See the last few lines of *Debi Choudhurani*: 'Now come Prafulla/ Appear in front of human society—let us see you. Come once again before this society and say: I am not new, I am traditional. I am that Word, I have come so many times, you have forgotten me so I have returned'—

Paritranaya Sadhunam . . . (from *Gita*)

Debi Choudhurani, op.cit., p. 872.

[35]Abhay Ashram, *Tritiya Barshik karya Bibarani* (Comilla, 1332).

[36]Mukunda Das, *Karmakshetra*, op.cit.

is to be derived from two sources alone—a knowledge of the epics, largely conveyed through the oral tradition, and their own work within the household. Religious instruction is thus identified with a popularised practical morality and the household itself is turned into a primary religious text. 'The household is the *Gita* so far as women are concerned.'[37] This is very close to the ideal education prescribed by the Gandhian leader Satish Das Gupta for the peasant: he must learn to read the Ramayana and a little bit of arithmetic, and that should be that.[38] We must remember, however, that there was, within Gandhianism, a generalised suspicion of all formal learning as divisive, empty and alienating. Higher education was the opium of the Indians, especially middle-class babus. There is, surely, a strong social inhibition, a desire to freeze power relations by forbidding access to sources of social mobility—of which higher education might be one. There is, at the same time, an equally significant strain of distrust for education as the stigmata of the privileged, a mark of distinction and division—a strain that the Gandhian mass movement, shaped by the tension between order and levelling, possibly inherited from medieval bhakti. We find in much of the bhakti canon the same suspicion of the book, the written word, or a closed and secret oral lore which makes knowledge the preserve of the Brahmin and which dooms the illiterate masses to a self-image of ignorance. Rebellion against the equation between knowledge and elitist education took the form, in both, not of a demand for equal access to education, but a delinking of the two, so that the possibility of true knowledge could equally well reside in the simple goodness and devotion and instinctive wisdom of the poor.[39] In colonial times the distrust of higher education was compounded by its alienness, which widened the gap between the learned and the unlearned in a deeper manner. The woman and the peasant, as ideal patriotic figures, had to be particularly careful in insulating themselves against the pretensions of this false knowledge.

The reordering of the categories of true and false knowledge according

---

[37]'Shiksha Bipad', a poem in *Bangabam*, 10 April 1930.

[38]Satish Chandra Das Gupta, *Bharate Samyabad* (Calcutta, 1930), p. 65.

[39]This note particularly strong in Kabir. See *The Bijak of Kabir* trans. Ahmad Shah (New Delhi, 1986).

to a criterion of the 'indigenous' was often concretised through a clinical metaphor: a foreign parasite that the host body must reject. This metaphor was applied to different kinds of impact that the West had upon the indigenous social body, Western and Indian medical systems being a very common field of giving it expression. Health and life depended, too, on the preservation of authentic past knowledge and skills of healing which now lay in the hands of the woman, in the interior space of the household. Command over this vital knowledge added a new dimension to the woman as life-giver and live-preserver, the lifeline of the future nation. If the goal of colonial exploitation is a ruinous drain of wealth and if the central purpose of the patriotic struggle is to reverse that flow, if freedom means, above all, the reappropriation of one's own fortunes, possibilities and destiny, then the woman occupied a strategic position within the scheme. With her ancient skills, she would liberate Indians from the expensive, futile and ultimately fatal trap of Western cure—which kills rather than heals.

She has to exercise her functions within this scheme, again, by promoting the boycott of foreign goods through which the drain operates. These are foreign bodies, again fatally grafted on to indigenous society; consuming them corrupts and eventually destroys the very fibre of the Indian way of life. Women decide on most items of consumption within the household: they must assume leadership in the struggle against foreign goods, habits and fashions. Labouring over the charkha, especially in Gandhian times, comes to complement the concept of boycott in a positive way. The routinised exercise of these two rituals was also to lead to a fundamental transformation in the very possibilities of a woman's being. The ignorant, self-centred, childish, giddy woman, fond of trifles, especially foreign ones, the butt of much popular satire and farce,[40] could mature into an austere, serious committed person, dedicated to a sober work ethic. She could end the waste and drain of both household as well as nation. At roving theatre performances, especially popular among village women and peasants, Mukunda Das

---

[40]For an account of farces on this theme, see Jayanta Goswami, *Samajchitre Unabingsha Shatabdir Bangla Prahasan* (Calcutta, 1974).

regularly exhorted women: 'Smash your [imported] glass bangles, women of Bengal, do not let yourselves be duped by delusions.'[41]

'Drain' was not simply a matter of financial worry. It was repeatedly linked up with a more serious moral concern: corrupting the sources of indigenous life. Through their special role at the charkha, and with boycott, women assumed a centrality within the nationalist enterprise. Other forms of the enterprise sustained this centrality. The device of social boycott was used to mark the boundaries between the pious and the godless—the nationalists and the loyalists, and the instrument of excommunication preserved the sanctity and ritual purity of the former. The snapping of social ties by women neighbours and relatives would be felt most keenly by women in loyalist families: unlike men, they had no professional world to escape to. The family metaphor was used repeatedly to define a new community of patriots; by implication women would have a larger scope of activities within it.

The ritual practices of nationalism made women's efforts particularly meaningful. The day of the partition of Bengal was observed as a day of mourning and ritual fasting. Women had to put out the hearth fires, the way they are accustomed to on the annual ritual occasion of *Arandhan vrat* (non-cooking *vrat*). To signify the indestructible unity of Bengalis, there were exchanges of the ritual wristlet (*rakhi*) among patriots. Traditionally, sisters receive this from their brothers. During the Gandhian movements women were required to save a small portion of food from daily consumption needs and donate this to Congress volunteers—the practice of *mushitibhiksha*. The charkha itself was once largely used by women for domestic needs: under Gandhi both men and women used it.

All such ritual, therefore, had meaning and resonance among the traditional practices of women, and then utilisation extended domestic, female ritual into the world of men and public affairs. There was a mingling of male and female spaces and practices. This sharing opened up possibilities for the reordering of gender relations. It was almost inevitable that patriotic literature returned compulsively to a review

[41]Mukunda Das, *Palliseva, Mukunda Daser Granthabali*, op.cit., pp. 48–9.

of women's location in society: at the heart of the nationalist discourse at this popular level there was a reopening of questions about widow remarriage, child marriage, polygamy, sexual double-standards and dowry. Major literary works that questioned conventional patriotic norms and practices—Tagore's *Ghare Baire* or *Char Adhyay* for instance—also did so through a depiction of their impact on women.[42]

Charkarani, a novel written by Jitendralal Pal during Non-co-operation, gathers up and knits together most of these themes and notions.[43] Binay, the Westernised son of a good-hearted rich peasant/usurer, returns to his village as an alien, uncomfortable figure. He encounters Shanti, a paragon of all patriotic and feminine virtue. She is fair, beautiful, a marvellous cook, a frugal housekeeper and the best wielder of the charkha in her village. 'Her pretty face, surrounded by strands of jet black hair, is intent on the charka rotating in front of her. She is Bangalakshmi herself.'[44] She and her mother criticise a Congress volunteer for accepting dowry. Her mother rebels when her father fixes her daughter's marriage with a widower and then holds up the marriage—this then means that Shanti has to remain a spinster all her life, for the ritual moment for the wedding is past. A reformed Binay eventually marries her. On the wedding night the shy bride whispers, 'I'll never let you use foreign cloth again.' Binay has to promise his agreement before he can kiss her.[45] The marriage is consummated on the basis of shared moral values. A new work ethic and a passionate commitment to a broad principle have reordered notions of feminine virtue and beauty. Women enjoy a large measure of self-determination and moral initiative. Yet a fair skin, a beautiful face and body and expertise in domestic chores retain their old importance. If the ritually fixed moment for the wedding is past, the mother's rebellion will doom Shanti to lifelong spinsterhood. In the end we find, perhaps, a conservatism that has nevertheless undergone some fundamentally important mutations.

[42]Tanika Sarkar, (Bengali), 'Middle Class Nationalism and Literature: A Study of Saratchandra's *Pather Dabi* and Rabindranath's *Char Adhyay*', in *Economy, Society and Politics in Modern India*, ed. D.N. Panigrahi (New Delhi, 1985).

[43]Jatindranath Pal, *Charakarani* (Calcutta, 1922).

[44]Ibid., p. 34.

[45]Ibid., p. 126.

The vocabulary of radical change—of any sort of anti-traditionalism to justify these mutations—was ruled out. Traditional social ideology and practices were regarded by most shades of nationalist as the one domain unmediated by foreign rule, the one independent space. Women and peasants, the only people as yet unpolluted by Western education, could preserve the purity of that domain. 'If our womanhood is made to lose direction, then the nation's defeat would be complete. If, like the so-called enlightened, Westernised Indian man, the Indian woman also takes its Western education and changes her own nature and religion then our subjection would be extended from outside to our innermost core.'[46] The woman's body was the ultimate site of virtue, of stability, the last refuge of freedom. Independence, like a hidden jewel, could be detached from external surroundings that spelt defeat and yet be concealed in the very core of the woman's body.

This is perhaps the reason why we note an obsessive preoccupation in early patriotic literature with sati—through her own self-destruction she preserves this concealed independence from being usurped.[47] Very often, an implicit continuum is postulated between the hidden, innermost private space, chastity, almost the sanctity of the vagina, to political independence at state level: as if, through a steady process of regression, this independent selfhood has been folded back from the public domain to the interior space of the household, and then further pushed back into the hidden depths of an inviolate, chaste, pure female body. There is then an implicit equation between a hidden and living freedom and chastity, traditionally the highest virtue of the Hindu woman; most powerfully demonstrated in sati and in *Jawahar vrat* (mass suicide by Rajput women in anticipation of defeat and death of their husbands in battle with Muslims). 'What does India have to fear? . . . When nobody except her women have the capacity to lie down beside their husbands on the funeral pyre with a laugh.'[48]

The woman, however, was the metaphor for both the unviolated, chaste, inner space and the possible consequence of its surrender. There

---

[46]Motilal Ray, *Bharatlakshmi* (Calcutta, 1931), Introduction.
[47]Bankim's romanticisation of sati has been seen in earlier chapters.
[48]Mukunda Deb Sarkar, *Nutan Vrata* (24 Parganas, 1925).

is something like an obsession with the signs of that final surrender, the fatal invasion of that sacred space: with the giving up of *sindur*, betelnut, deference towards husbands and in-laws, and religious faith; with the aping of foreign fashions and any insistence on greater leisure time for herself which might be misspent reading novels and developing a discordant individuality.[49] There is a tie-up with a whole range of themes made popular in pulp literature and bazar paintings from the nineteenth century[50]—the Westernised, tea-drinking, novel-reading, mother-in-law-baiting wife as a kind of a folk devil on whom are placed all the anxieties and fears generated by a rapidly changing, increasingly alien social order.

Up to the moment of Gandhian mass movements, the figure of the new patriotic woman did not generate major complications or tensions: given the definition of a new patriotic community in familial terms, the woman's patriotic enterprise would still be located within the family. The privacy of the interior domain also need not be violated since much of the ritual of nationalism—even the charkha of Gandhian struggles—could be performed within the home. There was, in fact, a linear continuity with the forms of nineteenth-century social reforms: the woman was to create a new kind of home which would be the nucleus of the new nation. Sarojini Devi, writing at the time of Non-co-operation, summed up the scope of such work: 'Whatever we can do from within our homes, we will do all of that.'[51]

Yet in their actual political practice Gandhians had embarked on a far more dangerous enterprise—bringing women out in public to engage in strident, militant protest, implying, ultimately, a violent erosion of the privacy of the female space and rough assaults on deep-rooted behavioural norms about modesty and propriety.[52] Mukunda Das often reflects on the advisability of such a step within the framework of

[49]Hemanta Kumari Guptabhaya, *Swaraje Bangamahilar Kartavya* (Sirajganj, c. 1921), p. 37.

[50]See the representations of the new vain middle class woman in Kalighat paintings, for instance W.G. Archer, *Bazar Paintings of Calcutta* (London, 1953), p. 13.

[51]Sarojini Devi, *Jatiya Sangeet* (Barisal, 1922), p. 22.

[52]Tanika Sarkar, 'Politics and Women in Bengal: The Conditions and Meaning of Participation', *The Indian Economic and Social History Review*, 21, 1, 1984.

moral development and gender relations. Ultimately he legislates against it.[53] Nor does there emerge a convincing literary representation of the militant woman who leaves the household, joins turbulent demonstrations and pickets, courts arrest, and spends long stretches of time in prison. There is thus a gap between political practice and its imaginative representation.

The reconstructed moral universe, created by the new sacred principles of nationalism, is one where the patriotic community becomes the family, where naked, fearsome shakti initiates a process of arousal and then transforms itself into nurture, where patriotic commitment reorders gender relations and revises notions of beauty, virtue and duties. Such a world cannot cope with the invasion of violently radical modes of action where different domains of patriotic activity are abruptly collapsed together, and where the actuality of equal choice and work in the political sphere makes a mockery of the language of traditionalism. Gandhians, perhaps, felt too uncomfortable with this figure because their own strategies had partially conjured up theories about it. Radical nationalists like Saratchandra in *Pather Dabi*,[54] and Pritilata Waddedar in her last testament, sought to grapple with the problem by casting it in the shape of an extraordinary sacrifice demanded of an elect few at a rare moment.[55] Gandhians had no easy way out. They were asking thousands of women, ordinary housewives and mothers, to engage in this project as a matter of everyday activity. The silence, the gap in articulation, indicates a failure of imagination to internalise adequately the extent of the ideological break that the movement had generated in its course, the possibilities of denying power relations and creating new terms of human relationships that it had opened up.

[53]Mukunda Das, *Palliseva, Mukunda Daser Granthabali*, op.cit.
[54]Tanika Sarkar, 'Bengali Middle Class Nationalism', op.cit. See also *Bengal 1928–1934: The Politics of Protest* (Delhi: Oxford University Press, 1987).
[55]Tanika Sarkar, 'Politics and Women in Bengal', op.cit.

CHAPTER NINE

Aspects of Contemporary Hindutva Theology
The Voice of Sadhvi Rithambhara

'*Khun Kharaba hona hai to ekbar ho jane do*' (If there has to be
bloodshed, let it happen once and for all.) Sadhvi Rithambhara,
a young *sannyasin* (female ascetic) spoke these words at a crucial moment during the Ramjanmabhoomi campaigns organized by Hindutva
forces between 1986 and 1992. A recording of her speech was made and
released shortly before 30 October 1990, when the Vishwa Hindu Parishad
(VHP), the religious façade of the Sangh combine, was about to lead its
first attack on the historic Babri mosque at Ayodhya. The speech was
repeatedly broadcast from temples across the Hindi belt and recited at
several *sadhu sammelans* (assemblies of ascetics) organized by the VHP.[1]
I shall attempt to lay out a conceptual grid with which to better understand the context in which Sadhvi Rithambhara's words were spoken.

Rithambhara has delivered a large number of speeches in different
parts of the country. She was, for instance, one of the chief speakers at
the historic VHP rally at the India Gate in Delhi on 4 April 1991, when
the VHP announced its decision to support the Bharatiya Janata Party
(BJP: the electoral wing of the Sangh combine) in the coming elections.
Slightly earlier, she was a leading speaker at the Dharam Sansad, the
apex body of sadhus affiliated to the VHP. Some of her speeches were

---

[1]On the movement and its organization, see S. Gopal, ed., *Anatomy of a
Confrontation: The Babri Masjid–Ram Janmabhoomi Issue* (New Delhi: Penguin,
1991); and T. Basu *et al., Khaki Shorts and Saffron Flags: A Critique of the Hindu
Right* (New Delhi: Orient Longman, 1993).

filmed on VHP video-cassettes, titled *Bhaye prakat kripala* and *Pran jaye par vachan na jaye.*[2] These speeches, originally delivered 'live', constitute only minor variations on her more famous audio-cassette. I will separate out these speech-acts from her career, her personality and her life-story, because her live appearances have been overshadowed by her recorded speeches. The details known of her life are few; at public appearances her physical gestures are minimal. Unlike Uma Bharati, another sannyasin active in the VHP cause, Rithambhara is no parliamentarian capable of suiting words to contexts. There is an immense austerity in her deployment of her figure: she is pure voice, bare words.

The importance accorded to this young female ascetic by Hindu religious institutions is unusual. Moreover, it is an honour exceptional inasmuch as it is vested in a sannyasin who ran only a minor ashram at Rishikesh and who, unlike Uma Bharati, had no reputation of great religious learning behind her. Even the precise sect that her ashram is part of seems largely unknown. The lack of information about her doctrinal affiliation is important: by such erasures the VHP attempts to obscure the considerable and significant sectarian differences among Hindus.

Rithambhara has amply justified the importance vested in her. Her ringing exhortations to Hindus to arise and kill Muslims have paid rich dividends in the form of anti-Muslim pogroms even in places earlier free of communal conflict. At the small western UP town of Khurja, for instance, the old lanes were strewn with nearly 200 Muslim corpses after two bouts of violence in December and January 1990–1. Interviewing some of the inhabitants we were told that though old habits die hard, and though peaceful coexistence had been one such old habit, repeated broadcasts of Rithambhara's cassette over successive days at local temples had finally done the trick.[3] Priests from Basti in UP informed us that they had suspended their normal programmes of recitation from sacred texts at temples in order to continuously play the cassette.[4] The Pesh

[2]Both were filmed at the J.K. Jain Studios, Delhi, in 1990.

[3]Interviews at Khurja, December 1990 and January 1991, conducted by Uma Chakravarti, Prem Chaudhuri, P.K. Datta, Zoya Hasan, Kumkum Sangari and Tanika Sarkar.

[4]Interviews in Basti, 1991, conducted by Sambuddha Sen and P.K. Datta.

Imam of the Babri mosque at Ayodhya pleaded with P.K. Datta, a member of our investigating team, to help ban the cassette via an agitation in Delhi. He said that this cassette had by itself 'erected a wall of hatred between hearts'. So widespread was the cassette's public use, he had no idea that a ban was already formally in place.[5]

In the voice of Rithambhara I hear a communal ideology that draws its force primarily, or at least considerably, from a religious vision. This vision depends on novel forms of support. Although it emerges as the utterance of a young ascetic—a conventional enough vehicle— the figure relaying the message is intentionally charismatic and forceful. Behind the voice lies a movement organized by an elaborate institutional complex for several years, successfully disguising the fact that the message derives its charge from something quite other than instant revelation. This is both an affirmation and a fundamental revision of the idea of the charismatic moment. The words of seeming revelation are, at one level, detached from the living presence of the charismatic person and, being endlessly and mechanically projected to listeners, seek to make them respond as to a direct and immediate command. The medium, instead of distancing the author and the message, merges with them. These are some of the new co-ordinates of contemporary bhakti, and they require serious analysis.

II

Communalism is shrugged off far too easily as plain politics masquerading as religion. This ignores much of the specific resonance that communalism has acquired among its votaries, and leaves unexplored some of its real sources of power. While communalism is certainly part of a political agenda, religion, however instrumentally used by certain politicians, possesses several separable cognitive categories and practices. I would therefore argue for a re-examination of the religious elements that go into the making of a communal movement.

The Ram-centred, RSS-led Hindutva movement is far too unprob-

---

[5]Pradip Kumar Datta, 'VHP's Ram: The Hindutva Movement in Ayodhya', in *Hindus and Others: The Question of Identity in India Today*, ed. Gyanendra Pandey (Delhi: Viking, 1993), pp. 46–73.

lematically held up as a telling example of something that effectively addresses godless, 'secular' modernity and which shows up the disenchanted and deracinated middle classes who have lost their former anchor in real, living faith. Faith supposedly lives on among the common people and can only return to higher levels in a distorted and repressed form. I would partially reverse this argument and suggest that modern Hinduism, over 200 colonial and post-colonial years, has systematically tried to absorb the public and political spheres within its fold; and that in fact this only continues its age-old practice of being closely connected with political processes in pre-colonial times. Moreover, it has been precisely the modern middle classes that have from the start been preoccupied with questions of faith; many have even derived their primary identity via such religious preoccupation. They have experienced and articulated their sense of changing times as a crisis of faith, and these have come with the cognitive disorders spawned by modernity through new religious resolutions.

The nineteenth century yielded a large number of cults, sects and orders whose understanding and uses of religion, or whose relationship with the sacred, were transformed away from traditional understanding in fundamental ways. Religious beliefs and practices have, similarly, gone through profound breaks and transformations in many previous historical periods as well, and what we have witnessed recently via the Ram movement is not therefore radically new.

One aspect of change in this sphere within the nineteenth century was, as we have seen, an enlargement of the discursive domain connected to the matter of faith, and an expansion of the scope of debates over its basic terms. Another change was manifest in the proliferation of social groups that participated in these debates, thanks to the growth of print and vernacular prose; the latter led to translations and popularizations of a far larger range of texts than ever before. Vernacular journalism began its career in Bengal with religious newspapers. Till the end of the nineteenth century, about three-fifths of all Bengali publications included in the National Library's holdings in Calcutta were on religious matters.[6] Fatwas issued by Deoband maulvis were printed and

[6]See chapter one herein.

widely disseminated, generating a second level of commentaries; and these in their turn produced yet another round of public speeches and debates or *bahas*.[7] Orality and print became thus interconnected and available as regularly handed down theological issues to large, popular audiences and readers. Lutgendorf has pointed out that sacred texts like the *Ramcharitmanas* now entered individual homes through print.[8] This created a deeper, more continuous and intimate relationship between text and devotee, a relationship that went beyond the occasionally collective listening to recitations and expoundings of texts. In a sense, therefore, Rithambhara's cassette reflects yet another moment in this process and promulgates a new dependence on the spoken word. We need to locate the Ramjanmabhumi movement within these long-term institutional and communication (media) changes within modern Hinduism.

Communalism is part of a process in which modern political concepts draw many of their valences from the realm of sacred meanings. We also need to remember a fact about communalism which is constitutionally embedded within it. This is the fact that communalism cannot ever name itself, it cannot articulate its authentic and specific agenda. Its agenda is to redraw the boundaries of religious identity and community in exclusively antagonistic and vindictive terms.[9] Deprived of the exact words for its own enterprise, it can only live as a parasite. I suggest that communalism inserted itself into and drew its life from two modern forms of bhakti: *deshbhakti* and Rambhakti. Of this duo, deshbhakti is a reflectively new form of devotion, while Rambhakti, an older tradition, was refigured through new usages during the anti-colonial movements.

III

In colonial times, both society and country were thought out and thought about very largely within the realm of the sacred. I use the word 'country'

[7]See Barbara Daly Metcalf, *Islamic Revival in British India: Deoband 1860–1900* (Princeton: Princeton University Press, 1982).

[8]See Philip Lutgendorf, 'Ram's Story in Shiva's City: Public Arenas and Private Patronage', in *Culture and Power in Banaras,* ed. Sandria Freitag (Delhi: Oxford University Press, 1990), pp. 34–61.

[9]I owe this observation to Pradip Datta's Introduction in *Carving Blocs* (Delhi: Oxford University Press, 1999).

deliberately because the ubiquitous words 'nation' and 'nation-state', which have emerged these days as the nearly exclusive terms with which to read nationalist or anti-colonial discourse, seem unsatisfactory in the context of such analysis. The *country* as birthplace, as homeland, as ancestral property, had meanings that are not collapsible within, nor historically or conceptually coterminous with, the vision of the modern nation-state. The latter has had a far more restricted, discontinuous and specific orbit of influence. It is important to recover the word *desh*, for desh was a visualization of the country as divine mother goddess, or as a deified motherland, and this was the term that created the first major form of modern bhakti—deshbhakti. The new deity rested on a synecdochical understanding—where the whole is greater than the sum of it parts—or as in this case where the deified motherland is detached from and valorized over the land and its people. From the late nineteenth century, deshbhakti began to acquire the character of a vivid icon which became an object of worship; a demonology; distinctions between believers and unbelievers; a holy chant; a mode of worship; and a concept which could demand acts of sacrifice.

More than anyone else, it was, as we have seen, the novelist-satirist-polemicist Bankimchandra Chattopadhyaya who, in his widely celebrated nationalist novel *Anandamath*, created the icon, elaborated the new bhakti, established its proper act of worship, and composed a sacred chant or mantra for this new deity—the chant of *Vande Mataram*. Bankimchandra, and especially his patriotic novel *Anandamath*, have been very significant resources for the Sangh combine. In the Sangh complex at Jhandewalan in Delhi, the VHP leader-cum-erstwhile BJP MP, B.L. Sharma 'Prem', talked about Bankim's inspirational writings. So did Asha Sharma, leader of the combine's women's front, the Rashtrasevika Samiti. The Suruchi Prakashan Bhandar, an RSS bookstall at Jhandewalan, sells cheap posters that depict the core song, *Vande Mataram*, taken from Bankim's novel. The song is chanted in full, at prescribed times, at all daily *shakhas* or training sessions of the RSS. To the combine, this remains the real national anthem. Rabindranath's song, *Jana Gana Mana*—the official anthem of the Indian state—is widely condemned as a paltry substitute. Rithambhara's speech pours anger and scorn over the substitution; changing one for the other was the ultimate betrayal of Hindu interest, she declares. It was forced on us by Muslim and pseudo-secularist pressure. As soon as the BJP government came to power in Delhi, it made *Vande Mataram* the compulsory anthem in all government-run schools.

The song begins in Sanskrit, then turns into Bengali, and ends with Sanskrit passages. It evokes the country in the form of the goddess of the motherland, but it breaks up the new goddess into three distinct and older divine forms. Each of these older forms is made to correspond to a different state of the land and its history—the bounteous land of the past corresponding to Annapurna, the giver of food; the starving, ravaged land of the colonized present, evoking the naked and angry Kali; and the triumphant yet gracious land of the glorious future, the state of Durga, the demon slayer. The future will belong to the Mother and her children only if the demon is slain.

Appropriately, the song first appears in the novel at the moment when a battle is about to commence. The novel itself is ambiguous about who the Mother is fighting against. It is set at a transitional moment in the eighteenth century, when the British ruled through a puppet Muslim sovereign whose misrule had led to a devastating famine. A band of ascetic warriors, helped by starving bands of villagers, has taken up arms against the political order. The rebellion ends the puppet Muslim dynasty, but instead of this being followed by the restoration of Hindu power, the British now assume direct government. The leader of the ascetics is heartbroken but a divine prophecy assures him that the transfer of power to the English is providentially designed. Later nationalists interpreted this conclusion as a reminder that the war was unfinished, and the leader still awaits the expulsion of the British. The RSS, which never participated in an anti-colonial struggle of any sort, reads this conclusion and the song as an exhortation to war against Muslims. Significantly, the song was later detached from the novel. It achieved a life of its own as a slogan in mass nationalist rallies. Ironically, it was also a slogan used invariably in times of communal violence.[10]

The song initially enters the novel as a sacred chant in Sanskrit which

[10]See Bankimchandra Chattopadhyaya, *Anandamath*, in *Bankim Rachanabali*, ed. J.C. Bagal, II (Calcutta: Sahitya Parishad, 1969), p. 726. Also the chapter 'Imagining Hindu Rashtra', in the present book.

is meant to be recited within a prescribed ritual sequence. However, a new mode of worship is soon composed around the song which introduces important shifts and breaks: in the first place, a few Bengali stanzas break through the Sanskrit. Second, it is actually first heard on the eve of battle, and not within the prescribed ritual sequence. War thus takes the place of a ritual act of worship. The song is chanted not by a brahmin priest but by a mixed crowd of ascetics and villagers and here resembles the congregational devotional music accessible to all in public sessions among Vaishnavas. Yet, instead of being sung as part of a peaceful contemplation of Krishna's *leela*—which is the normal purpose of Vaishnavite congregations—here it mobilizes the spirit of war and violence which are simultaneously introduced as aspects of ritual sacrifice, compulsory in the worship of the goddess. In spirit therefore the song is closer to the *Bhagavad Gita*, where Krishna is an inspiration for holy war, rather than to the erotically playful Krishna of Bengali Vaishnavism. Rithambhara's inaugural words in the cassette too invoke the spirit of the battleground as a new mode of worship, requiring a new order of sacrifice: she too encapsulated the mood of both the *Gita* and *Anandamath*. In the song devotional music is loosened from its original form as a chant and made to sacralize war through a politic displacement or transference of its context. At the same time, this hymn/song becomes the battle-cry that transforms a congregation of devotees into the single body of a disciplined army. If a Hindu community is here being imagined, then from the very start it is conceived as a community of people at war.

These imaginative resources towards a violent agenda are immensely enriched and extended, paradoxically, by the simultaneous evocation of gentle and peaceful images as aspects of the very same deity. Bankim introduces dramatic juxtapositions of lush, flowing sounds as well as harsh and jagged ones; images of bounty and nurturing alternate with those of fierce violence; deep piety is placed beside aggression. These rather shocking and astonishing transitions are held in place within the brief and continuous duration of a single song.

The rhetorical charge and power of the Hindutva project are often trivialized by assuming that this project has made a simple transition from the gentle quietism of past religion to the violence of the present. But *Vande Mataram* widens and complicates that notion and suggests, rather, a binary movement between tolerant Hinduism and violent Hindutva. And in this binary focus the song is not alone. Violence is related, even by Hindutva spokespersons, to quietism and gentle religious beliefs in multiple and complex ways. Rithambhara's speech, perhaps the purest condensation of the violent impulse, still retains the supple movement between the two domains of peace and aggression: Ram is intrinsically *udar* (tolerant), and so are Hindus. Yet the actions of demonic Muslims necessitate a violence which requires the transformation of Ram's fundamentally tranquil character.

Further, priests in Ayodhya told Datta that the ordinary *sevak* is mistakenly enthusiastic about the destructive dimensions of the movement. Rithambhara asks insistently for unadulterated violence, yet like the priests she too needs to frame this demand within an overarching principle of benevolence. The weaving together of the *madhur* (sweet) and the *krodhit mudras* (angry gestures) of Ram are thus enabled by the organizing principles of the song. And so it transpires that it is the Muslims—a factor extrinsic to Hindus and their peaceable worldview—who call forth violence in a fundamentally peaceful Ram and his Hindu community.[11]

Bankim gives deshbhakti its entire imaginary as well as its devotional and rhetorical repertoire. Bhakti is now directed towards a feminized figure who contains the tripartite aspects of *shakti* (divine life-force or energy), namely nurturing, violence and power. These aspects are embodied in the three different manifestations of the goddess—Annapurna, Kali and Durga. The three aspects are pulled together to compose a 'historical' narrative of India—her glory, her decline, and her future triumph. Bankim describes this bhakti as a fusion of the three forms of yoga or religious practice—*jñanayoga, karmayoga* and *bhaktiyoga*—the paths of knowledge, action and devotion. By this he lays claim to the entire resources of self-discipline and self-cultivation within all yogic forms.

Bankim also introduces two crucial departures in older forms of bhakti, both of which were destined to influence Hindutva theology. The devotee now expresses his bhakti ideally and with optimum

[11]See P.K. Datta, 'VHP's Ram'.

effectiveness through a war against the Muslim. The devotee becomes the demon-slayer himself, performing an act that the theory of divine incarnation or *avatarvad* has reserved for the avatar alone. At the same time, by so doing the devotee participates actively in the life of the divinity. In Vaishnava theories of leela or divine sport, the bhakta can do this in two ways. He can identify with a companion or associate of the deity and participate in the leela through an assumed persona. Or alternatively, as in *tathastha bhakti* enjoined upon Bengali Vaishnavas, he can stand transfixed at the shore of the leela and watch it as a spectator in rapt contemplation. In the new bhakti of Hindutva, however, he is given access to divinity via an immensely more activist and intrusive mode. He can enter the divine life in his own earthly being and, indeed, intervene in the life of the deity and even transform it through an act of war. He can become the saviour hero.

It is an immensely empowering mode. I was privileged to read out a paper on the RSS at a session organized by a Delhi women's organization for their area activists, who came from slums dominated by the RSS/VHP. I asked them why the Ramjanmabhumi message was so powerful, even though this theme is absent from all major textual traditions. They replied, 'We are always asking God for so many things. When he comes to us and asks for his home, who can resist?'

The appeal is heightened by some of the visual images used in the VHP media. Their video-cassette *Bhaye prakat kripala* deploys a lovely, dark child in the sequence when the deity is miraculously supposed to have manifested itself in the Babri mosque in order to reclaim it. Instead of the more widely-used visuals of the warrior Ram, this sequence shows a child playing hide-and-seek in his old home, in the birthplace he has lost. It is a long sequence. It builds itself on the beauty and pathos of an irresistible appeal—the appeal of a homeless male child.

IV

The RSS makes other, more extended uses of *Vande Mataram*. In its shakhas the hymn is always chanted *in toto* and in the original language. The RSS thus restores the song to its old status as a sacred chant, not a word of which can be altered. Neither the Bengali nor the Sanskrit passages may be translated, since the original words are supposed to contain sacred energy. When I asked why the song is never abbreviated, members of the organization told me that it is symbolic of the integrity of the Motherland. It is always displayed against a map of undivided India, expressing the organization's refusal to accept the partition of the subcontinent.[12]

Partition—always described by them as the result of Muslim culpability—comes to acquire new and more terrible meanings when it is filtered through the grid of this theological understanding. It is no longer a human disaster or a territorial division: it is the mutilation of a sacred body, an act of desecration committed by Muslims. The mutilation can be symbolically healed by chanting the hymn—the image of the undamaged body—in its entirety. In this way the chant sanctifies the divinity of the land and embodies its essential integrity. Simultaneously, it underscores the gross violation of its integrity.

Integrity emerges here as a condition of the sacred. Integrity and sacrality are conjoined in the single body of the Motherland, and by this semantic leap the political is absorbed into the religious, and political acts become imbued with religious significance. This sacred frame then goes on to refigure other political acts as desecratory. Rithambhara's speech abounds with figures of fissiparous, centrifugal politics: she evokes the horror of disintegration. Central to this horror is a disintegration of the wholeness of divinity. The images deployed to this end include reactions of the majoritarian Hindu/Hindu heartland to the separatist movements in Kashmir, Punjab and the North East, as well as to the dismantling of the highly centralized national polity now increasingly influenced by regional parties.

The map of India becomes the divine idol—at once sacred and vulnerable, and this explains the anger against Rabindranath's anthem *Jana Gana Mana*.[13] The latter detaches divinity from the body of the land and transfers it to the heavenly father. The country, now demystified, reverts back to the land and its people. More immediately, the synechdochal

[12]Interview with Asha Sharma, Rashtriya Seva Samiti, Delhi 1990.
[13]For the full text of the song, the Indian national anthem, see Tagore, *Sanchaita* (Calcutta: Viswabharati Publications, 1931, 1943), p. 697.

operation is undone and Tagore's India is invoked through a recitation of its many parts—the different and separate regions, the many peoples, the diverse geographical features. Rabindranath's map of the country, once again, represents a territorial region which can go through many histories and be redrawn in different ways. But in his vision the magical wholeness which, since Bankim's hymn, had reduced the diversity of the parts to insignificance, is unpacked. In that very literal sense, the Indian national anthem is in fact an act of 'disenchantment'.

Reification and mystification of the country have been fundamentally necessary for the political project of Hindutva nationalism. The premise of this project is an authoritarian, militaristic and overcentralized polity. The image of threatening neighbours outside and of treacherous Muslims within—both of whom are united by a common Muslim identity—is intended to keep the nation an aggressive and unstratified whole.

There is also a necessary spillover of meaning from the territorial to the social. Internal divisions of class and caste are seen as forms of divisiveness that desecrate the wholeness of the *desh*. These divisions, therefore, are not to be interrogated but submerged under a political piety that suspends all manner of criticism which might expose social hierarchies. Such criticisms, whenever encountered, elide into the metaphor of a divided and mutilated yet sacred body which has to be reconstructed as non-stratified so that it can continue singular and integrated. The sacrality of an integrated and aggressive yet perpetually threatened female body is the organising principle that holds the edifice together. The argument loses its power, its charge, if the country is allowed to be seen as a piece of land with flesh-and-blood people living within it. The power of this vision is further undone if the mystical description of people as soldiers in a holy war lapses into one in which they are social beings with very real social problems. Rithambhara warns untouchable dalits against violating the sacred unity of Hindus by the lure ('candy') of the Mandal issue. The problems of territorial diversity and social division require endless transcendence; a replay on many registers of the long history of past mutilations and desecrations of an inviolable, sacred body. The loss of Ramjanmabhoomi, Partition, Hindu disunity, lower-caste protest—all these are ranged together as enactments of the same terrible sin.

V

This new mode of bhakti through which the devotee actively participates in the life of a deity makes it necessary to fuse the mythological
and the historical, the time of Muslim invasions and the time of the
epics, and *voila!*—the devotee restores the birthplace to the deity and
Babur becomes the real adversary of Ram. There is indeed a semantic
conjuration at work in all this. Rithambhara is the magus who blurs
boundaries between communally-constructed history, epic and present-
day politics so completely and with such perfect ease that, today, Ram's
children can be beheld as locked in combat with Babur's sons.

Before Gandhi, the icon of the sacred Motherland had long sunk deep
into the nationalist imaginary through successive phases of the anti-
colonial struggle. It had left a deposit of images, symbols, rhetoric and
belief. With the advent of Gandhian mass movements, the attention
shifted away a little from desh as a feminine icon to the formulation of
the same concept as a sacred and ideal post-colonial political order. Ram
and his realm, the most popular objects of worship in India's north,
emerged as the dominant inspirational resources, dimming the lustre of
the mother goddess a little. Ram was invoked as the rebel who fought
against royal power with an army of monkeys and squirrels. He was also
king himself, the great lawgiver. As Gandhi chanted the name of Ram
as monarch, peasant leaders such as Baba Ramchandra, struggling in
autonomous ground-level movements, simultaneously had more in mind
than the rebel figure of Ram. Anti-colonial and popular movements
thus stretched out the boundaries of Rambhakti, grounding it in popular
political action and, in turn, reinscribing political action as acts of worship
and sacrifice.

The RSS used the aura of Ram as well as the aura of the Goddess by
founding its first shakha on the day of Vijaya Dashami, when Ram is
supposed to have received the blessings of the mother goddess in his
war against the demon.[14] Nationalism had already fused these two
forms of bhakti. With Hindutva the inspiration was initially male-
centred: the RSS is an exclusively male organization and until the 1990s
women were not allowed into its political movement. In fact, a women's

---

[14]Tapan Basu *et al.*, *Khaki Shorts*, p. 5.

wing was only founded in the RSS eleven years after the organization's own foundation. And as for the VHP, its present and future movements are oriented by three male deities—Ram, Krishna and Shiva. Savarkar had defined Bharat as the *pitribhumi* (Fatherland) of all Hindus, departing insistently from the *matribhumi* (Motherland) ideal.[15]

VI

In post-independence north India, however, there were important currents of change in devotional patterns. Most significant among these changes was a proliferation of female cults in a region that had been markedly bare of them. The Vaishno Devi temple at Jammu, dedicated to a goddess, emerged as the most popular pilgrimage for affluent devotees. Religious sessions dedicated to Bhagavati became standard, and a part of regular neighbourhood activities. A film expounded the cult and ritual for an instantly-invented goddess—Santoshi Ma—and immediately her worship became routinized among various middle-class and lower-middle-class households. A new penchant for devotional music is now abundantly fed with cassettes dedicated to Jai Mata Dei, Bhawani Ma, Mamta Ma, and Shakti Ma. The icons of these various goddesses have generated an abundance of calendar art, small images and posters. Everyday audio-visual spaces have been saturated with celebrations of goddesses. New film-created goddess-centred mythologies and miracle-lore have filled up the devotional imagination. At a VHP satyagraha at Ayodhya in January 1991, women *sevikas* spun out their own theories about the superior significance of Sita within the Ramayana.[16]

The Sangh combine needed to absorb all these reorientations in order to keep up with the times and appeal to a changing Hindu audience. Shakti has special connotations for women in electoral constituencies as well as in violent campaigns against Muslims, where women have been very active in recent years. It also has rich inspirational meanings for men who are about to initiate violence. So far, the only female icon to have reigned with her glory undiminished has been the Motherland. The Rashtrasevikas, however, have their own icon of an

[15]Ibid., pp. 12–55.
[16]See P.K. Datta, 'VHP's Ram'.

eight-armed Ashtabhuja Durga, whose weapons are objects of devout contemplation.[17] She presides over women's shakhas alone. From the 1980s, the VHP deftly set about appropriating these new icons. The Ramrath—re-created by a DCM Toyota touring India with L.K. Advani as chief charioteer—was preceded by *rathyatras* to honour Bharatmata and Ganga. The huge Ekatmata Yajna rallies used the icon of Jai Mata Di, worshipped at the Vaishno Devi temple. The VHP also constructed the towering Bharatmata temple at Hardwar.[18] Gradually therefore the goddess has worked her way up and percolated: she features in recent RSS *Vande Mataram* posters as well. These are topped by an identical two-armed, lion-riding goddess in a pink and gold sari, holding aloft a saffron flag. Sangh hymn-books are replete these days with songs dedicated to various goddesses, and Savarkar's term pitribhumi is now abandoned for a revitalized matribhumi.[19]

Rithambhara's centrality is partly responsible for restoring the female inspiration with a movement led by the Dharm Sansad and the RSS, which otherwise remains scrupulously male. Yet she is delineating not simply the significance of the sacred as female, she is relocating it within a particular order. Ram has definitively emerged, as a result of VHP campaigns, as an all-encompassing icon who dwarfs the emergent goddess cults and annexes them as auxiliaries within a movement strongly centred around him. VHP priests explain that Ram's aspects sum up all possible diversity in religious texts, beliefs and practices. Recent pilgrimage manuals at Ayodhya make the Ram temple coextensive with every significant moment in the entire history of India.[20] Ram encompasses in this view the entirety of both religion and country.

This movement has managed to stitch up the two forms of bhakti,

[17]See my 'Women's Agency Within Authoritarian Communalism: The Rashtrasevika Samiti and Ramjanmabhoomi', in Gyanendra Pandey, ed., *Hindus and Others*.

[18]See Lise McKean, *Divine Enterprise: Gurus and the Hindu National Movement* (Chicago: University of Chicago Press, 1996), chapter 5.

[19]See recent RSS texts such as Krishna Behari's *Pranamya Matri Devata* (Lucknow: Lokhit Prakashan, 1994); *Sangh Geet* (Jaipur: Gyan Ganga Prakashan, 1997); *Vande-mataram* poster published by Suruchi Kala Niketan (Delhi, 1997).

[20]P.K. Datta, 'VHP's Ram'.

for Ram and for desh, in a terribly potent brew. With an admirable husbanding of existing resources, it has combined the various energies associated with Ram and the motherland into a singular and composite noun—Ramjanmabhoomi. In fact, the insistent projection of Ayodhya as Ram's birthplace is intended to appropriate the emotional-devotional weight associated with the term '*janmabhoomi*' (birthplace) as a synonym for desh. According to a pilgrimage guide of 1893, written for Bengali pilgrims, Ayodhya's sanctity derived from the fact that it was the place where Ram *died*. It was also referred to as Ramgaya, since the association with his death and funeral meant that pilgrims were required to perform their ancestral rites here, as in Gaya.[21] It is in order to link up with the older deshbhakti and its reliance on the motherland being the *birthplace* of us all, that Ayodhya now, in contrast, needs to be beheld primarily as a birthplace.

This 'spatialization' of the object of devotion, i.e. the sacred as a specific place or space which needs to be recovered through a struggle, moves the struggle for sacred country into the more bounded notion of struggle for a sacred birthplace—not of the people, but of Ram. In the video-cassette *Bhaye prakat kripala*, the map of India has a green blinking light to indicate the birthplace of Ayodhya. If Christianity has its Bethlehem and Islam its Mecca, the green light of Hindutva shines with saffron favour upon Ayodhya. The techniques of propagating Hindutva are frequently borrowed paradoxically from the very religions that are being opposed. The map of India is still sacred, but now it is made more a protective larger covering which guards the sacred heart that is the birthplace. Ram's birthplace now sheds its sanctity upon India. Through this process of reworking old material, and through a series of transferences and displacements, India's sacredness is simultaneously emphasized and yet made derivative of Ram's birth in the country. The struggle for the country is replayed within a narrower territorial confine as the struggle for Ram's birthplace. Rithambhara's voice brings back the call for desh, the feminized sacred force. Yet she dedicates the country itself to Ram—'*yah des Ram ka hai, yah parives Ram ka hai.*' This country belongs to Ram, this environment belongs to Ram.

[21]Tirthamukur (Calcutta, 1893).

VII

Rithambhara gives this divine hierarchy an earthly counterpart. As a sannyasin she embodies shakti within herself. But she also calls Hindu men to action, to vengeance—'*vir bhaiyo jago!*' (Brave brothers, awaken!) She uses emasculation and eunuchs frequently as tropes while relying on images of combative masculinity. Women are also invoked, and there are things for them in her speech: anecdotes about other brave women; images drawn from food and cooking; homely and humorous tales referring to domestic concerns; the domestic politics played out among daughter, mother and sister-in-law. There are heroic images too with which women can identify, and Rithambhara reverently refers to *matrishakti*— the shakti that specifically resides in the mother goddess and, by extension, in mothers. Women must internalize the Ramjanmabhoomi agenda, they must fill their hearts with anger and take their place in the struggle. She leaves them in no doubt about what role they should play. Their hearts angry, their bodies hard with the desire to avenge, they must produce sons who will kill Muslims. She begins by calling them mothers, she ends up addressing them as wombs (*kokhs*). This is a form of motherhood that almost brutally transgresses the known forms of emotion and gesture associated with motherhood. In her story, Bhagat Singh's mother weeps after her son's execution not because her only child is dead, but because she has no other son who can die in the holy war. She hungers to re-experience her loss. Reproduction and mothering are reviewed primarily as acts of anger, and this represents a crucial departure from the known emotional universe. The woman in this vision of Hindutva conceives and nurtures her sons as instruments of revenge; she gives birth to masculine violence; the space for this violence is reserved for men: 'Make yourselves into a clenched fist, my brothers!'

VIII

Rithambhara's voice is distanced from the combatants, yet her words, when it is time for action, will speak through the bodies of these combatants. The rhetorical use of repetition is therefore necessary, for the call to violence has to be embedded within the body via exhortation. Violence is transgressive, and therefore its necessity can be most powerfully communicated when the demand for it emanates from an agent who is seemingly and conventionally distanced from it—an ascetic and a woman. Her appeal seems all the more cogent because she seems to stand to gain nothing from it: in fact, her hortatory voice seems to transgress her calling, to make a sacrifice of her own need for ascetic peaceableness, and thereby gains all the more credibility. The VHP claims that *sadhushakti*—the sacred energy of ascetics—leads the movement, but it deploys every communicative technique to ensure that the urge seems both holy and universal. The presence of the *sadhvi* (the female ascetic) is both an example to men and an indication that no-one is immune from the desire for violence. To make it a pure desire, sadhushakti is made to appear detached from all aspirations that sadhus might have for themselves: it conceals material incentives, which are considerable. The Ramjanmabhoomi made ashrams, *akharas* and temples, run by *mohunts*, sadhus and priests, a most lucrative real-estate investment at Ayodhya, and thus added vast financial power to the resources of organized religion. Shortly after Independence, the state had imposed various forms of financial control on religious establishments that were irksome to mohunts and priests. The 1957 electoral manifesto of the Jan Sangh (predecessor of the BJP) had promised such people protection.[22] As a matter of fact, the *maths*, the mohunts, the older pilgrimages—the older religious leadership, in short—had somewhat lost their importance with the proliferation of new temple networks, media-produced cults and godmen. The VHP has forefronted this old guard and vested them with renewed claims to supremacy, power and resources.

This link-up is part of an old agenda based on mutual benefit. But in the present movement no mention is heard of such mundane calculations—in contrast with what had been candidly expressed in the 1957 manifesto. Sadhushakti now came out to demand the birthplace for the sake of Ram: other motives were piously discounted or absent. This time the sadhus were held up as an alternative to the corrupt political order that Rithambhara denounced with revulsion. The image of the sadhu as a form of pure disinterestedness and complete innocence of worldy gains was recovered in order to oppose it with dirty trade-offs in the political world. Rithambhara reclaims sadhus as the guardians

[22]McKean, *Divine Enterprise*, p. 100.

of pure religious passion: images of greed and corruption, in her speech, encompass merely the entire world of electoral politics. Sadhus, guided by Ram, are held up as leaders of the good society. The cassette was produced before the VHP decided to publicly support the BJP in the elections, and before the BJP depoliticized as well as sacralized its electoral slogan: *'Ramrajya ki or chalem, BJP ke sath chalem.'* (Move towards Ramrajya: Move with the BJP) This seems to introduce the concept of rule by sadhus, and sure enough the sadhus did soon publicly nominate the BJP as their agent. By October 1990 everyone knew that this was going to happen. Rithambhara, however, made no mention of this possibility in her cassette, thereby positing sadhushakti as a disinterested alternative to the corruption of the electoral system. The nomination of the BJP by this disinterested sadhushakti seeks then to divest the BJP of the taint of politics.

Rithambhara's speech carefully distances itself from a political address. Rather, it uses some of the conventions of the *katha* mode, or the public recitations and explanations of sacred texts. These techniques include what in music would be called a rondo movement, i.e. repeatedly coming back to the same point from a variety of discursive paths. In Rithambhara's case these discursive routes take the form of exhortations, homilies, anecdotes and stories, and couplets that embed the moral ineffably in the memory. The linguistic range behind the speech is remarkable—chaste, Sanskritized Hindi is used when reciting names of holy places and people, Urdu-dominated Hindustani for the couplets, a domestic and homely Hindi for the stories. The tone moves quickly from tremendous passion to humour to nearly obscene and earthy parables. The overriding impressions is that of sustained anger, passion, continuous urgency, but it is deftly broken up by this wonderfully level variety of narrative modes.

Sacred myths alternate with communalized histories, folk-tales and proverbs to reiterate the same points. However, there is not even one full citation from any of the sacred texts, not one complete recall of any mythological event. This is not simply the deliberate evacuation of real religious content; it is also the making of a new religious mode. Ram is entirely detached from the epic frame and a novel and original VHP theology is crafted with ingredients drawn largely from the new form of deshbhakti. There is a surprising omission of sacred texts in RSS books, printed discourses, and in the VHP's religious material. Though the VHP does recognize the Bhagavad Gita as the canonical text of Hindus, they make little use of it. What we really see is a return to sacred orality, the eviction of older canonical traditions to clear the space for a new mythology and canon of bhakti. This is not a canon that would bear scrutiny if examined in the light of the established religious texts. This is the theology of instant bricolage, an arsenal of on-the-spot fragments. Any coherent totality of text and myths is conspicuous by its absence here.

Rithambhara's speech sums up the entire wisdom of the new theological discourse and renders it accessible and memorable. The great utility of the cassette is its effacement of all trace of technological manipulation, its metronomic cadences of complete spontaneity. Freshly recaptured each time before new audiences who hear the cassettes under very different circumstances, and who bring their very different experiences and understanding, the cassette infinitely stretches out the meanings of the original words to spur listeners to action and enlist allegiance to the new Hindutva.

If, as I suggested at the start of this essay, communalism is structured by the unsayable, if it has to seek homes in the discourses of others—deshbhakti and Rambhakti—then there is the real risk that it may not be able to adequately preserve its own distinct identity, thereby losing its purpose in a different discursive world. Rithambhara's function is to enunciate and preserve what is normally, or most often, unsayable—to spell out the agenda of violent aggression that distinguishes communalism from its two foster homes. A VHP sannyasin can best give homespun credence to communal violence via representing the private face, the intimate domain of the Sangh combine. Her excessive speech, her 'feminine unaccountability', her hysterical emotiveness—the inner domain where religious life is conventionally assigned—are thus most effectively and powerfully deployed to mobilize the world that lies outside, namely the masculine world of political, communal action. The disguise, the masquerade of a supposedly peace-loving renunciant who has been awoken from godly slumber into divine fury—these are accomplished theatre. The words of self-revelation, of self-description, cannot be spoken by all; they can be uttered only at very special circumstances of sustained violence. For that very reason, even as they are *enacted*, they need to be *enunciated* with absolute clarity, with unambiguous stridency, with an undisguised declaration of intent. That is why the charismatic utterance seems so single-mindedly, purely and divinely violent—'*khun kharaba hona hai to ekbar ho jane do.*'

APPENDIX
Vande Mataram: Text and Translation[23]

Text
vandemataram
sujalam suphalam
malayajasiitalam
sasyasyamalam
mataram

subhrajyotsnapulakitayaminim
phullakusumitadrumadalasobhinim
suhasinim sumadhurabhasinim
sukhadam varadam mataram

saptakotikanthakalakalaninada karale
dvisaptakotibhujairdhrtakharakaravale
avala kena ma eta bale
bahubaladharinim namamitarinim
ripudalavarinim mataram

tumi vidya tumi dharma
tumi hrdi tumi marma
tvam he prana sarire

[23]Translated by Sri Aurobindo and republished by permission of the Sri Aurobindo Archives, Pondicherry.

bahute tumi ma sakti
hrdaye tumi ma bhakti
tomari pratima gadi mandire mandire

tvam hi durga dasapraharanadharini
kamala kamaladalaviharini
vani vidyadayini
namami tvan

namami kamalam
amalam atulam
sujalam suphalam
mataram

vandemataram
syama saralam
susmitam bhusitam
dharanim bharanim
mataram

Translation
I bow to thee, Mother
richly-watered, richly-fruited
cool with the winds of the south
dark with the crops of the harvests
the Mother.

Her nights rejoicing in the glory of the moonlight
her lands clothed beautifully with her trees in flowering bloom
sweet of laughter, sweet of speech
the Mother, giver of boons, giver of bliss.

Terrible with the clamorous shout of seventy-million throats
and the sharpness of swords raised in twice seventy-million hands
who sayeth to thee, Mother, that thou art weak?

Holder of multitudinous strength,
I bow to her who saves
to her who drives from her the armies of her foremen
the Mother.

Thou art knowledge, thou art conduct,
thou art heart, thou art soul,
for thou art the life in our body.
In the arm thou art might, O Mother
in the heart, O Mother, thou art love and faith,
it is thy image we raise in every temple;

For thou art Durga holding her ten weapons of war
Kamala at play in the lotuses
and speech, the goddess, giver of all lore,
to thee I bow.

I bow to thee, goddess of wealth
pure and peerless
richly-watered, richly-fruited
the Mother

I bow to thee Mother,
dark-hued, candid
sweetly smiling, jewelled and adorned
the holder of wealth, the lady of plenty,
the Mother.